Alexander W. Dreyfoos

PASSION & PURPOSE

Published by The Raymond F. Kravis Center for the Performing Arts, Inc.

First printing, November 2015
Copyright © 2015 Alexander W. Dreyfoos
All rights reserved

Unless otherwise noted, all photographs copyright © 2015 Alexander W. Dreyfoos

Library of Congress Cataloging Data: 2014952622
"Alexander W. Dreyfoos: Passion & Purpose"

Acknowledgment and appreciation to the four major photographic studios of Palm Beach and their staffs, which undoubtedly created many of the photographs herein, though they cannot be linked individually after so many years. Thank you for graciously allowing publication of your work.

> **Davidoff Studios**
> **Lucien Capehart Photography**
> **Corby Kaye's Studio Palm Beach**
> **Mort Kaye Studios**

Summary: The authors chronicle the life, enterprises, and adventures of the American inventor-entrepreneur-philanthropist Alexander W. Dreyfoos, approved by their subject.

ISBN: 978-1-56352-9009

Manufactured in Canada

Book and jacket design by Burtch Hunter Design
Front cover photo by Graham McGill
Back cover photo by Alex Dreyfoos

To Renate, the love of my life
Alex

Alexander W. Dreyfoos
PASSION & PURPOSE

Lise M. Steinhauer and David Randal Allen

KRAVIS
CENTER
FOR THE PERFORMING ARTS

Contents

Acknowledgments

Thank you to the many people who contributed to this book, and apologies to any whom we have been remiss in naming:

Karen M. Allen
Kate Alvarado
Ilene Arons
Rena Blades
Catherine Dreyfoos Carter
Bard S. Crawford
Robert W. Dreyfoos
Renate Destler Dreyfoos
Don Duso
E. Llwyd Ecclestone
George T. Elmore
William J. Gilbreth
Shannon R. Ginn
Connie J. Graham
Paul Gray
Cindy Odum Harris
Michael Hawley
Amin J. Khoury
Dr. Richard Lerner
Garrison duP. Lickle
Dr. Jack Liggett
Stephen Martin
George G. Matthews

Graham McGill
George J. Michel Jr.
Robert B. Millard
James P. Mitchell
Judith A. Mitchell
D. E. "Josh" Murray
Marjorie Murray
Henry "Rip" McIntosh
Barbara Suflas Noble
Rosanne B. Odum
Gayle Pallesen
R. Carroll Peacock
William B. Peterson
Thomas R. Pledger
Will Ray
Donald R. Riehl
Stanley M. Rumbough Jr.
AnEta Sewell
Bernard Shlossman
Susan Schuyler Smith
Evelyn Dreyfoos Spelman
Lee Spencer
Ellen Van Arsdale

The authors would especially like to thank Judy Goodman for her significant contribution in compiling information.

Any errors should be attributed to the authors.

Foreword

What can you say about someone you have known for more than 60 years? We've lived in the same house, eaten together, listened to hours of his 10-meter ham radio chatter, double-dated, and had many great times together. We've kept up contact through all the ups and downs of life over 40 years, and then I've had the privilege of working with him on building a great performance center for another 20 years. What can anyone say about him that hasn't already been said?

About 10 years ago, talking with a business acquaintance, Alex's name came up. "What kind of a guy is Dreyfoos?" he asked. "Well, he's an MIT guy," I said. Okay, that puts us in the nerd bandwidth of the social spectrum, but I digress. "He's very bright," I continued. "He started Photo Electronics Corporation, won an Academy Award, he's a photographer, flies his own jet, owns a boat, and owned a TV station. He's a really nice guy. Take my word for it, you would really like him."

Now that doesn't tell you who Alex really is. So, how do you describe someone you know well? It bothers me when we describe people by what they have done or what they own. Rather than list accomplishments, let me offer some insight into Alex Dreyfoos.

Everything Alex does has a purpose. Even with things that appear frivolous, there is a purpose. Other people go scuba diving for recreation; Alex does it to take pictures. Correct that: *I* take pictures; Alex takes *photographs*. You may have seen him with his 3-inch-by-5-inch cards. He's not jotting down something so he won't forget it; he is taking notes and making a "To Do" list. When he asks a question or asks me for advice, I know he has a purpose in mind.

Now maybe you can say, lots of people do things with a purpose, but I don't know anyone who does so with more passion than Alex. Everything he has ever done, he has been passionate about, including helping others. I have seen people ask him a question, then watched their eyes glaze over as he gives them as complete an answer as possible. Many people witnessed his passion through the building of the Kravis Center; it honors the good works of Ray Kravis, but to me it will always be "The House that Dreyfoos Built."

There is much more I could say, but I would like to offer a few words by John Wayland, written in 1899. Alex knows these words. "The True Gentleman," Wayland wrote, "is the man who does not make a poor man conscious of his poverty or any man of his inferiority; who does not flatter wealth, cringe before power, or boast of his own possessions or achievements; whose deed follows his word; and who appears well in any company—a man with whom honor is sacred and virtue safe."

Alex Dreyfoos is many things, but most of all he is a true gentleman.

George Michel, March 24, 2012
On Alex Dreyfoos' 80th birthday celebration at the Eunice and Julian Cohen Pavilion, The Raymond F. Kravis Center for the Performing Arts, West Palm Beach, Florida

Alexander W. Dreyfoos

PASSION & PURPOSE

The Night of Stars

Dreyfoos took this photograph on the eve of the
Kravis Center's dedication, September 1992.

November 28, 1992 . . . As darkness fell on West Palm Beach, Florida, the once utilitarian thoroughfare of Okeechobee Boulevard became the glamorous corridor for a parade of limousines and luxury cars. The boulevard's new crown jewel, the shimmering Raymond F. Kravis Center for the Performing Arts, was making its official debut, and the glitterati were there to christen it. They milled around the plaza, taking in the sculpture and architecture of the new building. Within, champagne and fine wines flowed freely in the 1940s Moderne interior. Silver trays offered Scottish smoked salmon and caviar. At the appointed time, the guests were seated for the main event: The Night of Stars. This was history in the making.

"Ladies and gentlemen! Welcome to the Gala Grand Opening of the Raymond F. Kravis Center for the Performing Arts!" With those words, the curtain rose.

Actor Burt Reynolds, Master of Ceremonies, introduced the Florida Philharmonic Orchestra, performing Leonard Bernstein's Overture to *Candide* under the direction of James Judd. The applause was deafening as the audience—lovers of the arts from Palm Beach, South Florida, the nation—indeed, the world—celebrated the moment.

Among them was an unassuming man, one more tuxedo blending into the well-heeled crowd, to whom this night belonged. It was Alexander W. Dreyfoos who had had the vision and fortitude to create this mecca for the arts. After 12 unrelenting years of hard work, on this night he could, just a short drive from his home, revel in the extraordinary performances of legends: Roberta Peters, Isaac Stern, Faith Prince, Ella Fitzgerald, Leontyne Price, Lily Tomlin, and Alvin Ailey American Dance Theater.

The procession of guests—ushered to the rooftop of the Kravis Center's parking garage for a sumptuous post-performance dinner of lobster salad, rack of lamb, and chocolate soufflé—was a tribute to Dreyfoos and to those who helped him achieve this triumph. The politicians were there: Florida Governor Lawton Chiles, US Senators Connie Mack and Bob Graham, numerous congressmen, and other local, state, and federal officials. Celebrities from the entertainment world abounded, among them Charles Nelson Reilly, Ossie Davis, Ruby Dee, and Loni Anderson. The Palm Beach social list was also well represented. The evening appeared flawless, the weather included. Warm ocean breezes gently fanned the guests who dined and danced to the Alex Donner Band.

The next day's reviews offered the ultimate benediction to The Night of Stars: "Spectacular." "Remarkable." "Grand." "A first." "Unprecedented." No such event had ever taken place in Palm Beach County. The bar had been raised for the performing arts in South Florida.

Alex Dreyfoos had spent his life raising the bar. In the Palm Beaches, it would seem to have required little effort to achieve this with a performing arts facility, as they were of limited existence. The Royal Poinciana Playhouse in Palm Beach proper had seen many big-name stars since 1958, but it was a small, intimate theater. Potential locations for a large construction project were scarce elsewhere on the island.

Across the Intracoastal Waterway on the mainland was the West Palm Beach Auditorium, built in 1967 and often called the "leaky teepee." In addition to having a perpetually dripping roof, its design was best suited for rodeos and gun shows. The interior was an open circle that was configured according to each use. There were no solid walls, but only heavy black curtains that outlined a performance area when needed. When a temporary stage was added, the hanging cloth absorbed sound, preventing any reverberation. Even so, the auditorium served as the primary local venue, by default.

Violinist Isaac Stern had played at the city auditorium many times, while acknowledging its "miserable acoustics." When Dreyfoos was promoting the Kravis Center, Stern taped a public service announcement to air on Dreyfoos' WPEC-TV12. Stern told all who listened that at the auditorium, "Beautiful music comes out of my Stradivarius and falls flat on the floor. This community needs a performing arts center."

Dreyfoos aimed high, for a center to rival some of the world's best. Ironically, the ultimate location would not be on tony Palm Beach but across the bridge in West Palm Beach, alongside a railroad line and adjacent to a well-worn commercial area. The place was overdue for a makeover, and the project was just what community leaders wanted to attract and anchor new development. The site did not present itself easily, however.

Dreyfoos and his fellow Kravis Center founders had set out to open an arts complex that served all members of the community. During the design and early construction phases, the *Palm Beach Post* had become skeptical of the center's goals, calling it an indulgence for the wealthy of the community, "a rich man's sandbox." Those predictions were quickly proven wrong when the center's management began booking musical and theatrical acts that paralleled the broad tastes of the socio-economic strata of greater Palm Beach County. As Kravis Center CEO Judith Mitchell put it, "We burst the elitist bubble" well before the opening.

Topping all of the superlatives about the beauty of the structure, the genius of its design, and the promise of its purpose was the fact that by the time of the Gala Grand Opening, the center was debt-free.

How the Kravis Center came to be—its architecture, its operating philosophy, and its financial structure—is far more complicated than most would imagine. Complications are not so unusual for a project of this size, but few people realize this: The venue would likely not exist in this time and place had it not been for a convergence of events in the life of Alexander W.

Dreyfoos—events that pushed him to passionately pursue the purpose of getting the center funded, constructed, and operating.

Before 1992 ended, Dreyfoos would be named "Man of the Year" by the *Palm Beach Post* and would take on new philanthropic efforts in South Florida. Most of the guests attending the grand opening knew him as the owner of WPEC, the local CBS Television Network affiliate. Some also knew that he owned Photo Electronics Corporation, LaserColor Laboratories, and the Sailfish Marina. But only a few understood that he had leveraged three decades of endeavors, which eventually placed him at the center of the auspicious Night of Stars at the Kravis Center Gala Grand Opening on November 28, 1992. ☞

Dreyfoos (right) introduces Master of Ceremonies Burt Reynolds on the opening night of the Kravis Center.

(left to right) Violinist Isaac Stern, Ray Kravis, and Dreyfoos.

Jazz vocalist Ella Fitzgerald at the press conference before the opening of the Kravis Center.

(left to right) Judy Mitchell (then Shepherd), Kravis Center director of development, promoted to CEO shortly after the opening; with actress Marilu Henner.

(left to right) James Judd, music director of the Florida Philharmonic Orchestra, and actor Charles Nelson Reilly, on opening night.

A celebration onstage: dancers of the Alvin Ailey American Dance Theater engage (left to right) soprano Leontyne Price, actress Loni Anderson and Burt Reynolds (then married), and Broadway actress Faith Prince.

(left to right) Loni Anderson with actress Ruby Dee and husband actor Ossie Davis on opening night.

CHAPTER 1

Backlighting

Mt. Ampersand, the view from the Dreyfoos summer home in New York's
Adirondack Mountains, not far from his childhood playground
on Burnt Island, which had a similar view.

Island Life

Twelve hundred and fifty miles north of West Palm Beach, from a comfortable leather chair at his Adirondack summer home, Alex Dreyfoos watches the sun dip below the horizon on Lake Kiwassa and cast an amber glow across the placid water and Mt. Ampersand in the distance. Save for the call of a single loon, there is absolute stillness. The peaceful setting is worlds away from the glamorous, frenetic social pace of South Florida, where Dreyfoos and his wife, Renate, spend much of their winters. His roots are here in the Adirondacks, where he is reminded of blissful summers with his parents and younger sister at a tent-platform camp on Burnt Island, on a nearby lake. For Renate, the Adirondacks are a reminder of her birthplace, the Black Forest of Germany.

Dreyfoos still enjoys visiting the site of the family campground, though it's now devoid of any sign of human habitation. To reach Burnt Island from their home on Lake Kiwassa, Dreyfoos navigates their pontoon boat through a series of waterways. He and Renate sometimes detour along the way, to pick up sandwiches at the Lakeview Deli across from the state boat launch. Then they wait their turn to go through a set of locks connecting Lake Kiwassa with Lower Saranac Lake.

The 2,285-acre Lower Saranac Lake is relatively pristine, with few signs of human development—a stark contrast to the 1930s and '40s, when the State of New York permitted families to build wooden platform-tented camps on the lake's shore. Dreyfoos motors close to the edge of Burnt Island and the spot for which his family had held the permit, evoking the years when they roughed it here every August.

Island life in the Adirondacks was a definite departure from the Dreyfoos family's suburban life in New Rochelle, New York. Dreyfoos and his younger sister, Evelyn—called "Evie" by family and close friends—claimed Burnt Island as their personal playground. Often, Dreyfoos' friend Don Duso would join them. Duso's father, Harry, owned the Crescent Bay Marina on Saranac Lake where the Dreyfooses stored their boat, furnishings, and canvas tents in the off-season. "Each winter," Dreyfoos recalls, "the Dusos cut ice blocks from the lake, which they insulated with sawdust and stored in a barn. When summer came, we picked up blocks each week for refrigeration. There was no electricity or running water on the island, and the lake doubled as our bathtub." Shortly before the family left New Rochelle for the camp, Harry and Don and their crew would set off for Burnt Island to furnish the camp and erect the canvas tents on their platforms. They would also pull out the 16-foot Lyman lapstrake-construction outboard, an open wooden boat that the Dreyfooses kept at the lake for transportation. Don would then wait anxiously for his summer companion, Alex, to arrive.

More than 60 years later, Duso recalled those idyllic days on Burnt Island. "Even back then, Alex showed signs of leadership. We played a lot of war games. We made guns out of sticks and chased each other around, pretending to shoot them. We'd terrorize the island. Evie was our target most of the time." Duso remembers Alex's parents as "good people, all very warm and friendly."

The Dreyfoos camp consisted of a sleeping tent for the children, a living-sleeping room tent for the parents, an outhouse, and a dock. An outdoor kitchen with a stone-sided, wood-fed fireplace and old-fashioned cooktop

DON DUSO

Don Duso lived in the Village of Saranac Lake his whole life. In August 1941, when he was nearly 10 years old, he was returning by motorboat from a visit to Alex at Burnt Island when he witnessed a sailboat capsizing on Lonesome Bay. Albert Einstein was in the water, his feet caught in the rigging. Duso dove under, untangled his feet, and "held him up by his hair until more help arrived," as he later related. "If I had not been nearby, he probably would have drowned." The world-renowned physicist had been a frequent guest to the village since 1936, along with other prominent Jewish-Americans. Such watery rescues were reportedly common, as both sailing and swimming were not among Einstein's talents.

After inheriting his father's Crescent Bay Marina, Duso became a community leader, serving for decades as fire chief. Each year he chaired the Saranac Lake Winter Carnival. Duso and his wife, Sandy, were the sole witnesses at the wedding of Alex and Renate Dreyfoos. Don died in 2010.

resided under a canvas fly. Dreyfoos Sr. built the fireplace himself and cooked most of the family's dinners. He stored perishable ingredients using an inventive refrigeration method, a wooden box in the ground with a cover over it. One of his son's chores was to take his first boat, a 14-foot Thompson rowboat with a small engine, to Crescent Bay for ice to stock the underground cooler.

When he wasn't in the kitchen, the elder Dreyfoos was teaching his son to love and respect the natural world. "My dad was relaxed in the outdoors," says Dreyfoos. "He loved to hike and fish and camp." Dreyfoos Sr. was also an excellent fly fisherman. Father and son would climb into Alex's rowboat around 4:00 in the afternoon, and Alex would row his dad around the island for an hour or so. Without fail, they would return with two or three smallmouth bass for the family's dinner, a guarantee of bounty that has since diminished. Many years later, Dreyfoos preserved, in frames on the walls of his summer home, some of the fly lures his father had tied.

Dreyfoos' mother, Martha, took a more genteel approach to the month-long family holidays. According to his sister, Evelyn Dreyfoos Spelman, "she read a lot, picked berries and flowers, and played board games with us. But mostly, she practiced her cello." A renowned musician, Martha Whittemore Dreyfoos often had only limited attention for her children.

Dreyfoos, in contrast, remembers the Adirondack retreat with fondness. He could run and play with wild abandon, accompanied by Don Duso or friends who would visit from New Rochelle. Here he first developed his love of photography—there has never been a shortage of images to capture in the Adirondacks. Much later, Dreyfoos would realize that part of the beauty of Burnt Island had been the feeling of spaciousness, which only existed because old undergrowth had been cleaned out by a fire in the 1800s; hence its name.

Best of all, young Dreyfoos had his father's undivided attention for a month straight. It was not that his father didn't dote on him the rest of the year, but August belonged especially to the two of them.

Early Family Portrait

The blueprint for Alexander Wallace Dreyfoos Jr.'s life was drafted long before his birth on March 22, 1932. The gene pool of previous generations contributed talents and interests that manifested themselves in his distinctively different parents. According to what is known about Alexander Wallace Dreyfoos Sr., his Jewish ancestors instilled in him a pragmatic approach to business, a strong work ethic, and a love for learning. Martha Bullard Whittemore had a New England Protestant pedigree, was independent, and put her classical music career above all else. By virtue of its cultural differences, this union may appear unorthodox, but history reveals the passions and strengths that would mix compatibly in their son, Alexander Jr. [See the Appendix for a chart of the direct lines in Alex Dreyfoos' ancestry.]

The Swiss Connection

Dreyfoos ancestors are found in the Swiss canton (state) of Aargau as early as 1453, when the family was called "Triefus," which evolved into "Dreifus." From 1622 to 1803, Jews were allowed to live in only two places in Switzerland: Endingen and Lengnau, in Aargau. In the early 19th century, when Switzerland went through a severe economic crisis, the Jews, who were traditionally merchants, were especially devastated. In addition, the so-called "Jewish Law" of 1809 abolished all Jewish rights.

In 1822 the government appointed Wolf Dreifus as rabbi for all of Lengnau. This individual is likely related to another Wolf Dreifus (1785-1840) of Aldingen, in the state of Württemberg, Germany, a direct ancestor of Alexander Dreyfoos.

The Guggenheims were also a prominent family in Aargau. In Lengnau, Simon Guggenheim's wife died in 1836, leaving him with six children. When he later married a widow with seven children, the authorities refused to authorize the marriage. In 1847 Simon, Rachel, and their many children boarded a ship for Philadelphia, a journey of two months. Simon's oldest son, Meyer (1828-1905), amassed a fortune in mining and smelting and became the patriarch of the celebrated Guggenheim dynasty.

Forty-six miles from Aargau, across the German border in Aldingen, there lived another part of the Guggenheim family, which had come from the city of Worms, 38 miles away. Though Worms was prominent in the Protestant Reformation of the early 16th century, its Jewish Quarter remained intact from the 10th century until after Dreyfoos' ancestors had left. Elizabeth S. Plaut, a distant cousin of Alex Dreyfoos, compiled a family history: *The Guggenheim/Wormser Family: A Genealogical 300-Year Memoir* (KTAV Publishing, 1996). Plaut begins her family tree with Isaac Samuel Guggenheim, born in Worms in 1703, who moved to Aldingen. His son Samuel Isaac (1739-1797) changed the family surname to Wormser, after their new neighbors kept referring to them as *die Wormsers*. Several Jewish settlements were located in the Ludwigsburg area that included Aldingen, but little remains except the Jewish burial ground.

Here the Guggenheim-Dreifus connection is clear. Samuel Guggenheim's daughter Zerla married Salomon Pappenheimer, whose daughter Dryka "Theresa" (1819-1908) married Samuel Dreifus (1815-1895). These are the paternal grandparents of Alexander W. Dreyfoos Sr.

Samuel & Theresa Pappenheimer Dreyfoos

Samuel and Theresa were both born in Aldingen; married in Philadelphia, Pennsylvania; died in Cincinnati, Ohio; and buried in the United Hebrew Cemetery there. Samuel immigrated to the United States about 1840, among the first to seek escape from the militarism and Prussian dominance of his homeland. The large wave of emigration from Germany that began at that time continued through the 1850s.

Samuel owned or ran a hardware store in Harrisburg, Pennsylvania, with Theresa's brother Leopold and sent for Theresa in 1843. Their wedding took place at a Jewish temple under the name *Dreyfus*, but shortly after, Samuel changed the spelling to *Dreyfoos*. He and Theresa raised nine children, living in Lancaster until about 1847. After some unclear business problems in Philadelphia, they moved to Cincinnati a few years later. In 1840 about a thousand Jews lived in Cincinnati, the majority of them from Germany like the Dreyfooses.

In 1850, Leopold and Samuel opened another hardware store, Pappenheimer & Dreyfoos, at 36 Pearl Street, Cincinnati. According to an extremely detailed report from what became Dun & Bradstreet, they amassed what was then considered a small fortune. Two notations mention that Dreyfoos and Pappenheimer were Jews; all comments are positive: "excellent character . . . attentive and economical . . . cautious and not about to take risks." In 1867, Samuel was convinced to put his profits into a shoe business with two sons-in-law. The riches were soon lost.

Samuel is described as "a lovable, gentle creature with, however, a far less strong character than his wife, who 'wore the pants' in their home." Theresa Dreyfoos is remembered as "a remarkable woman, a real pioneer." She had the first sewing machine and the first Steinway piano in Cincinnati, apparently purchased during their affluent period. She was community-minded, helping the Bauer sisters from Stuttgart to establish what would grow into the Cincinnati Conservatory. Although he did not play an instrument, Samuel also loved music, like many of his family. In response to a nationwide call by a rabbi in 1863 to aid victims of the Civil War, Theresa joined other Jewish women in founding and sustaining the Cincinnati branch of the Widows and Orphans Asylum Association.

William Wallace & Rachel Jacobs Dreyfoos

The oldest son of Samuel and Theresa, William Wallace Dreyfoos, would become the grandfather of Alexander Dreyfoos Jr. Wally, as he was called, served in the Civil War at the tender age of 16, and was considered a talented violin player and a fine carpenter. In his youth, he represented imports for the family's linen mills in Zurich and Stuttgart. He celebrated his 27th birthday by marrying Rachel Jacobs, born in England, though her parents, Lionel and Caroline Hess Jacobs, came from Amsterdam, Holland.

Alexander Wallace Dreyfoos (Sr.) was Wally and Rachel's first son, born in 1876. It was about this time that this branch of the family appears to have ceased practicing the Jewish faith; no historical records have been found of the family in synagogues near their homes, or of a Bar Mitzvah for Alexander. Wally moved his family to New York to be president of Dee & Dee Embroidery Co., his father's fancy goods business, then back to Philadelphia and on to Chicago—now with five children in tow—evidently for the sake of young Alexander's education. In the end Alexander would have two brothers and three sisters and was particularly fond of his youngest sister, Laura. She would later marry Dr. Walter Jacobs, a member of the Rockefeller Institute for more than 50 years, who aided in the development of cortisone and a drug to combat sleeping sickness. ⚭

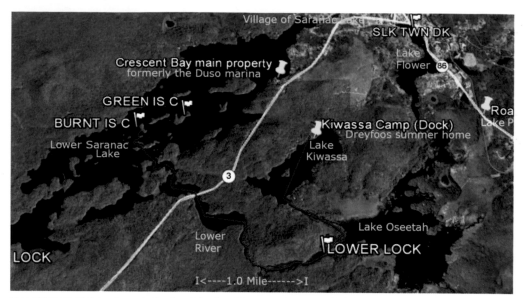

The red line traces the water route Dreyfoos takes from his summer home on Lake Kiwassa, through the locks of Lower Saranac Lake, to visit the family campground of his childhood at Burnt Island. Image © 2014 New York GIS, USDA Farm Service Agency.

Alexander Dreyfoos Sr. sitting in the family's 16-foot Lyman in the 1940s.

Dreyfoos with his mother and sister, Evelyn, camping at Burnt Island about 1940.

The Dreyfoos family's Burnt Island campsite showing the main tent, 1930s.

The Dreyfoos family's cook station on Burnt Island.

Alexander Dreyfoos Sr., catching dinner in the 1920s.

Dreyfoos at the wheel of the family's 16-foot Lyman, at Burnt Island about 1940.

Harry Duso, who took care of the Dreyfoos family's needs for their Burnt Island campsite.

Lionel Jacobs, great-grandfather to Alex Dreyfoos, by Apeda Studios, 1906.

Rachel Jacobs Dreyfoos, grandmother to Alex Dreyfoos.

William Wallace Dreyfoos, grandfather to Alex Dreyfoos.

A family photo in what appear to be nightclothes, taken by Alexander Dreyfoos Sr. between 1918 and 1930, including his mother (center, seated), four of his siblings, and one of their husbands.

CHAPTER 2

Alexander and Martha Whittemore Dreyfoos

(left to right) Evelyn, "Don," Martha, and Alex, posing for family Christmas card, 1946.

The Photographer

In 1891 Alexander W. Dreyfoos Sr. graduated from the Sulzer Street School in Chicago, then completed a two-year course at the Chicago Manual Training School, where the director called his behavior "inapproachable." The well-rounded academic curriculum was augmented with hundreds of hours of mechanical and free hand drawing, woodwork, and time in the foundry and forge. This seems a natural progression, considering all the time his father had spent in the basement of their home teaching him how to use tools—a gift that he would also pass on to his own son, Alexander Jr. He briefly worked for Cowles & Ohrenstein, Architects in Chicago, who were sorry to lose his quality work, finding him "reliable, honorable, and ambitious."

Building on his structured education, Alexander taught himself photography. He tried following in his father's footsteps, selling lace and embroideries

APEDA

Following is the history of Apeda during the years of ownership by Alexander Dreyfoos Sr., as written by David Shields of the University of South Carolina:

Location: 33 W. 34th St.; 102-104 W. 38th St.; 212-216 W. 48th St. . . . Apeda was a diversified corporate studio located in New York City and organized in 1906 by partners Alexander W. Dreyfoos and Henry Obstfield. From its organization it pursued two business strategies: shooting original portraiture and reproducing uncopyrighted images by other photographers of newsworthy scenes or celebrities under its own trade name. Dreyfoos was the head photographer and to him goes credit for developing sports portraiture beyond baseball and boxing imagery into a wide-ranging field analogous to theatrical portraiture in its treatment and promotion. . . .

Apeda would buy up the entire production archive of photographers who had business difficulties or were moving to other parts of the country. . . . Dreyfoos remained head photographer, lensing sittings himself, and overseeing a small staff of event photographers and college yearbook portraitists. During the mid-1930s and 1940s, Apeda left off performing arts work, turning to advertising imagery, industrial photography, High School class portraiture [including his son's New Rochelle High School], and Armed Services portraiture. . . .

The several photographers who contracted for work with Apeda over the years were conversant in very contemporary portrait styles, often imitating [signature] features of the name photographers of the day. If there was any discernible ability characteristic of the company's photography, it was the ability to portray the whole body of the subject. While whole body portraiture was normal in sports and dance photography, it grew infrequent in 1920s theatrical portraiture, whole body shots being associated with production stills. Apeda photographers bucked the trend, producing whole body non-production portraiture after it went out of fashion in Manhattan.

in the United States, but he soon tired of the traveling life. In 1906, he opened a one-room photographic studio on the top floor of a small building at the corner of 55th Street and Sixth Avenue, New York. He called this business "Apeda," an acronym for Art/Photography/Etchings/Drawings and Architecture. (Later he would also use an acronym to name the family boat.)

After a year in the business, Alexander Sr. realized he had to do something unique to be really successful. He was inspired by seeing thousands of photographic postcards imported from Germany by a wholesaler client, and considered how he might provide that service locally. He reasoned that if he could buy photographic paper at deeply discounted prices and devise a method to print thousands of them each day, he would have a profitable commercial art and advertising business. He found a way to purchase the supplies inexpensively from the Haloid Photographic Company in Rochester, New York. (Haloid became Haloid Xerox in 1958, and then just Xerox in 1961.) Within a week, the entrepreneur had $12,000 worth of orders on his books.

The senior Dreyfoos conceived ways to produce photographs in great quantities. (See sidebar, page 25.) He invented, built, and patented a mass production high-speed semiautomatic contact printer and a large photographic drying machine. He created production lines for airbrushing, finishing, mounting, and packaging photos.

In 1913, White Studios obtained an injunction to restrain Apeda from reproducing photos taken by White that actors brought to Apeda to copy. After three years, an appellate court decided unanimously that the injunction could not hold. This landmark case declared that, in the absence of a copyright, the customer/sitter who employed a photographer also owned the resulting product.

In 1928, the company occupied five floors of the Apeda Building west of Times Square on West 48th Street, and employed nearly a hundred people. Employees both took the photos and processed them. The business produced more than a quarter of a million prints monthly.

Dreyfoos' methods enabled him to profit from the new moving picture industry, which was highly prosperous with silent films in the 1920s. Starting in 1927, when movie attendance was $60 million, it cashed in on the novelty of the new "talkies," which drove attendance to $110 million in the next two years.

The 1930s became the Golden Age of Movies, with the production of blockbuster musicals, horror, and gangster films. Then the Great Depression triggered by the crash of 1929 cooled the fever somewhat, but Americans sorely needed an escape and theaters went to great lengths to draw them in. The film industry did not suffer as badly as many sectors of the economy, but total company profits of $54.5 million in 1929 gave way to losses of $55.7 million in 1932. The most notable films came from the Big Five studios that owned theater chains; they felt the crash because of their investments. Of the five, only Metro-Goldwyn-Mayer (MGM) continued to make a profit, albeit smaller: $1.5 million in 1930 compared to $4.3 million in 1931. MGM was the top studio from 1931 to 1941 and billed itself as having "more stars than there are in heaven," referring to its A-list movie stars under contract.

Fortunately for Dreyfoos, it was MGM with whom he and his then partner, Irving W. Goldfield, held a contract. Besides decorating the display cases outside of theaters and in their lobbies with photos of film stars, Apeda created batches of copies for the performers to supply to their fan clubs.

By 1934, box-office receipts had begun to rebound. In 1940, an estimated 42 percent to 46 percent of Americans saw a movie weekly. In 1946, after World War II, the figure was 64 percent.

The prosperity of the film industry that was a large part of Apeda's business through the '30s and '40s eventually met its demise. In the late 1940s, the number of traditional movie theaters declined, while drive-ins increased. But the greatest and permanent effect was from the arrival of television.

Dreyfoos' father returned to other types of portraiture, as well as developing new ideas. He aspired to modify Kodak's Wash-Off Relief (later renamed the Dye Transfer process) to make consistently high quality color photographs in large quantities, so he could supplement or replace the part of his business that required airbrushing. Wash-Off Relief could produce beautiful results with the help of a skilled technician, but because there were so many variables in the process, there was no guarantee of ever getting two pictures that looked the same. The research project eventually became prohibitively expensive, and Dreyfoos put it aside.

When Apeda was young, in 1909, Alexander had married Ella Rosina Seligsberg, a librarian from Baltimore, Maryland. They adopted a daughter, Ethel, who they raised in Mount Vernon, Westchester County, outside New York City. Eventually the family moved into Manhattan to be near Alex's business. Daughter Ethel married Lewis Leo in 1931, and graduated from Wellesley College the following spring.

The 1930 US Census also lists in this household a son named Alexander Dreyfoos, age 18, born in New York State. This mysterious son is not mentioned in his supposed mother's (Ella's) obituary; she died that December. In fact, no further identification of this Alexander is known.

ALEXANDER W. DREYFOOS SR. PATENTS

The senior Dreyfoos passed to his son a strong belief in the role of inventiveness as an impetus to progress in business and industry. He modeled his beliefs, placing importance on precision design and patent registration as required steps in securing economic rights to one's ideas.

In Patent 1,051,567 for a "Photographic Printing Apparatus" issued on January 28, 1913, the elder Dreyfoos wrote that "in printing multiple copies from a (black and white) negative . . . it is necessary, in order that the prints be uniform and alike in appearance, that the printing exposure, the distribution and the intensity of the light, be substantially the same for each copy printed." A similar objective for an advanced photographic color device would be echoed in a patent issued to his son 50 years later.

The patented "apparatus" was used at Dreyfoos' Apeda studios in New York, primarily to turn out multiple black and white photographic prints of actors and actresses used in advertising displays at local theatres. Dreyfoos was clearly pleased with the results his devices provided, writing in one patent description: "By means of the nicety of regulation and the standardization afforded by my invention, I am enabled to accomplish the objects specified, as well as others not hereinbefore enumerated."

Over time, Dreyfoos' father added more equipment to his operation and secured several more patents:

Patent 1,099,694 (dated 1914) improved the Photographic Printing Machine for "automatically producing photographic prints in large quantities."

Patent 1,118,640 (dated 1914) was for a Vignetter, a device that could be fitted to the front of a camera to obtain a variety of visual effects by arranging the moveable Vignetter parts in front of the lens.

Patent 1,385,365 (dated 1921) secured the rights to a Photographic Drying-Machine, which could run continuously—drying, burnishing, and giving a glossy finish to large quantities of prints.

Like his father, Wally, another of the entrepreneur's passions was music. He was an amateur cellist and enjoyed playing chamber music with various non-professional groups, so he shared interests with the musicians who came to Apeda to be photographed. One in particular would change his life permanently.

The Whittemore Line

While both Alexander and Martha Whittemore Dreyfoos came from families to be proud of, it was Martha who remained more conscious of her roots. Her ancestor Thomas Whittemore migrated from Hitchin, in the county of Hertfordshire, England, to Charlestown (the nucleus of Boston), Massachusetts, in 1642, shortly after it was settled. Seven generations of Whittemores followed Thomas to America before one of his namesakes, Martha Whittemore's great-grandfather Thomas, was born in Cambridge in 1800. This well known Universalist minister was a prolific writer and musician who played the violincello (successor to the viola da gamba). Whittemore represented Cambridge in the legislature and was president of the Vermont and Massachusetts Railroad and the Cambridge Bank. In 1858, three years before he died, he was honored with a doctorate in divinity by Tufts University.

Thus began a line of overachievers. This included Thomas Whittemore's grandson Charles Alexander Whittemore, who would become Dreyfoos' grandfather. He was educated at Harvard (A.B., 1885) and Harvard Law School (1888). On graduation, he married Evelyn Cutting Bullard, the daughter of the president of the East Cambridge Savings Bank and a descendant of an impressive line of colonial New Englanders. This Evelyn Bullard Whittemore was admitted into the National Society of the Daughters of the American Revolution in 1890, by virtue of her descent from Samuel Bullard, John Cutting, and Isaac Loker, for their material aid to the cause of American independence during the Revolutionary War. Evelyn was artistic, and inspired a love for art history, antiques, and music in her daughters: Elsie, Elinor, and Martha (b. 1898), who would become Alex Dreyfoos' mother. Dreyfoos would one day apply for and receive membership in the National Society, Sons of the American Revolution.

The Musician

Martha Whittemore graduated from the Child-Garden Music School at age 12, when she performed her first solo. Her cello instruction began with Miss Laura Webster at the school of Miss Lillian Shattuck, who had been a celebrated violinist in her youth, in the Pierce Building, Copley Square, Boston. She was also educated at Miss Webster's School on Appian Way in Cambridge, on a site later occupied by Radcliffe College. The poet e. e. cummings also attended Miss

Webster's in 1902-1903, and his biographer wrote: "Classes began with the Lord's Prayer and a reading from the Bible (as required by Massachusetts law). [They] were conducted in a very informal way and the emphasis was on the three R's with a lot of creative play in arts and crafts."

Martha and her elder sister Elinor, a talented violinist, performed at social and charitable events throughout New England. In 1914, the two began billing themselves as the Whittemore Trio, enlisting various musicians as their third, usually a pianist such as Arge Gerry or Amee List.

Beginning with her childhood recital, Martha gathered a collection of clippings of her performances, and recorded each in her diary, phrasing the duo's work much like social announcements for young ladies of good breeding at that time: "The Misses Elinor Whittemore, violinist, and her sister Miss Martha, 'cellist, assisted at a vesper service" and "The Misses Whittemore are the talented daughters of Mr. and Mrs. C. A. Whittemore, formerly of Lexington."

By 1917, the Whittemore Trio was represented by the Redpath Lyceum Bureau, a national booking service, and Martha no longer needed to invent her own accolades. Redpath described the group as

> . . . a Boston instrumental trio of note, and one of the most successful of the younger entertainers . . . recognized by the critics and leading musicians of Boston as one of the thoroughly artistic musical organizations of that city. The artists of the Whittemore Trio are not only musicians of high order but possess the personality which makes their concert a success in every detail.

Arthur Foote, known as one of the "Boston Six" composers, wrote to the young ladies: "There is nothing that a composer can feel more deeply than that others should like his work to put the amount of interest and care into its performance that you all did."

Martha's family rented a Boston apartment in 1920, possibly a floor of a three-story home. Her father practiced law, Elsie worked as a Christian Science obstetric nurse, and Elinor and Martha were professional musicians. Although Martha's parents took in a boarder, presumably for income, they were able to travel to England, France, and Italy on the SS *France*.

Martha studied with several celebrated cellists, including Alfred Wallenstein in New York and the Portuguese Madam Guilhermina Suggia (second wife of her idol, Pablo Casals) in London. At concerts she played not only the cello (then known as the 'cello, an abbreviation of its full name, violin-cello) but also the viola da gamba, an ancient six-stringed instrument that preceded the cello and was the chosen instrument of her great-grandfather Thomas Whittemore. Fliers describe Martha's 17th-century viola da gamba, made by luthier Richard Meares of London, which she purchased from W. E. Hill & Sons of London in 1931. From the time she married Alexander Dreyfoos, Martha also performed with his cello, which was said to have been made in 1610 by Maggini of Brecia, Italy.

A handsome young woman with distinctive flaming red hair, Martha dressed in 16th- and 17th-century costumes to complement her instruments. She performed in Carnegie Hall, Town Hall, Symphony Hall, and the Metropolitan Museum in New York, and in the Museum of Fine Arts in Boston, but Europe was where she longed to be.

Martha's sister Elinor, five years the elder, paved the way, spending several summers with Miss Lillian Shattuck in England and Brittany. In 1924 Martha finally joined them, performing regularly there while studying strings. When it came time to return home that October, Martha remained behind—for three glamorous years. Her mementoes include photographs of famed cellist Paul Bazelaire, with whom she played in Paris, signed to Martha "with affection." Her 1926 diary, written in French, details her classes with Armenian cellist Diran Alexanian, and then with Bazelaire. This instruction was "to get ready for Casals," she wrote to her sister Elsie, as Martha's dream was to study with the "king of violin-cellists."

Martha documented many highlights of her European sojourn through correspondence home, such as a party she and Elinor attended in Madrid, hosted by the King and Queen of Spain. In another epistle, she recounted a tale about stopping off at Cartier's in Paris with General T. Coleman DuPont, then in his 60s. He purchased a diamond watch for Martha and another to take to her sister, Elsie. For Elinor, he purchased a sapphire brooch.

Martha would later tell her daughter, Evelyn, "You'd be amazed at what I did" while living abroad. Despite her exciting life, however, she had difficulty supporting herself solely from her cello performances. She supplemented her musical income by taking tourists shopping, earning a percentage of what they purchased. When her visa ran out in 1927, she reluctantly returned home.

Martha continued to correspond—in French—with friends she had made in Europe. Her Russian friend Tobotchka, who had toured Spain with her in 1925-1926, wrote Martha from the Café La Perla in Paris in November 1929 to bring her up to date on how her musical friends were faring. She reminded Martha that they had all pledged to commit themselves to a life of music and freedom—but suggested that if they were going to be realistic, they might need to marry.

When Martha's father died in 1930, the family lost whatever affluence they may have had. Her mother and sister Elsie, still a nurse, did without servants, and took in a middle-aged female boarder. Martha was a boarder herself, residing in New York with another unmarried woman and employed as a cello instructor.

High Contrast Gene Pool

At some point Martha Whittemore visited the Apeda studio of Alexander Dreyfoos, in all likelihood to sit for promotional photographs. A photo of Pablo Casals from 1927, inscribed to her "with kind regards," may have been gifted in Europe, although it bears the Apeda mark. Martha met Alexander's wife, Ella, there, before Ella died of cancer just before Christmas 1930. Seeing the Great Depression under way, Martha would have appreciated that Alexander not only valued good music, but also that he owned a successful business. Dreyfoos, never having set foot outside the United States, was smitten with this glamorous, worldly musical artist. Just six months after Ella's death, the widowed husband married Martha Whittemore.

Interfaith marriage was uncommon in the US at the time, and would remain so until after World War II. In 1930 when a Protestant married, 78 percent of the time it was to another Protestant, and Jews married other Jews 97 percent of the time. Still, religion was not a high priority in Americans' lives from the 1920s until the late 1930s. Though Martha was proud of her lineage, her choice of husband had little relevance to the Jewish practices of his ancestors.

Ten months after his second wedding, when Dreyfoos was 56, his first and only son was born: Alexander Wallace Dreyfoos Jr. When Martha Dreyfoos, 34, delivered this healthy baby boy, her husband was ecstatic. His first wife would only agree to adopt a girl, and he had longed for a son ever since. A baby sister, Evelyn Whittemore Dreyfoos, would arrive a year and a half later. Evelyn says her father could never do enough for Martha. "He had this beautiful wife with flashing red hair, 22 years younger than him, who always took center stage. He put her on a pedestal and promoted her career."

The younger Alexander was destined to inherit his love of music from both sides of the family. His inventiveness, entrepreneurial sense, and photographic talent are Dreyfoos traits. The Whittemore bloodline of New England would give him a worldview and fuel his desire to experience life at its fullest.

Appearances

During the earliest years of their children's lives, Martha and Alexander Dreyfoos raised Alex and Evelyn in a Manhattan apartment, close to the music and theater world to which both of the parents had a strong connection. Dreyfoos has few memories of that period. His picture of family life comes into sharper focus after the family moved to Westchester County, New York, in 1937, about the time Dreyfoos started attending Henry Barnard Public Elementary School, where he stayed through seventh grade.

Their house at 19 Wildwood Circle straddled the boundary between Larchmont and New Rochelle. "Everybody thought we were rich," he muses, "because the house was so big. The truth of the matter was that my dad purchased it in the depth of the Depression, so he was able to get an incredible deal. Dad made a relatively good living with the movie industry during the '30s and '40s, but we were never wealthy." In fact, as his business declined after World War II, Dreyfoos' father tried to maintain his family's living standard and provide them with the pleasures of those successful years.

The Dreyfooses were a typical suburban family that celebrated holidays like Easter and Christmas as social occasions. The family placed no value on religious rituals, focusing instead on ethical and moral behavior as requirements for participation in society. Dreyfoos recalls, "It was about gift-giving, Santa Claus, stockings, decorations, and holiday guests. There was no religious discussion in my childhood home. The little I learned about Judaism as a child was from a Jewish classmate. I also had a favorite playmate who was Catholic. My mother sent me to Sunday school at the Christian Science and Presbyterian churches. I enjoyed it, but nothing I learned there about religion stayed with me."

The definition of being Jewish has traditionally been maternal; a child is a Jew if his or her mother is a Jew. In 1983 the Jewish Reform movement officially broadened that definition to include either parent, but only if the child was raised with a Jewish identity. Dreyfoos was not.

Based on the extensive photo documentation by his father, Dreyfoos appears to have led an idyllic childhood. However, Dreyfoos points to a picture taken for the family's annual sitting during the Christmas season. Under the glare of studio floodlights, their beloved Irish setter, Don, is curled up in the foreground of a beautifully appointed room. Behind the dog, Dreyfoos' mother poses at the piano as if she is accompanying her children, though she did not play this instrument. Evelyn draws her bow across the violin, and her brother holds the cello. "My mother *wanted* me to play the cello," he says, "but I totally rejected both the cello and the piano, though I loved the music they made. I had too many other interests." While Evelyn did not possess the same interests as her mother, she was conscientious musically and continued to play the violin throughout her life. She concedes that she and the dog were the only two genuine articles in that photograph in terms of the roles they played. Appearances were critical to her mother, who, Evelyn says, liked to put on airs. "I remember her asking us if we had brushed our teeth—in French," she laughs.

Dreyfoos has vivid memories of his mother leaving the family at home as she and her friend Blanche Winograd went off in their period costumes to play their ancient instruments. Martha performed on the viola da gamba, with Winograd accompanying her on the harpsichord. Martha was on the faculty locally at Wolfe Conservatory, but also spent time away from home to teach at Turtle Bay Music School and Tally-Ho Music Camp.

While Martha devoted minimal time to her family, they were in the capable hands of a German housekeeper, Greta Gerstman, who lived in the Dreyfoos home with her husband, John, until Dreyfoos' father sent them away at the start of World War II. Evelyn speculates that her father believed it would not be wise to have Germans living under their roof during that time.

Even when Martha was at home, her husband did most of the cooking when there was no domestic help. Evelyn remembers how her grandmother

Apeda Studio INC.

PHOTOGRAPHERS

APEDA BUILDING

212-214-216 WEST 48TH STREET

PHONE BRYANT 1455-1456-9625

NEW YORK

Letterhead for the business of Alexander Dreyfoos Sr.

An early imbibition print, an example of experimentation with the dye transfer process by Alexander Dreyfoos Sr.

A photo produced by Apeda Studios of actress Mae West, promoting her 1921 revue, *Whirl of the Town*.

Alexander Dreyfoos Sr. as his son remembers him most.

Photo by Alex Dreyfoos Sr. of Fifth Avenue, New York, during World War I, with the spires of St. Patrick's Cathedral in the distance.

Alexander Dreyfoos Sr. playing cello.

A movie house of the 1930s showing the 8-inch-by-10-inch marquee photographs Alexander Dreyfoos Sr. had invented a way to produce inexpensively.

One of Dreyfoos' favorite photos taken by his father, of the family's Irish setter, Don, in 1937.

Ella Dreyfoos, the first wife of Alexander Dreyfoos Sr.

Ethel Dreyfoos, adopted daughter of Ella and Alexander Dreyfoos Sr.

Thomas Whittemore, great-great-grandfather to Alex Dreyfoos.

Charles Alexander Whittemore, grandfather to Alex Dreyfoos.

Martha Whittemore, from a brochure by the Redpath Lyceum Bureau, which represented the Whittemore Trio.

Playing on her
Viola da Gamba
a beautiful
early english instrument.
Its tone plaintive and
intriguing.

She uses the old style of
technique
and she wears the
quaint costume
of the period.

Her violoncello
is one of
unsurpassed
tonal quality
and brilliance.
It is the
work of
Maggini
of Brecio
about 1610.

From a brochure by Apeda Studios.

Cellist Pablo Casals, writing to one of his biggest admirers "with kind regard" in 1927, well before Martha married Alexander.

MARTHA WHITTEMORE

AFTER four years in Europe, with steadily increasing prestige as a concert artist, Martha Whittemore returns to her native America for a new series of recitals and with a mature command of her instrument. This young violoncellist, with the advantages of training under such masters as Madame Suggia, Alexanian and the great Casals himself, has already won real success both as soloist and ensemble player. She has played in Europe and America with many of the most noted artists of both continents.

Miss Whittemore's art is characterized by a strong yet natural individuality, with an unusual beauty of tone added to a fine, straight-forward and unpretentious musicianship. She is becoming more and more widely known and is undoubtedly making her place among the leading violoncellists of the country. American audiences are sure to welcome her contributions to the musical life of her country and her return will no doubt arouse much interest.

Press Comments

NEW YORK GLOBE—Aeolian Hall was packed when Martha Whittemore played. She was heard in the Variations Symphonique by Boellmann, which she rendered with unusual skill, and lived up to the reputation she has earned.

NEW YORK SUN—Over two thousand people heard Martha Whittemore last evening playing the Saint-Saens concerto. She played with fine musicianship, and her tone was large and beautiful.

NEW YORK GLOBE—Martha Whittemore proved to be an instrumentalist of exceptional ability. She well deserved the great applause which rewarded her efforts.

MUSICAL LEADER, CHICAGO—Heard Martha Whittemore, a delightful young violoncellist, on Saturday. After four years abroad she has come back with lovely artistry.

BOSTON EVENING TRANSCRIPT—One of the leading women violoncellists of the country.

ROCHESTER POST EXPRESS—Martha Whittemore is a violoncellist of undoubted artistic attainments, fine interpretative ability, and has something individual to give to her hearers.

LEWISTON DAILY SUN (MAINE)—A violoncellist of sure touch and pleasing personality. Her tone was very pure and her phrasing delightful.

HARTFORD DAILY TIMES—Martha Whittemore plays with assurance and an exceptionally beautiful tone. Her technical resources are ample.

ANGLO BELGIAN TIMES (BRUSSELS)—The American ambassador entertained at the embassy to afford the opportunity of hearing Martha Whittemore. Undoubtedly every artist should put a certain amount of personality into all works and in last evening's recital it was this personality which enhanced the program. Miss Whittemore showed the gifts of a true born artist.

LE MONDE MUSICALE (PARIS)—The Rachmaninoff sonata was played with fine spirit and perfect understanding by the Misses Roberts and Whittemore.

NEW YORK HERALD (PARIS EDITION)—Of unusual interest to music lovers was the concert by Martha Whittemore, the American violoncellist, well known to Paris audiences.

CHICAGO TRIBUNE (PARIS EDITION)—An enthusiastic audience greeted Martha Whittemore at her concert last evening. She was in fine form and made a most pleasing impression.

EL PUEBLO GALLEGO (VIGO, SPAIN)—Martha Whittemore is a fine musician, with flawless technique and beautiful tone. In the Lalo concerto she showed a remarkable understanding of melodic and rythmic form.

A short bio of Martha Whittemore and comments on her performances from critics in the United States and abroad.

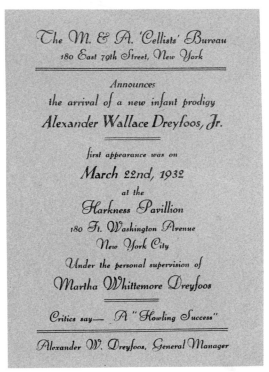

The M. & A. 'Cellists' Bureau
180 East 79th Street, New York

Announces
the arrival of a new infant prodigy

Alexander Wallace Dreyfoos, Jr.

first appearance was on

March 22nd, 1932

at the

Harkness Pavillion

180 Ft. Washington Avenue
New York City

Under the personal supervision of

Martha Whittemore Dreyfoos

Critics say— A "Howling Success"

Alexander W. Dreyfoos, General Manager

Announcement of Dreyfoos' birth.

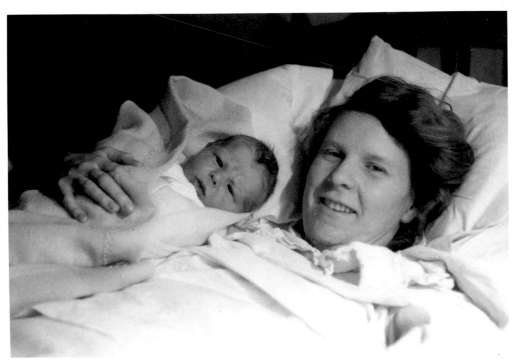

Dreyfoos, 36 hours old in 1932, with his mother.

Martha's cello in the Dreyfoos' New York City apartment, 1930s.

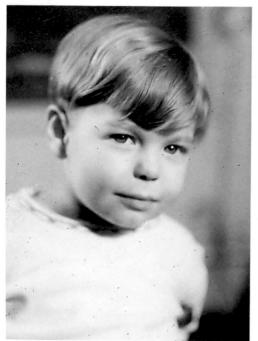
Young Alex Dreyfoos in 1935.

Evelyn and Alex Dreyfoos, in 1936 at Rye, New York.

The Dreyfoos home, 19 Wildwood Circle, New Rochelle, New York.

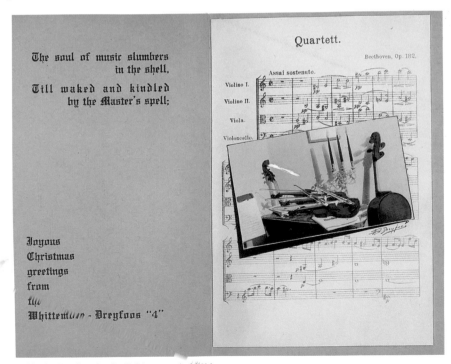

The soul of music slumbers
in the shell,
Till waked and kindled
by the Master's spell;

Quartett.

Beethoven, Op. 182.

Assai sostenuto.

Violino I.

Violino II.

Viola.

Violoncello.

Joyous
Christmas
greetings
from
the
Whittemore - Dreyfoos "4"

Inside the Dreyfoos family Christmas card of 1940.

43

Evelyn and Alex Dreyfoos, 1945.

PACK 1

New Rochelle, N.Y.

GRAND OUTING
Saturday, February 20, 1943

Trip to New York — see and hear
Broadcast of "GAME PARADE"
Lunch   ---   Then a Surprise

INSTRUCTIONS

1. Wear Cub Uniform
2. Meet at Larchmont Station-9.15 A.M.
          New Rochelle " 9.20 A.M.
 - Den Dads will be there.
3. Parents release must be at School
   Office for Mrs. Serphos by Thursday
   February 18th.
4. You will need $1.00 for expenses;
   give it to a Den Dad at station.
5. Parent should let us know whether
   they will meet their boy at station
   or whether he will go home by himself. Trains arrive at:
          New Rochelle Station-4.01 P.M.
          Larchmont   "   4.06 P.M.

                    A. W. Dreyfoos
Telephone: Cub Master
New Rochelle 6-4199

Notice of a Cub Scout outing, prepared by Dreyfoos' father.

Three generations: (front) Dreyfoos' aunt Elsie Whittemore, grandmother Evelyn Cutting Bullard Whittemore, and mother; (rear) Dreyfoos and sister Evelyn, on her 16th birthday, in 1949.

Dreyfoos (first row, far right) with his Boy Scout troop.

Dreyfoos shows his support of the Boy Scouts of America in Palm Beach County. The poster close-ups are of his Scout days. Photo by Ron Oats.

CHAPTER 3

Developing

(left to right) Phil Brooks, secretary, and Dreyfoos, president,
presiding over an SAE chapter meeting in 1954.

Pursuing a Prophecy

Alexander Sr. had lofty aspirations for his son, if not for his daughter. He assured Alex Jr. that someday he would attend the Massachusetts Institute of Technology. "Dad also told all of his friends," Dreyfoos remembers somewhat sheepishly. "He liked to show me off." Relentlessly preparing his son for the prestigious institution, the elder Dreyfoos encouraged him to take on technical challenges. Dreyfoos would pick out projects in electronics magazines, and his father would purchase the required parts at Harvey Radio (a forerunner to Radio Shack), which he passed on his workday commute between his studio and Grand Central Terminal. Other parts, Dreyfoos and his friend Graham McGill scavenged from scrap dealers on Canal Street in Manhattan.

"This approach preceded the ready-to-assemble Heath Kits," explains Dreyfoos. "In 1947, at 15, I built a TransVision TV from a pre-packaged kit.

In fact, it was the first TV set in the whole neighborhood. All our neighbors showed up to watch it!"

In addition to building electronic devices, while still in high school, Dreyfoos earned an amateur radio license. With his father's help, Dreyfoos was aiming himself toward an MIT education.

According to his high school guidance counselor, however, he had forgotten something important. "At our first meeting, I went waltzing into her office to talk about my plans after high school. 'I'm going to MIT,' I told her confidently. She looked at my grades, laughed, and said, 'Oh no, you're not. Not with these grades.' I always had dozens of hobbies and projects in progress, so I suppose I hadn't paid enough attention to my high school work. I received mediocre grades." Fortunately, it was not too late for Dreyfoos to raise his average.

Dreyfoos also made time for lasting friendships, such as with Graham McGill, whose mother was a beloved English teacher at New Rochelle High School. Dreyfoos met McGill there in the eighth grade and saw him regularly until McGill died in 2011. Earlier he shared some remembrances: "We didn't have time to think about our home lives in those days. We were too busy growing up. We were at the age where the world is so interesting to you that you get involved in all kinds of things. We both loved aviation. Alex was into chemistry, radio, and electronics, and once he could drive, we went all over the place." The young Dreyfoos was also an excellent athlete, and he and McGill competed on the high school swim team. "In sprint races, I could wax his butt, as we used to say," recollects McGill. "But in distance races, like across the lake, I didn't stand a chance against him."

Sometimes their swimming ability helped during adventures, like the night they went skinny-dipping in the Kensico Reservoir, which was prohibited. A ranger spotted them and demanded that they come to shore. Instead, they swam further into the darkness. Eventually they reached a small island, where they stretched their naked bodies out on smooth boulders and studied the constellations overhead. During their swim in the inky darkness, they had lost their bearings and at first weren't sure what direction to swim in to find their clothes, but Dreyfoos successfully charted the course of their return swim by studying the stars. McGill says, "This guy was a navigator before he ever owned a sextant."

Though Evelyn Dreyfoos cherished Alex, she also remembers him as that mischievous older brother who "sometimes let his electronic urges get the better of him." He amused himself by using electronics to literally "bug" his sister, such as hiding a microphone at their front door to eavesdrop when dates kissed her goodnight. Perhaps his most egregious prank was during a pajama party she hosted for her girlfriends in the family's living room. Evelyn says she warned everybody that her brother might try to bug them. "We checked everywhere and could not find any suspicious wires. Unbeknownst to us, Alex had run a wire from his upstairs room down the outside of the house and inside the living room window behind a curtain." He also invited a bunch of friends to his room to share in the eavesdropping. At some point the high jinks were discovered, but only after the young women had confided in each other about their teenage heartthrobs.

Even with all his interests, as many parents can imagine, Dreyfoos eventually became aware of "the fumes"—gasoline and perfume. When he turned 15, his father gave him the family's 8-year-old blue 1939 Oldsmobile. The deal was that Dreyfoos would have to rebuild the old car's engine and repair its brakes before he could drive it. His goal was to complete the work by the time he turned 16 and got his driver's license. After school, Dreyfoos rode a city bus that he disembarked at an Amoco service station on the Old Boston Post Road (US Route 1), half a mile from his home. "A mechanic there took me under his wing and, through a series of conversations, explained how to do a valve job, ring job, brake job, and even a full replacement of engine bearings. I learned how to do a tune-up, install an ignition system, rebuild a carburetor—truly everything that makes a car work!"

His efforts reaped great rewards for many, according to Graham McGill. "With that car, Alex became the *de facto* taxi service for his wide circle of high school friends, which, fortunately, included me. I got well acquainted with his back seat on many double dates," chuckles McGill. He says Dreyfoos dated several girls, but one that stands out in his mind was Roddy McDowell. "She was the most gorgeous gal in the high school. She had black hair and blue eyes and an 'ooh-la-la' figure. She was something." During the summer of his junior year, while Dreyfoos was in the Adirondacks with his family, he met and was smitten with Ann Carlough. She was a year older and soon went off to Simmons College.

Dating was made easier for both Dreyfoos and McGill as members of their high school's top fraternity, Tau Pi. "Jocks were first choice to get accepted, but Graham and I were on the swim team, at least. I'm sure my car played a role for me, and the popularity of Graham's mother for him." Looking back, Dreyfoos feels the organization provided good leadership and social networking training.

Although Tau Pi had no African American members, growing up in the north at that time, racial hostility was not prevalent in Dreyfoos' world. The first black person that Dreyfoos knew well was at New Rochelle High School. Jesse Arnelle was a talented athlete who later achieved greatness in college and pro basketball, before becoming a high-profile attorney and a board member for several major corporations. This relationship of mutual respect created a positive foundation for Dreyfoos' attitude toward minorities.

While Dreyfoos enjoyed his peers, he remained close to his father. Shortly after the end of World War II, when Dreyfoos was 14, his father had purchased a 26-foot Steelcraft cabin cruiser and named it *EVALMA*, an anagram for Evelyn, Alex, and Martha. He joined the Horseshoe Harbor Yacht Club in Larchmont and kept the boat there. Dreyfoos reflects, "Our family spent a lot of time on the *EVALMA* until Dad sold it, just before my senior year in high school."

In high school, Dreyfoos put his technological know-how to work to make extra cash. He ran the sound and light board backstage at the New Rochelle High School auditorium for assemblies and theatrical performances, and served as the deejay at school dances, using his own homebuilt audio equipment. This led to outside paid jobs as a deejay. He also started a car radio repair business, which he advertised by distributing promotional cards his father printed for him. His first project, quite naturally, was his 1939 Oldsmobile.

Towards the end of Dreyfoos' senior year, in May 1950, his mother joined a charter flight to France to attend the naissance of Pablo Casals' Prades Festival, now known as the Pablo Casals Festival. After a decade during which Casals had refused to play in public, the audience was in joyous tears. Martha Dreyfoos heard nearly all of the concerts of the festival before her thrills were ended by a cablegram. Back home, her husband had had what he thought was a heart attack, though the doctor called it an anxiety attack. Nonetheless, that summer the elder Dreyfoos, then 74, was not up to setting up the Burnt Island camp for the family's annual retreat. Instead,

PLUMMETING OVER THE FALLS

After graduating from high school, Graham McGill attended Wesleyan University, but got restless and left to join the US Air Force, serving as a fighter pilot during the Korean War. A skilled journalist, he went on to become an editor at the Schenectady Gazette. *He has written two books and numerous articles, among them this rollicking adventure story about Dreyfoos and himself that appeared in the August 2008 issue of* Adirondack Life *magazine.*

The two high school juniors rented a canoe in the Adirondacks with the goal of taking it from Long Lake to Lower Saranac by way of the Raquette River. On the Raquette, they encountered a sign that informed them they would have to portage their canoe 1.3 miles around the waterfalls that were just ahead of them. Seeing that the portage route, which was saturated from recent rains, had become "boot-sucking slop," the young men considered whether they might be able to go further along the river before hauling out to avoid the falls.

McGill wrote, "[T]he river was slow and wide and we couldn't see or hear a waterfall. I wondered if we might just paddle on a little ways, pull over when we heard the falls, shorten the trek, and ease the workload.

"'Hey, Alex, whaddya say we see how far we can go on this flat water before we start carrying? Maybe we can stop above the falls and start our portage from there. Might make this grind a lot easier.'"

Before long the two were sucked into the unrelenting current from the falls with steep vertical walls of stone on both sides. There was no way out, according to McGill's narrative: "Our exertions became furious. Swinging our paddles from one side and the other, trying to avoid boulders, we shifted into overdrive, but the Raquette took over, assumed control, shoved us, slammed into us, hurtled us to the left and the right. Against its awesome power, we seemed irrelevant. Our craft became a speck, a metallic fleck of flotsam. Suddenly, we rounded a bend and the drop-off was upon us. Our bow extended beyond it, out into space in apparent defiance of gravity with Alex still flailing helplessly away in thin air. Then his torso pitched downward and he, the canoe, and I were engulfed in a whirling cauldron of froth. And for one brief, agonizing moment we were dissolved in the river. . . .

"Instantly, I was toppling about in a bubbly spume, a mishmash of suds, clawing my way toward the light. When at last I surfaced, I was alone. Where was my friend? Had he drowned? What would I say to his parents? Where the hell was the canoe? Had it sunk? Then, the top of Alex's head appeared! Then his face! Then the canoe, shooting skyward like the breach of a small whale, falling upside-down with a thump beside us."

The intrepid travelers hauled their canoe to shore and took inventory of their wet supplies. Everything could be dried in the sun, save for a box of soggy Saltines. "Other than that, not counting our moxie, we'd lost nothing," McGill reported.

McGill remembers relating the tale to Alex's father, and that he laughed hard.

they rented a motel room for a week. "During that trip," remembers Dreyfoos, "Dad purchased me a used 19-foot 1937 Chris-Craft. I would later learn he had borrowed the money to buy it. If I had known then, I might have worried about being able to afford an MIT education." Instead, he kept his eye on the path to fulfilling his father's prophecy, which had become his own dream as well.

As for his grades, says Dreyfoos, "New York State had Regents Exams that covered several years of math and science. If you did well on them, your classroom grades didn't penalize you. I managed to do well enough to get into MIT."

MIT: Gateway to the World

Five years after the end of World War II, in 1950, Alex Dreyfoos arrived at the Massachusetts Institute of Technology in the 1939 Oldsmobile he had rebuilt. Harry S. Truman was president, and the Korean War had just started. Senator Joseph R. McCarthy was investigating alleged Communist spies inside the US State Department, and his congressional hearings monopolized network television programming. "Goodnight Irene" and "Mona Lisa" were the top popular music recordings, by the Weavers and Nat King Cole, respectively. Conductor Arturo Toscanini led the NBC Symphony Orchestra on a transcontinental tour. The FCC adopted the CBS Field Sequential Color Television System as the first color standard for television in the United States. (See sidebar, page 53.) New ideas and technology were being eagerly embraced by a nation intent on seeking the good life. The times could not have been better for Alex Dreyfoos, a man still called "remarkable in his inventiveness" 60 years later by his friend, industrialist Stan Rumbough. Dreyfoos was on a trajectory that would lead him to change the world of color photography reproduction, and MIT was to be his launching pad.

"Alex and I were both in ROTC at MIT," remembers Paul Gray, who was in Dreyfoos' graduating class of 1954 and would become MIT's president from 1980 to 1990. (The National Defense Act of 1916 created the federal Reserve Officers' Training Corps, ROTC. MIT started the country's first Army ROTC in 1917, and its Air Force program, AFROTC, in 1947.) Although they had been too young to serve in World War II, it was this war more than anything that influenced the spirit of the nation during their MIT studies.

CBS FIELD SEQUENTIAL COLOR

The CBS field sequential color system, engineered by Peter Goldmark, was a mechanical method for capturing and viewing a color television picture. Comprised of a rotating wheel of red, green, and blue filters in front of a monochrome camera, the system transmitted to a black and white cathode ray tube (CRT) receiver that was viewed through a second rotating color wheel. The two wheels had to be synchronized so that each successive field was viewed using the same color filters as the camera. The field rate produced was a slightly flickering 24 color frames per second.

To accommodate the increased field rate within the standard 6 MHz television broadcast channel, the lines per frame were reduced from 525 to 405. This made the CBS color system incompatible with the existing black and white 525 line standard. No standard monochrome receiver could present a viewable picture when color was broadcast.

The first color broadcast by CBS using its Field Sequential Color System took place on August 28, 1940. The 1949 version of CBS's system was the third time its field sequential technique was presented to the Federal Communications Commission (FCC) for adoption as the US standard.

In October 1950, RCA brought suit against the FCC to prevent the start of CBS color broadcasts. RCA took its case all the way to the US Supreme Court, which, on May 28, 1951, affirmed a lower court ruling in favor of CBS. In the process, RCA had delayed the implementation of the CBS system, continuing to sell black and white sets that could not receive the CBS color signals. Weak advertiser and viewer acceptance forced CBS to abandon the system. Critics of RCA charged that its tactics were purely economic, pressing for CBS's failure all along. The last commercial CBS field sequential system color broadcast was a college football game on October 20, 1951.

Ultimately, the US color television standard was decided by the National Television Standards Committee and approved by the FCC on July 22, 1953. The new standard was supported, and partly designed by, RCA.

Gray elaborates: "With the great crunch of American GIs coming back from the war and many of them going to college on the GI Bill, there were a lot of veterans in our class. They set the pace, because they weren't there for the social life or to party—they were in school to get a degree and a job as quickly as they could. That affected the intellectual and academic climate for the rest of us. It was pretty intense."

Students who got poor grades in the first semester were soon gone. According to Gray, "Those first terms filtered out the folks who perhaps should

THE MIT WAY

At the instigation of William Barton Rogers, Massachusetts Institute of Technology was chartered in 1861. Recognizing that America's "classical" learning institutions were fixated on studies of the liberal arts, Rogers set out to establish an institution where the curriculum directly addressed the new and complex challenges brought about by the Industrial Revolution. Delayed by the American Civil War, the college first opened in 1865 in Boston's Mercantile Building. Rogers, a natural history scientist, had three guiding principles for the new technology institute: recognition of the value of "useful knowledge"; learning by doing; and integration of professional and liberal arts for undergraduates.

MIT's slogan of *mens et manus* (mind and hand) is rooted in its history. The institute believes, "You must understand foundational topics at a deep level (*mens*) and be able to execute the practical application of these concepts (*manus*)." As a "shared ethic," *mens et manus* says to students: Use your hands and your brain to examine a problem and invent a solution, and then do something to bring your solution to reality. This principle would become a guiding presence in Dreyfoos' future endeavors, as would the work ethic that prevailed during his time at MIT.

have gone somewhere else. The great lesson of the freshman year at MIT for all the high school valedictorians and high achievers is that there's a bottom half of the MIT class, and it's not a disgrace to be in it." For Dreyfoos, mindful of how his high school guidance counselor had told him he didn't have a chance of getting into MIT without better grades, the MIT pecking order was irrelevant. What mattered was that he had achieved his and his dad's dream. He was ready to work hard.

Sigma Alpha Epsilon

By its very demanding and competitive nature, the MIT culture has always encouraged close teamwork and sharing, which created enduring friendships and loyalties between students. Dreyfoos would amass a large cadre of lifelong friends at MIT. "The camaraderie was principally around your residence and secondarily around your academic major," Gray explains. "If you lived in a fraternity, you had 30 or 40 friends from there. If you lived in the sole dormitory, you had a set of friends there."

Student housing at MIT in the post-World War II years was limited. To ease the demands on dormitory space, the school counted on a certain percentage of the freshman class to join a fraternity and live in a "frat" house. Since fraternity membership required an invitation, many disappointed young men ended up instead in the dormitories. To become a fraternity member, students had to show up a week before school started. Dreyfoos was among the first to sign up during rush week and was accepted into the Sigma Alpha Epsilon house at 484 Beacon Street, Boston, just across the Charles River from MIT in Cambridge.

Sigma Alpha Epsilon, or SAE (fondly referred to by Dreyfoos and his fraternity brothers as "Sleeping And Eating Society"), was founded in 1856 at the University of Alabama. Among some of the most notable SAE members are President William McKinley, law enforcement "G-man" Elliot Ness, author William Faulkner, World War II aviator Joe Foss, and former Joint Chiefs of Staff Chairman General Richard Myers.

"The True Gentleman," creed of Sigma Alpha Epsilon, is often recited by SAE pledges, actives, and alumni, and is quoted in part in the Foreword herein. With these words, John Walter Wayland won a writing contest conducted by the *Baltimore Sun* in 1899. The piece was also printed in a manual used at the US Naval Academy in Annapolis, Maryland. It is said to best exemplify the ideals of the SAE fraternity:

> *The True Gentleman is the man whose conduct proceeds from good will and an acute sense of propriety, and whose self-control is equal to all emergencies; who does not make the poor man conscious of his poverty, the obscure man of his obscurity, or any man of his inferiority or deformity; who is himself humbled if necessity compels him to humble another; who does not flatter wealth, cringe before power, or boast of his own possessions or achievements; who speaks with frankness but always with sincerity and sympathy; whose deed follows his word; who thinks of the rights and feelings of others, rather than his own; and who appears well in any company, a man with whom honor is sacred and virtue safe.*

In Dreyfoos' time at MIT, the brothers at the Sigma Alpha Epsilon house on Beacon Street all aspired to live up to the gentleman's creed.

His SAE brother George Michel acknowledges that there were lapses in judgment. In those days, Michel says, pranks were regular fare, often between the students at MIT and Harvard. "Every day something would happen. The thing was, there was usually a technical challenge to the mischief. You had to do calculations, exercises, draw up plans—and then, not get caught!

"In the winter, we got into a lot of trouble playing a game we called 'tonk.' It involved thumping the tops of automobiles with snowballs from the roof of the SAE house, causing traffic jams on Beacon Street." The students would roll snow into a huge ball as for a snowman; along with the snow would come gravel from the flat roof. Then they would heave the very heavy ball off the roof, usually aiming for a taxi, where it would make the sound "tonk." Several SAE brothers ended up in Roxbury Criminal Court after successfully tonking a passing automobile. It did not help that the occupants of the car were policemen. The group managed to get out of a very tight spot when the judge who heard their case turned out to be an SAE brother. They got off with paying a small fine for damage to the car and an officer's uniform.

George Michel, who would become Dreyfoos' best friend for life, even saved his life once. During college, Dreyfoos lost consciousness when a piece of meat became stuck in his throat. Michel performed essentially what would become known as the Heimlich maneuver, dislodging the morsel and restoring Dreyfoos to consciousness.

Michel was Dreyfoos' SAE pledgemaster in 1950. Six months older than Dreyfoos, he was a sophomore at the time, and could always draw a crowd to tell a story or propose an idea. Michel had graduated from Admiral Farragut Academy, a strict naval boarding school in St. Petersburg, Florida, which he had attended from age 12. (Dreyfoos' grandson, Michael Aron Carter, would graduate from Admiral Farragut Academy in 2001.) He fit in perfectly with the abundance of military types at SAE after World War II, who were up to 10 years older. In his freshman year, he roomed with two veterans, one a B-24 Liberator bomber pilot, the other a Navy commander.

The next fall, in walked Dreyfoos. "And, well, he's a nerd!" Michel describes the freshman Dreyfoos as wearing big, black, horn-rimmed glasses, white shirt, and dark tie and trousers. "We didn't know what to make of him. He seemed immature. We had to build him up to help him fit in," Michel fondly muses. Dreyfoos speculates on how poorly it might have gone for him if he had not had the experience of Tau Pi fraternity in high school.

Dreyfoos credits Michel with refining his manners and tastes, which would serve him well in later years. In 2007, a former classmate wrote, "You are the living proof that MIT grads are not nerds!" Also about this time, Dreyfoos showed his MIT yearbook to his younger friend Garrison "Gary" duPont Lickle, president/CEO of Chilton Trust Management, who laughed. "There he was with his classmates, wearing lab coats and black-rimmed glasses, looking like lab rats. Today Alex exudes an entirely different impression— you wouldn't know he's an eccentric genius."

Dreyfoos arrived at SAE lugging a huge box, says Michel. "Of course, we looked at it real hard and said, 'What *is* this?'" "Loudspeaker" was the terse response. The speaker box was a low frequency "woofer," guaranteed to deliver a powerful bass response. Built into the box was what Dreyfoos called a "Klipschorn," which he had built himself. "Now this device was really ahead of the curve," Michel explains. "This was something you couldn't buy." The Klipschorn was the best sound device at the time, providing true high fidelity, the full range of frequencies audible to the human ear. In those days, Klipschorns were normally only found in movie theaters and the homes of a few wealthy audio enthusiasts. It was invented by audio pioneer Paul Wilbur Klipsch, patented in 1946, and changed little in 60-plus years of production in Arkansas.

"You have got to realize," says Michel, "we didn't even have stereo then, and Alex was walking in with the finest high fidelity system for the whole SAE house to enjoy. 'Okay,' I remember thinking, 'so now we have a nerd high fidelity freak.'"

The next thing to come through the door was Dreyfoos' amateur (ham) radio system. To make his radio station function, Dreyfoos needed an antenna on the roof, a good earth ground connection, and a place to set up his transmitter, receiver, and monitoring gear. He piled his ham rig on his desk in the study room. Michel remembers how, especially on weekends when he and his fraternity brothers would be studying at their desks, "Alex would come storming down from the bunk room on the fifth floor, walk over to his desk, and turn on this ham radio system. He would keep repeating, 'CQ, CQ, CQ 10, CQ 10-meter phone, this is K2BLH-slant-one in Boston. What say someone?' while carefully tuning the band. Following this strange announcement would be a long period of loud static—'SSHHHHH'—with Alex listening intently for the slightest sound of a human voice. Every once in a while he'd get somebody. It was the same every weekend: 'Click. CQ, CQ, CQ 10, CQ 10-meter phone, K2BLH-slant-one in Boston,' Click. SSHHHHH."

Michel gradually understood the meaning of the call sign K2BLH-slant-one (K2BLH/1): K2 indicated to receiving stations that his license was in the New York district. Adding "slant-one" told them his station was temporarily operating in the K1 district in New England (Boston). Michel was intrigued, and could see how wrapped up his friend was in making his system work properly. Contacting other ham operators around the world was like a game to Dreyfoos. Michel asked him, "Why do you do this?"

"We're talking to people in Holland, Belgium—all the way down in Africa. We pick up places all around the world," Dreyfoos explained.

"But what do you talk about?" Michel persisted.

"Not much," admitted Dreyfoos. "We mostly just log in the location and signal quality and exchange 'QSL' postcards, written confirmations acknowledging our contact." No wonder it was important for receiving parties to know his transmission location.

Michel was clueless about what made ham radio attractive, but enjoyed listening in. "They had lots of little codes. A far-off radio operator shrouded in static would refer to an XYL. That meant a married young lady. Alex would often talk about his YL, or young lady—his girlfriend."

After arriving at MIT, Dreyfoos had seen Ann Carlough from high school a few times, now at Simmons College, but he concentrated more on Joan Jacobson, whom he had dated during his last six months of high school. Joan followed him to Boston in his sophomore year, also attending Simmons, with Dreyfoos' sister, Evelyn. Dreyfoos and Jacobson often double-dated with George Michel and his girlfriend, Paula Frei, whom he would later marry. According to his sister, Dreyfoos also found time to help his fraternity brothers find dates, and would call Evelyn for help setting up dates with the women at Simmons. (Evelyn later had a career as a social worker and in 1964 married Harvard graduate Henry Munson Spelman III, a noted philatelist and postal historian. They had two daughters, Laura Elizabeth and Carol Louise.)

Michel was intent on helping Dreyfoos fit the mold of the MIT culture. "Alex was basically coming from suburbia to MIT. He wasn't much of a drinker, so he had to learn a bit about drinking." He also didn't smoke or drink coffee, but he made a point of joining Michel and his buddies every morning at 1 a.m. at Spoon Train, a Boston café. Dreyfoos enjoyed their company and conversation and drank an occasional Coca-Cola while his pals downed coffee and smoked cigarettes for an hour. "It was a pressure-packed environment," says Michel. "Our heads would be spinning, and we couldn't just go to bed. We needed this comforting routine."

Michel and Dreyfoos spent a lot of time together at the SAE house during Dreyfoos' freshman year. The group also often included Franklin M. Jarman, whose father, W. Maxey Jarman, was a leading socialite in Nashville and ran the footwear and apparel retailer, General Shoe Company, which became the conglomerate GENESCO, the world's largest apparel firm. (From *Time*, August 13, 1951: "'Every well-dressed man should have at least 30 pairs of shoes in his closet,' says Nashville's debonair W. Maxey Jarman, 47. He talks that way because he makes the famed Jarman shoe and 23 other brands.") George Michel's father was vice president and general manager of H. Boker & Co., manufacturer of high quality hand tools and cutlery. It was unlikely that Frank's and George's families were struggling to pay their sons' tuition; Dreyfoos' was. Due to his father's failing health, Dreyfoos also never received visits from his parents while at MIT. He was on his own.

Dreyfoos was known as mild-mannered, unassuming, and considerate. He was not the kind of person to dominate the conversation or try to be the center of attention. Former classmates most often describe him as even-tempered, cheerful, and unflappable. Always carrying a camera, Dreyfoos became SAE's resident photographer, and even built a darkroom in the basement of the fraternity house, but he was outgoing, not the sort to hide behind his camera. Michel quickly recognized Dreyfoos' leadership skills and was his biggest promoter.

Another student Dreyfoos met on his arrival at the SAE house was Bard Crawford. They shared the ordeals of being pledges during their freshman year but were not especially friendly. Then, on the first day of their sophomore year, Dreyfoos and Crawford found themselves as assigned roommates. Crawford remembers the fall day when they moved into the SAE house. Dreyfoos marched into their room with all of his possessions and opened everything up, a scene reminiscent of George Michel's initial observations a year earlier. First he assembled his ham radio equipment on his desk. Then he sat down and turned it on. He opened the microphone switch and announced, "This is K2BLH-slant-one, carefully tuning the band. CQ, CQ. What say someone?" Crawford was amazed at how Dreyfoos called out into the airwaves, inviting anyone who could hear his voice to chat. He was further amazed by how easy Dreyfoos made it look. "It was sort of like people today on the Internet in chat rooms, but this was 40 years earlier and far more complicated."

Crawford also recalls Dreyfoos' interest in music and his joy in listening to it on his hi-fi system. "He talked about musical theater and often played his favorite classical records and show tunes."

Because Dreyfoos was the SAE house treasurer during the first term of his junior year and Crawford was the assistant treasurer, the pair remained roommates. Theirs was the only two-person room with a safe. "Alex and I had a lot of work to do to keep up the books on the house," says Crawford. "During the first term of our senior year, Alex was president of the house while I was vice president. I was president the next term, and Alex was still on the executive committee. So we both spent the last four or five terms on the executive committee running everything for the house." Dreyfoos still marvels at his ascent to the fraternity's leadership. "Most of the brothers were jocks with quite different interests and hobbies than mine. I didn't do much with sports or get involved in their pranks. I spent my time in the darkroom or improving my hi-fi and ham rigs."

Crawford saw part of Dreyfoos' charisma as his vast knowledge and willingness to share it with others. "Alex had all these things that he could do, and I kept being surprised and delighted by that—just being able to watch him and talk with him about these things. Alex was very interested in learning about and sharing his understanding of technology. I was learning technology in an academic sense from MIT, but I was learning many other related things from Alex. For instance, Alex had just learned about transistors. He described them as smaller, faster, and more reliable than vacuum tubes. He was convinced they would replace vacuum tubes and have a big effect on the world in years to come. I learned that first from Alex, not from MIT."

Crawford and Dreyfoos spent a lot of time talking about radio. "He described the whole phenomenon of radio to me, especially shortwave frequencies that ham radio people use and how they bounce off the ionosphere and zigzag all around the curved globe. I remember once when Alex had a conversation with a man in Australia. He was very excited about that, in terms of how the signal worked."

A Great Loss

On November 22, 1951, during the Thanksgiving holiday of Dreyfoos' sophomore year, Alexander Dreyfoos Sr. died. He was 75. His death certificate gave the cause of death as chronic nephritis (inflammation of the kidneys), chronic myocarditis (inflammation of the heart muscle), and arteriosclerosis (hardening of the arteries).

"I had driven down from Boston to New Rochelle the day before Thanksgiving," recalls Dreyfoos, "my first return home since school had begun in September. My father was not well. My mother was convinced that he had kept himself alive to see me one more time. We were together that evening and had a nice chat. He didn't seem that bad off. When he was obviously tired, I went to bed. We talked of chatting more in the morning, but he passed on at 3:00 a.m. By the time I woke up, my mother had had his body removed from the house." The next day the elder Dreyfoos was cremated at the Ferncliff Crematory in Ardsley, New York. A few days later, after a brief memorial service, Dreyfoos returned to MIT to live out the dream he and his father had shared.

His father's death had changed that as well. "I learned that my father had been borrowing money from his company to finance our lifestyle. His partner, Irving Goodfield, purchased my dad's stock in Apeda from my mother." In hindsight it became clear that Dreyfoos' father always expected to precede his wife in death because of their age difference. He knew his partner would buy him out to clear up his debts. Martha Dreyfoos sold the family home. While reorganizing her finances, she was disappointed to learn that her husband's cello, which they had believed to be very valuable, held little resale worth for her. Dreyfoos suddenly found himself on the MIT student loan program.

This sample of the eulogy given by a friend of his father hits home the similarities between father and son, and how much Dreyfoos' father influenced the man he would become:

Alex symbolized to me a man who lived his life fully every day. He had a real zest and enthusiasm for life and a love for people. He was genuine and real, with a dynamic personality and a true sense of the proper values in

*life. He was sincere, loyal, generous, and not given to ostentation. . . . Alex
enjoyed an unusually rich and full life due to his many and varied interests.
. . . a lover of music [and] of nature and of the out-of-doors, an ardent fisherman, adventuring where one could go only with a guide. . . . a gracious
and charming host. . . . A life as full and rich as Alex's never dies. It lives
on in the hearts and minds of all who knew him, especially his children,
who have been nurtured by his love and will carry on in this spirit.*

The Widow Dreyfoos

Martha Whittemore Dreyfoos had maintained her professional music career during her marriage. Just two months before her husband died, she attended the Zermatt Summer Academy of Music, Switzerland, where her idol
Pablo Casals was holding master classes in the interpretation of cello litera-
ture. She wrote home: "Casals is so wonderful in every way, and the lessons
have been a real inspiration."

When Martha became a widow, while her son relied on university financing, she managed to resume traveling internationally for her music. In
1955 she wrote her sister Elsie from England, where she was taking master
classes with cellist Maurice Eisenberg: "We all practice at least four hours a
day, [and] have class lessons four times a week besides lectures and concerts,
so there's never a dull moment!" Martha had arranged to return to Casals'
classes in Zermatt again, then to visit friends in Frankfurt, she said, "and
maybe get to Boston before Evelyn leaves college."

In 1968 Martha took a three-week excursion under instructor Mildred Alfred to several big cities of Europe where, Elsie says, "she knew people." The
following summer, she went with two vocalists on a Scandinavian tour where,
again, Martha had friends. This was the world she felt most comfortable in.

The highlight of her later career came in 1970. She was honored as one
of "The 100 Cellists" invited to New York to pay tribute to Pablo Casals by
performing his composition, *La Sardana*, under his direction. She conveyed
her thrills while still fresh to "Dearest Elsie":

*Well, Casals has come and went home today. I'm not down to earth
yet! It was so wonderful and exciting! The 100 cellists were invited to play
by Leopold Stokowski. He's the founder and conductor of the American*

Orchestra. He started this program by conducting Leonore number 3 by Beethoven, then [Rudolf] Serkin played Beethoven's 5th piano concerto also conducted by Stokowski. Then Beverly Sills sang Bellini, Rossini, and Donizetti. Then we were the last on this program.

This concert was an occasion with Parquet Tickets $125.00 each (and gross of $151,000 was taken in). The head music critic was there. They practically never go to benefit concerts, but this surely was very very special! He wrote in his review "above all those cellists." Every seat was taken. I heard one man saying, There's not room enough even for a sardine!

Casals had many standing ovations, and when we played his composition "La Sardana" there was so very very much applauding, Casals took his baton and indicated that we would play it again. More applause!! And cheering. I never have heard so much thunderous applause or Happy Cheers! . . . We all felt most honored to have been asked to play. . . . Yes, I saw Casals just long enough to tell him how happy [I was] to be playing in that wonderful concert. So much Love, dear. Martha.

In a souvenir book, Casals, Stokowski, and Serkin autographed photos of themselves for her, for what was surely a special remembrance. Casals had moved to Puerto Rico, and Martha attended his 1971 festival there with fellow musicians. A few months later she joined the European Organ Study Tour of five countries.

During another Organ Tour in 1972, Martha Dreyfoos suffered a stroke while in Rome. She spent the remainder of her life in Christian Science nursing homes—Tenacre in New Jersey, and Fern Lodge in California, where her daughter, Evelyn, was on staff. When she died in 1977 at age 79, Martha's family had her ashes spread over the Pacific Ocean.

Because of developments in medicine, it only became clear to Dreyfoos later that his mother had probably suffered from Alzheimer's disease, which he might inherit. Martha Dreyfoos had taken care of herself, but not well, until the mid-1960s. Though she still traveled overseas, her son had to keep her checkbook. By the time she moved from Tenacre to Fern Lodge, she had ceased to talk or to recognize people.

As a widow in 1956, Martha had been very disappointed to learn upon appraisal that her cello, previously her husband's, was not valuable after all, though she loved its tone. She returned to Hill & Sons in London and purchased a cello with a body by Carlo Tononi of Venice in 1723, and a head by a different maker circa 1800. After her death, this cello sold to a musician in Berkeley, California, for seven times the amount Martha paid for it. Her restored cello bow sold for more than $60,000.

Martha Whittemore Dreyfoos' name lives on as one of the first Americans of the 20th century to undertake the study of and gain proficiency on the viola da gamba. She passed on her viola da gamba to her son, who presented it to the Yale University Collection of Musical Instruments in 1984. After a major restoration in 2013 by the distinguished firm of Andrew Dipper Restorations and Museum Services in Minneapolis, Thomas MacCracken of Yale informed Dreyfoos: "After cleaning the paper label glued to the inside of the back-plate, Mr. Dipper was able clearly to read the date correctly as 1664, which makes it the earliest dated viola by Meares out of the 10 that I now know of."

Permanent Inspiration

The financial troubles of Alexander W. Dreyfoos Sr. were not part of the obituary in the *New York Times*, which documented his contributions as a photographer in New York City's theatrical and musical communities. Its publication, however, would change the course of his son's life.

MIT ensured that every student experienced, for at least one semester, an instructor of considerable reputation. In Dreyfoos' case, it was Professor Arthur C. Hardy for sophomore physics in Room 250 on the second floor of Building 10 (the Great Dome), known as the 10-250 lecture hall. Hardy has been described by a former student as "a charming, dapper, courtly gentleman, … senior (and, I'd argue, superior) in every way to [other professors]. His tweed jackets were a trademark. We also recognized him by the flower in his lapel."

When Dreyfoos was at MIT, everybody spent time in 10-250, the amphitheater-shaped room beneath the dome. Stairs rose up from the lecturer's pit. The entrance to the hall was at the same level as the lecturer, so entering and departing students had to pass by the lecturer, but they had no reason to be acquainted, since teaching assistants dealt with the undergraduates. Yet on Dreyfoos' first day back in school after his father's death, as he was leaving 10-250 after his regular physics lecture, Professor Hardy addressed him. "Are you Dreyfoos?"

"Yes, Professor," he answered, surprised at being recognized. How Hardy managed to identify Dreyfoos will forever remain a mystery.

Hardy expressed his condolences on the passing of Dreyfoos' father—he had obviously seen the obituary—and asked about his own interests in photography.

"I have cameras, and, yes, I take pictures," said Dreyfoos. "I also have a darkroom, but my father was an artist, and *my* real interest is electronics. I'm going to be an electronics engineer." Hardy surprised Dreyfoos again, asking him to make an appointment with his secretary to meet at his office. Lecturers like Hardy rarely took time with undergraduates.

At the time, Dreyfoos was contemplating a career in improving and advancing high fidelity sound systems. In 1950, electronic light meters built into cameras were considered futuristic. Light meters had no relationship to cameras; they were separate devices carried in a photographer's pocket. During the many meetings that followed, Hardy convinced Dreyfoos that he expected electronics and photography to have "a lot of interaction" over the next two or three decades, and that this marriage would shape his career.

Together, Dreyfoos and Hardy mapped out a curriculum for him at MIT that combined physics and electrical engineering. Dreyfoos approached both of these departments and explained what he wanted to do. Both responded that their respective programs were too stringent for Dreyfoos to get a degree if he took time away to study in another department. Then Hardy had an idea. The School of Industrial Management—established in 1952 with a charge of educating "the ideal manager"—was expanding. It had been given a building by Alfred P. Sloan (Class of 1895), then chairman of General Motors, which became the Sloan Business School, an effective competitor for Harvard Business School. A new degree, Business and Engineering Administration, had been announced at Sloan, to be run by Professor Erwin H. Schell. Hardy believed Schell would allow Dreyfoos to study anything he wanted as long as he completed the core business courses.

Hardy was right. Dreyfoos was able to take all of the courses he selected in physics, optics, photographic theory, and electrical engineering. The result was a perfect balance of what he needed to create a successful business enterprise, built on the combined foundations of photography, electronics, and business. In addition to his Sloan education, Dreyfoos worked under the tutelage of Professor Hardy, who happily shared the body of knowledge he had amassed over his career.

MIT required an undergraduate thesis, and Hardy advised Dreyfoos on his, which explored the various color processes that existed at the time, and analyzed the pros and cons of each. Dreyfoos got to know the professor well and continued to turn to Hardy for his valuable guidance. Dreyfoos often observed Hardy's interaction with his secretary, Miss Elizabeth "Betty" Beaman, and suspected they had a strong romantic attachment. Sure enough, Hardy and Beaman later married after his first wife died. Even after Dreyfoos left MIT, Hardy kept up with his progress. "He would send me little notes," says Dreyfoos, "saying, 'I see you have gotten a patent for x. Congratulations.' I imagine his wife may have had something to do with that."

The Dreyfoos Tower of MIT's Stata Center was a gift to the institution by Dreyfoos in honor of Professor Hardy. At the dedication in 2004, Dreyfoos said, "My gift to MIT is a thank you to Arthur Hardy for being a great mentor and for being there, for me, at a critical time of my life. I hope the interplay that this building is designed to encourage leads to many new mentor relationships of the kind I was so fortunate to have."

Norbert Wiener

As MIT is a hub for technical genius and academic brilliance, Dreyfoos was exposed to other great minds of the era besides Arthur Hardy. Another who left a lasting impression was mathematics professor Norbert Wiener, who had been born in Columbia, Missouri, in 1894. His father was a professor of languages who tutored his son at home until it became clear the child was a prodigy in not only languages, but mathematics and more, yet to be seen. He went to high school at age nine and attended Tufts College at age 11, graduating in three years. Subsequently, Wiener studied a range of subjects at a variety of schools, including Harvard, where he began teaching philosophy in 1915. In 1919, he joined the math department at MIT, where he taught until his death in 1964.

At least once a year, SAE would invite Wiener to dine with the 40 brothers at the fraternity house. "Norbert Wiener's visit was a tradition," recalls Dreyfoos. "I don't know how many other fraternity houses he visited, if any." At SAE, typical of fraternities of the time, the brothers were required to dress

ARTHUR C. HARDY

Arthur Cobb Hardy, PhD, was an optical physicist. He is recognized most for creating the field of colorimetry by inventing the recording spectrophotometer, for which he received a patent in 1935. His "photometric apparatus" (US Patent No. 1,987,441) was designed to measure two million different shades of color in degrees and frequencies, then chart and record the results. His invention, by defining colors for the first time, was a major scientific innovation, creating the new field called "colorimetry," moving the discipline from guesswork to science. He licensed his patent for the invention to the General Electric Company, which sold the first machine in May 1935.

The recording spectrophotometer measures the intensity of light as a function of color frequency creating a record of its intensity as a function of its wavelength, or location, on the electromagnetic spectrum. The precision in color identification offered by the Hardy invention made colorimetry essential to industrial applications in printing, textiles, ink, paint, and photography. In science, the device is utilized in everything from chemistry and geology to remote sensing satellites and the space program.

For many years, Professor Hardy was secretary of the Optical Society of America, also serving one term as president. He served the Society of Motion Picture and Television Engineers on its Progress Committee and chaired the organization's Standards and Nomenclature Committee in 1930. Around that same time, Hardy wrote the "Optics" section of the Encyclopedia Britannica.

Professor Hardy's original books on colorimetry and optics continue to be referenced today by anyone seriously involved in the field. He became an assistant professor at MIT in the 1920s, working in the development of quantum theory. Hardy received the Frederic Ives Medal in 1957, an award made annually by the Optical Society of America "for distinguished work in optics."

PUBLICATIONS BY ARTHUR C. HARDY

"Color Correction in Color Printing" *Journal of the Optical Society of America*, April 1948.

Handbook of Colorimetry (MIT Press, 1936)

The Principles of Optics (McGraw-Hill, 1932)

"A Recording Photoelectric Color Analyser," 1929

"A Study of the Persistence of Vision," *Proceedings of the National Academy of Sciences of the United States of America*, Vol. 6, No. 4 (April 15, 1920), pp. 221-224.

The Journal of the Society of Motion Picture and Television Engineers published many writings by Hardy from 1922 to 1930 on his advanced studies involving optics and their application in the motion picture industry.

for dinner in a jacket and tie. All of them sat at one large table.

Dreyfoos explains, "The first thing Dr. Wiener would say is, 'All right, who is non-native American?' We had a Cuban, a Frenchman, a Greek fellow, and a couple more nationalities. They'd hold up their hands, and Dr. Wiener would say, 'Please, only talk to me in your native tongue.' He would carry on conversations with all of them, no matter what their language was. That made for an interesting dinner.

"After eating, we all moved up to the chapter room, where a dozen chess boards stood ready in a circle for 12 of SAE's best players. Professor Wiener would go around the inside of the circle from one board to another. After several rounds, he'd have checkmated everybody. We loved it, and we tried hard to beat him. It was terrific."

Driving toward the MIT campus one cold and snowy morning, Dreyfoos spotted the professor walking along the street wearing no coat or hat. When Dreyfoos offered him a ride, Dr. Wiener readily accepted. The professor talked about some aspect of one of his many areas of study, which included noise and stochastic (random) processes, electronic communication, and mathematics. Norbert Wiener is best known as the founder of cybernetics, a result of his studies concerning the phenomenon of feedback and how it relates to biology, human organizations, computer science and engineering.

Summer Boat Trip up the Hudson

As dedicated as Dreyfoos was to his studies, he never lost his love for the outdoors. Toward the end of the summer of 1952, before his junior year began, he was ready for an adventure in the 19-foot Chris-Craft that his father had purchased for him. His MIT roommate, Bard Crawford, recalls the invitation to come along: "Alex asked what I thought about quitting our summer jobs a week early and taking his boat on a cruise up the Hudson River through the Champlain Barge Canal to visit Lake Champlain. He thought it would take about three days to get to the lake. We would spend a day or so there and then three days coming back."

The excursion would take them past Albany on the Hudson River, entering the Champlain Canal at Fort Edward just before Glens Falls. At the end of the canal—Whitehall, New York—they would enter the southern end of the Champlain-Richelieu River watershed, passing Ticonderoga and

Crown Point before entering the widest expanse of the lake, just past the Split Rock Lighthouse. Once on the lake they could visit Port Henry and Plattsburgh in New York; and Burlington, Vermont, if time allowed. Before turning back for New York City and home, they might ponder what it would be like to sail farther north. Like 18th-century French traders or Iroquois Indians, they could dream of following the lake on into Quebec onto the Richelieu River, eventually meeting the Saint Lawrence River and the North Atlantic—if they only had the time.

Crawford told Dreyfoos he didn't know anything about boating, but he did own a sleeping bag. "That's all you'll need. I'll supply the rest," assured his friend. Crawford's mother dropped him off at the Dreyfoos home early on a Saturday morning in late August to begin their adventure. "Alex had told me that he was in the process of overhauling the boat's engine," explains Crawford. "The meaning of that did not become clear until I stepped into Alex's basement. There was the engine, totally in pieces, neatly laid out on the floor. Alex was ready to put it back together. I didn't think we would be leaving on our trip any time soon."

Crawford watched Dreyfoos reassemble the engine, hoist it onto a dolly, and wheel it to the backyard, where the boat was waiting on a trailer. Together they inserted the engine into its housing. "I'd say that within a couple of hours from the time my mom dropped me off, the boat was in the water," remembers Crawford. "With the engine humming, we set off."

Dreyfoos piloted the Chris-Craft along Long Island Sound toward New York City, then up the East River. They turned into the Harlem River and followed it to the Hudson, just above the George Washington Bridge. Crawford says, "I remember cruising past the location where they had started [in March] to build the Tappan Zee Bridge. We also saw the mothballed World War II Navy fleet, anchored just north of the new bridge."

Late in the afternoon of the second day, they had trouble weaving through a series of buoys as they passed through Mechanicville, New York. Crawford recalls, "You were supposed to know whether to go to the right or left of the buoy based on the color, but these buoys had been there a long time and were rusty. We came on one right in the middle of the river and couldn't tell what color it had been. We guessed wrong and hit a rock. The boat kept running, but it was vibrating badly."

Dreyfoos had a good idea what the problem was, so they pulled over to a place where they could assess the damage. Again Crawford watched Dreyfoos go to work: "Alex went through this operation, which still amazes me. Wearing his bathing suit, he opened up a toolbox and got out this big, heavy wrench. He dove underwater at least eight or 10 times where it was dark and the current was flowing." Dreyfoos handed up a cotter pin, a nut, a key, and then the damaged prop to Crawford. Eventually he extracted a bent drive shaft, as Crawford stuffed a rag into the "stuffing box" that otherwise would have been open to the water. Dreyfoos handed up the heavy, six-foot brass rod to his friend.

Straddling the Hudson River 150 miles north of New York City, Mechanicville is home to the Springfield Terminal freight yard, connecting with the Delaware and Hudson and the New York Central Railroad lines in nearby Schenectady. In the 1950s, the presence of the freight yard made Mechanicville a bustling community of railroad support services, including a number of machine shops.

Out of the water, Dreyfoos hiked to a pay phone. In a few minutes, he located a machine shop about a mile away, but it was 10 minutes before five and the shop was about to close. "Alex handed me the shaft. It was time to put *my* skills to work," says Crawford. "I'd been on the track team in high school, and the MIT varsity lacrosse team. The next thing I know, in my bathing trunks, tee shirt, and sneakers, I was running down the main street of Mechanicville, New York. After about a mile I reached this machine shop with this weapon in my hand." Crawford handed the shaft to the waiting lathe mechanic, who expertly straightened it. Then he jogged back to the boat, where Dreyfoos—during eight or 10 more dives into the river—reinstalled the shaft and a spare prop, and started the engine. "It purred smoothly and quietly when he put it in gear," Crawford remembers. "It was quite an illustration of Dreyfoos' hands-on mechanical ability and technical knowledge."

Dreyfoos and Crawford camped out that night in a small cove on the western shore of Lake Champlain. Until then, they had been eating crackers and Spam, but that night, while Crawford gathered firewood, Dreyfoos pulled out a fishing rod and, in a few minutes, caught a smallmouth bass for dinner. "That meal was elegant," recollects Crawford. "I remember it as the best tasting meal I had ever eaten."

The First Knot

Since his father's death, Dreyfoos had been treated like a son by Aron "A. J." Jacobson, the father of his steady girl, Joan. A. J. did not, however, understand the younger man's interests in electronics and would ask, "Where do you think you are going with this technical stuff?" He preferred that Dreyfoos take business courses. One summer Dreyfoos worked for A. J. as a chauffeur. "He was trying to groom me to go into his business, AJ Contracting Company in New York City, which included a lot of renovation work for banks, offices, and stores. It was successful, because he worked hard and did a good job. He also knew exactly who to pay off and who to deal with. In those days, you could not get anything done in Manhattan without paying a lot of 'gratuities.' The practice was abhorrent to me. I wasn't interested in that kind of work, so I disappointed A. J. in that regard." Nonetheless, the two already had the foundation for a lifelong close relationship. A. J. admired Dreyfoos' intelligence and his record at MIT, and saw in him the makings of a perfect son-in-law.

Dreyfoos felt pressured towards a wedding immediately after his graduation from MIT. "Joan wanted us to have kids right away," says Dreyfoos. "Her mother had given birth later in life and was not an example Joan wanted to repeat." A. J. was poised to help him realize what he thought should be his dreams. It was as if Dreyfoos' destiny was already scripted. On June 27, 1954, less than a month after his graduation, Dreyfoos "did what was expected." He and Joan Jacobson were married in a non-religious ceremony outdoors on her family's estate at Rye, New York. George Michel served as best man. Bard Crawford, other SAE fraternity brothers, and a high school friend were the ushers. Graham McGill, on active duty as an Air Force pilot at the time, was unable to attend.

On reflection, Dreyfoos admits that this first marriage was one of convenience. "Her father made life easier for me, and in many ways, so did Joan. She was bright, talented, and very eager to be helpful." The cover letter of his 1954 MIT thesis acknowledges this: "To my fiancée, Miss Joan Jacobson, who has spent so many hours in editing and preparing this thesis in its final typewritten form, I owe a sincere vote of thanks." In another era, Joan probably would have forged a successful career of her own, but this was the '50s. She left college without graduating, to marry, start a family, and provide backup for her husband's dreams.

Eventually the couple came to lead parallel lives, with Joan running the household and providing clerical support, and Dreyfoos devoting nearly all of his time to fulfilling the vision that he and Arthur Hardy had crafted at MIT. Dreyfoos recognized how different he and Joan were. "I saw problems, but I had a high energy level. When she was unhappy sometimes, I had other interests to distract me." Looking back, Dreyfoos realizes that his work was his central interest: "I was so aimed at my job and engineering that family life couldn't play a major role. Getting married was what we were expected to do in those days, but not my main focus." As happens with many young marriages, the couple's lives would veer off in opposite directions, but not before some significant events took place.

If life had changed dramatically for Dreyfoos in his four years at MIT, so had the world beyond. Dwight D. Eisenhower succeeded Harry Truman as President of the United States, and the Korean War was over. The US Senate censured Joseph McCarthy for his unsubstantiated claims of Communist in-filtration in American government. An ailing Arturo Toscanini conducted his last public concert for the NBC Symphony Orchestra on April 4, 1954, orig-inating from New York's Carnegie Hall. Television was fast becoming the focus of American culture, and industry giants hotly competed for its audi-ence. In 1953 the Federal Communications Commission reversed its deci-sion to use Peter Goldmark's CBS Field Sequential Color System as the national color television standard and replaced it with a system engineered mostly by RCA, parent company of the CBS competitor, NBC Television.

Goldmark's long-playing (LP) microgroove 33⅓ rpm vinyl phonograph discs introduced by Columbia Records in 1948 became the new standard for home audio, overtaking the brittle but longstanding 78 rpm. The record-ing industry stopped releasing 78 rpm discs altogether in 1954, substituting smaller, more durable 45 rpm microgroove records, marking the beginning of the rock 'n' roll era. "Rock Around the Clock" by Bill Haley & His Comets and "That's All Right Mama" by a new singer named Elvis Presley were among the top hits of 1954.

Mass production of the first all-transistor consumer device, Regency's TR-1 Portable Transistor Radio, began in November 1954 in a joint venture with Texas Instruments. Change was coming, as described in 2013 by the Norwegian company Esato, a mobile phone content provider: "(A) little known Japanese company which finished third in the race to put a transistor radio on the market did so approximately 12 months later, making a smaller product, used six transistors (compared to the TR-1's four) and used half the power of the TR-1. It air-freighted 20,000 units into the US which sold for $39.95 (compared to the TR-1's $49.95) under the Totsuko brand. A year later, it decided to change its name . . . to SONY."

Also in 1954, the federal government put an end to Eastman Kodak's monopolistic practice of bundling film sales with photofinishing services, allowing more players to enter the field. Suddenly technological innovation had become the essential means for staying competitive. Vital ingredients of Alex Dreyfoos' future were falling into place. ✎

Young Dreyfoos built the electronics project shown on the cover of this electronics magazine.

(left to right) Dreyfoos, Evie, and their mother aboard *Evalma*, the Dreyfoos family's 26-foot Steelcraft cruiser.

New Rochelle High School.

Dreyfoos' business card during high school.

Dreyfoos beginning a 100-yard practice sprint for the New Rochelle High School swim team.

Dreyfoos' senior picture, New Rochelle High School, 1950.

Graham McGill in 1950.

Dreyfoos in his 1937 Chris-Craft in 1950. See also Chapter 18.

Dreyfoos' photograph of a party at his Sigma Alpha Epsilon (SAE) fraternity house at MIT.

Dreyfoos' photo of MIT, viewed from his SAE fraternity house and showing the Great Dome (Building 10) at center.

Dreyfoos (left) with George Michel at MIT, in the early 1950s.

The SAE fraternity house, Dreyfoos' home at MIT.

George Michel and his future wife, Paula Frei, at MIT in the early 1950s.

Paula and George Michel at the Kravis Center in 2003.

Dreyfoos' MIT ROTC unit at summer camp, 1953.

MIT Professor Norbert Wiener.

Dreyfoos' desk at the SAE fraternity house, showing his ham radio and audio gear.

Cartoon of Dreyfoos at the SAE house.

Bard Crawford at an SAE chapter meeting, early 1950s.

Dreyfoos' SAE chapter in 1954.

(left to right) Alex and Renate Dreyfoos, Bard and Jane Crawford, and Dan Lickly, at Lake Tahoe in 2000.

Martha Dreyfoos and daughter, Evelyn, at Evelyn's 1955 graduation from Simmons College.

The MIT logo including "Mens et Manus."

Pablo Casals
Bucaré 3, Punta Las Marias
Santurce, P. R.

February 10, 1958.

Dear Mrs. Whittermore,

Thank you very much for you good wishes.
Please accept ours.

Do you continue studying cello with
Maurice ? It was so lovely to see him in Paris
and beeing with him a few days.

With our most cordial greetings,

Sincerely yours,

Pablo Casals

Pablo Casals

A letter to Martha Whittemore Dreyfoos from her idol, Pablo Casals, in 1958 mentions the classes she took in England with cellist Maurice Eisenberg.

Walt Disney with a recording spectrophotometer in 1938, invented by Arthur Hardy and marketed by General Electric Co.

Professor Arthur Hardy and his wife, Elizabeth "Betty" Beaman, who Dreyfoos knew when she was Hardy's secretary.

MIT Professor Arthur C. Hardy.

A.J. and Lillian Jacobson, Alex and Joan Dreyfoos, and Martha Dreyfoos, at Alex and Joan's wedding in 1954.

CHAPTER 4

Expanding the Depth of Field

Lt. Dreyfoos at Sembach Air Force Base, Germany, in 1956.

Reporting for Duty

For the first four months of their marriage, the young Dreyfooses lived with Joan's parents. A. J. and Lillian Jacobson provided the newlyweds with a secluded second-floor bedroom suite in their home in Rye, New York. While A. J. held out hope that Dreyfoos might want to join the family business, his son-in-law still had his heart set on working with electronics and photography, and was pleased when Hazeltine Corporation offered him an engineering job. "They knew I was about to head off to the Air Force, and wanted me to come back to them afterward." Hazeltine's historic role of inventiveness in radio and electronics and its involvement in establishing color television standards greatly interested Dreyfoos. He accepted their offer as he waited to be called into military service.

On November 4, 1954, Dreyfoos entered the US Air Force. Having been in ROTC at MIT, he had been deferred from the Draft and the Korean War and started his service as a second lieutenant. In the summer of 1953, between his junior and senior years at MIT, he had received six weeks of military training at Griffis Air Force Base in Rome, New York. Dreyfoos was assigned to Sembach Air Base, near Kaiserslautern, West Germany. Its location was strategic, near the borders with France, Belgium, and Luxembourg, in the southwestern state of Rheinland-Pfalz.

The Photo Lab

Dreyfoos figured the Air Force made him a supply officer because of his MIT degree in business and engineering administration. As he sat waiting in the adjutant's office at Sembach to report for duty, he overheard the adjutant speaking on the telephone about finding a replacement to command one of the base's three photographic laboratories, critical components of Sembach's reconnaissance mission: "It's been weeks! I really need somebody," the adjutant complained to the officer on the other end of the phone.

When it was Dreyfoos' turn to speak with the adjutant, he could not resist asking about the opening. "Pardon me for eavesdropping, sir," Dreyfoos stated, adding confidently, "I don't know anything about supplies—or being a supply officer for that matter—but I do know quite a lot about photography."

"Job calls for a major," the adjutant bluntly declared.

"Well," Dreyfoos boldly asked, "who do you have running it now?"

"A couple of sergeants are holding down the fort."

"Why don't you let *me* hold down the fort until a major shows up?"

Dreyfoos got the job, and no major ever showed up to replace him.

The 22-year-old commanded a 40-man photo lab; nothing fancy, but highly specialized and well equipped for its mission. Two types of cameras were used aboard the aircraft flying the photographic missions. The film was nine inches wide and 250 feet long. The cameras either took a 9-inch-by-9-inch picture or a 9-inch-by-18-inch picture. "There were no enlargers in the lab," Dreyfoos explains, "and the PI (photographic interpretation) guys examined the negatives with magnifying glasses. The rule for the lab was to turn the film around and get it to PI within 30 minutes of wheels-down for each mission. So long as we were able to meet that standard, we could do just about anything else we wanted with the rest of our time."

Dreyfoos rapidly built up an on-time record that helped establish his reputation on the base. "One of my sergeants, who could 'moonlight requisition' just about anything, acquired some unauthorized aerial reconnaissance color film and matching processing chemicals," Dreyfoos remembers. "With it, we created some beautiful shots of the squadron planes over the Swiss Alps and with some castle in the background. That stuff made us really popular with the pilots and senior officers."

When the lab was on standby, waiting for the next photographic flight to land, Dreyfoos kept himself occupied. He examined ways to improve the consistency of the dye transfer process. "It was like having my own lab and darkroom. I explored how to make dye transfer less expensive and more repeatable. I finally decided that it would be difficult, maybe impossible, to significantly improve it. I was also interested in improving prints from 35 mm slides. The quality was terrible back then, except for dye transfer and a few more complex processes." The biggest problem, Dreyfoos concluded, was consistency in the colors of prints from slides.

While accumulating knowledge and experience, Dreyfoos often thought about what he had learned from Arthur Hardy. Except for physics, he had never taken a course from Hardy, but the professor had casually taught him the whole field of colorimetry, color spectrum, the tricolor theory, and how vision works. Nathaniel H. Pulling, another former student and friend of Hardy, wrote in 1958:

> [These] do not seem to be the most important things he taught us. They were rather the capacity for purposeful analytical thinking, and the ability to formulate significant and worthwhile questions before trying to find any answers. In this respect Hardy's philosophy reminds us of what another scientist wrote in Alice in Wonderland:
> "Would you tell me, please, which way I ought to go from here?"
> "That depends a good deal on where you want to get to," said the cat.
> . . . All the while [Hardy] was discussing the premises of the problem and the general nature of its solution, his slender gold pencil was flicking back and forth formulating the relevant equations on a pad of yellow paper. "And the darn thing doesn't even have an eraser!" one student was heard to remark. The clarity and precision of his thinking is legendary.

Pondering these lessons, Dreyfoos started to define how he would approach improving the consistency of color reproduction in photography, and owning and operating a photographic business.

Sembach Air Base

The work of Dreyfoos' photo lab was of great value to his country. The National Museum of the US Air Force at Wright-Patterson Air Force Base declares: "One of the most important and dangerous missions during the Cold War era (1949 to 1991) was electronic and photographic reconnaissance." In what is called the Cold War's "bloodiest period," between 1950 and 1962, twenty US aircraft, most on reconnaissance missions, were destroyed by the Soviet Union.

Before Sembach Air Base became a primary target of the Soviet Union, it was a French airfield used by occupation forces after the 1919 Armistice. When the occupation of Germany ended in 1930, the French troops withdrew from the left bank of the Rhine River, and the land returned to farming. The Third Riech's Luftwaffe began using Sembach as a fighter base in 1939, abandoning it to farming after conquering the French in 1940.

Throughout the Cold War, Sembach Air Base was a front-line NATO air base hosting several USAF Close-Air Support, Tactical Reconnaissance, and Tactical Air Control units. The base was designated for NATO use in 1950, with construction of new facilities and runways completed by summer 1953. Shortly before Dreyfoos arrived a year later, the USAF moved its 66th Tactical Reconnaissance Wing to Sembach from Shaw Air Force Base in South Carolina. A new, 8,500-foot concrete runway would service three Tactical Reconnaissance Squadrons (TRS): When Dreyfoos arrived, the 30th TRS was flying RB-57Ds. The 302nd and 303rd were flying RF-80 Shooting Star jets, and transitioned in late 1955 to RF-84F Thunderflash jets.

The Cold War role of Sembach is difficult to measure, because much of its post-World War II history remains cloaked in secrecy. Even so, the basic facts are clear: There was a tremendous need for information about Soviet weapons development and deployment. Equipped with the most sophisticated cameras and high-resolution films available, the aircraft based at Sembach probably carried out reconnaissance missions that included many nerve-wracking incursions into Soviet territory. Considering the activities originating at Sembach, the Soviets most likely had listed the air base as a primary initial target, should the Cold War suddenly turn hot.

During Dreyfoos' time at Sembach, President Dwight D. Eisenhower announced his concern that the USSR would consider an overflight by military aircraft to be an act of war, and proposed an "Open Skies" treaty in 1955. When the Soviets rejected the treaty in 1956, the US Central Intelligence Agency commenced reconnaissance flights using Lockheed U-2 aircraft. This continued in secret until the U-2 flown by Francis Gary Powers was shot down over Soviet territory in May 1960. These covert missions flew out of Landstuhl Air Base, the NATO strip adjoining Ramstein Air Station. The U-2's sophisticated optics required processing by equally sophisticated equipment back in the US Sometimes weather conditions raised the question of whether the footage was good enough to send home. Since there was no photo lab at Ramstein, it was brought to Dreyfoos' lab at Sembach for a determination: Keep it, or do over?

Dreyfoos concluded his military service in the fall of 1956. By 1959, Sembach had become a primary American missile base in Europe, adding a Tactical Missile Wing equipped with short range MGM-1 Matador and MGM-13 Mace ground-to-ground missiles. The importance of the base escalated with the addition of major communications and radar facilities. In 1971 the 17th Air Force moved its headquarters from Ramstein to Sembach Air Base.

With the Cold War over, in 1995 control of the Sembach flight line was given back to reunited Germany. The base is now an annex of Ramstein Air Base, renamed Sembach Annex. Administrative control remains under the command of the USAF-Europe. The runways have been dismantled and much of the former base has been turned into an industrial park.

The aircrews based at Sembach—along with their ground support and photo processing facilities—played critical roles in the gathering of intelligence necessary for maintenance of global security during the Cold War. Dreyfoos served among those Cold War veterans who quietly performed their assigned tasks, protecting the US from the threat of nuclear annihilation by the Soviet Union.

What's the Air Force Without Flying?

Dreyfoos has always had a passion for flying. It strongly influenced his choice of Air Force ROTC at MIT (although, if they had offered a Navy ROTC program, that would have been his first choice). With a small sum left over from his college loans, he had started flying lessons at MIT. "The lessons were inexpensive," he says, "so I had logged about seven flight hours on the flying club's Cessna 120 before I graduated."

Second Lt. Dreyfoos believed he could not meet the high vision standards to become an Air Force pilot, nor probably even the less stringent requirements for navigators, but he decided to give it a try. "I thought that if I didn't wear my glasses during Air Force summer camp, my eyesight might improve enough to pass the navigators' uncorrected-vision requirements. It worked, and I passed the flight physical during the last few days of camp." Then he returned to wearing his glasses. Apparently he had passed the test only marginally, because when they called him in for a retest, he failed. Dreyfoos considers that was probably a good thing. "Flight training would have required a four-year commitment instead of the two years I needed to serve without it."

One evening at the Sembach Officers' Club, Dreyfoos was relaxing with fellow officers and pilots when the subject of his interest in flying came up in the conversation. As he revealed his passion for aviation and his flight training at MIT, he also revealed his knowledge, and his respect for the experience and skill of the aviators. While his vision could not qualify him as an Air Force pilot, it was fine for general flying. One of the pilots stepped away from the bar and addressed the young officer: "Dreyfoos, do you want to go flying?"

"You bet."

"Then meet me tomorrow morning for radar training," commanded the pilot, clearly following the 8-hour "bottle-to-throttle" rule concerning alcohol consumption.

The reconnaissance pilots were known "hot shots" who were bored by ground-controlled approach (GCA) radar training. The purpose of the exercise was to provide the controllers with live radar images, using real aircraft, repeating real-time maneuvers over and over for the radar students. Having Dreyfoos aboard to do most of the repetitive flying made the experience a little less annoying for the pilots.

As he climbed into the jet waiting on the flight line, Dreyfoos was amused to see the pilot put on his oxygen mask and turn up his oxygen to 100 percent to rid himself of the hangover from the previous evening. Then he sternly ordered Dreyfoos, "Do *exactly* what radar control tells you to do."

In minutes, they were off the ground in the two-seat Lockheed T-33 Shooting Star, a modified training version of the Lockheed F-80.

"In those days," Dreyfoos explains, "there was no ILS (instrument landing system). There was nothing in your cockpit to tell you how to land. When visibility wasn't good, you turned to GCA (ground control approach). The controllers used radar to tell you what degree heading to take, and when and at what angle to descend. Then as you came closer, they would tell you if you were too low or too high on the glide slope or too much to the left or right."

This scenario repeated itself several times while Dreyfoos was at Sembach. Although he could not log the time toward his pilot's license, he learned to fly jets and enjoyed many hours at the controls before leaving the Air Force.

The Domestic Front

Joan Dreyfoos joined her husband at Sembach in December 1954. Although new housing was under construction at the base, as new arrivals they didn't qualify for it right away. The base assigned them living quarters in nearby Kaiserslautern in an old German building that Dreyfoos describes as "cold and cramped—not very nice." Though he wanted his wife to be comfortable, Dreyfoos did not give much thought to the quality of their living quarters. He was in the Air Force and in Europe, facing a whole new set of challenges and experiences. The following spring, the couple finally moved from their drafty, old accommodations into newly completed officers quarters on the base.

The Dreyfooses made the most of their location. The Air Force shipped over Dreyfoos' 1949 Oldsmobile Rocket 88, which he had purchased in 1951 with money from his summer job. "In our first year, we took our 30-day leave in 15 Fridays and Mondays, giving us 15 four-day weekends," Dreyfoos recalls, "with taking photographs as my main objective." Sembach's location close to the center of Western Europe made it possible to travel widely without buying expensive European gasoline. It cost 10 cents per gallon on the base, so he would fill the tank of his car and load the trunk with jerry cans full of extra fuel; the luggage went into the back seat. While touring, the Dreyfooses stayed at small, inexpensive hotels and family-owned pensions. The couple visited most of the major West European cities, but because of Dreyfoos' top-secret security clearance, they were not permitted to visit Berlin or any place east of the Iron Curtain.

Dreyfoos enjoyed touring with Joan and was okay with serving in the military, but was concerned that his wife seemed depressed. Her life was much different from her days as his sidekick at MIT. As a military wife, she was now expected to be a modern 1950s homemaker, focused on cooking, cleaning, and decorating. This role expanded suddenly on March 22, 1956 (Dreyfoos' 24th birthday), when Joan gave birth to their daughter, Catherine Marcia Dreyfoos, at Wiesbaden Army Hospital. ⚬⟜

Lt. Dreyfoos, first row seated, third from right end, at Sembach.

Dreyfoos (second from left) training NATO officers at Sembach Air Force Base in 1956.

Dreyfoos' photograph of a member of his team, on guard duty at Sembach Air Force Base.

The living room of Dreyfoos' on-base quarters, Sembach.

JOAN *AND* ALEX DREYFOOS

ARE HAPPY TO ANNOUNCE THE ARRIVAL OF

CATHERINE MARCIA

AT THE

WIESBADEN AIR FORCE HOSPITAL, GERMANY
ON

MARCH 22, 1956

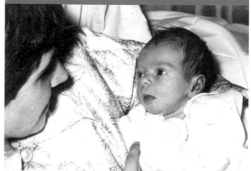

Announcement of Dreyfoos' first child in 1956.

Dreyfoos enjoying the balcony of his quarters at Sembach Air Force Base.

Dreyfoos' flying machines, in order of ownership:

(1) Cessna 310.

(2) and (3) Cessna 421 Models B and C; this is the 421C, the first of several registered as N12TV for WPEC.

(4) Cessna Conquest 441 turbo-prop, shown here at Merrill C. Meigs Field, Chicago.

(4) Dreyfoos in his Cessna Conquest 441.

(5) Cessna Citation II.

(6) Cessna Citation Ultra, taken by *Silver Cloud's* chef as Dreyfoos circled the boat.

(6) Interior of Citation Ultra.

(6) Instrument panel of Citation Ultra.

(7) Bell Jet Ranger owned by Dreyfoos and used as the news helicopter for WPEC. The station's helipad was round and surrounded by trees, so takeoff was straight up, requiring full power. Servo-controlled microwave equipment mounted under the copter allowed broadcasting direct from the air, putting the vehicle at maximum weight. These two factors meant the occupants had to forego air conditioning, an uncomfortable situation in South Florida.

(8) After seeing Miami WPLG-TV's air-conditioned AStar 350-B3 helicopter, Dreyfoos bought one for personal use after selling WPEC.

(8) Instrument panel of the AStar helicopter.

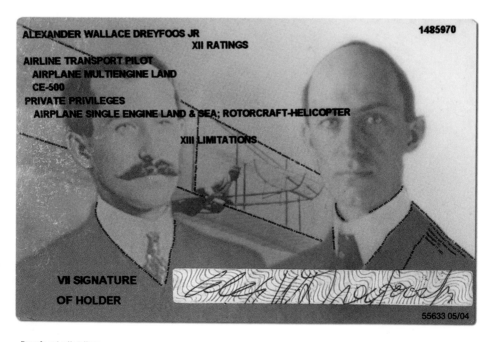

Dreyfoos' pilot license.

Dreyfoos flying an F16 out of Homestead Air Force Base, Florida, in 1981, later commenting, "Exciting adventure! I got sick during the synthesized dog-fight maneuvers, but amazing closing speeds, high G's."

Brigadier General George Doriot (1899-1987), a French immigrant and Harvard MBA graduate, was chosen to head the first public venture capital firm, American Research and Development Corporation (ARDC), in 1946. He also kept one foot at Harvard, teaching in the business school. In 1957, while he was Dreyfoos' instructor, he led ARDC to invest in two

---

A HEAD IN THE CLOUDS

From the time Dreyfoos left the Air Force, he had been eager to earn his pilot's license. The GI Bill then allowed applicants to make only one change in their educational program after approval. So, to calculate his GI Bill funding, he told the Veterans Administration that he wanted to get a PhD in Business Administration at Harvard. Then upon completing his master's degree (MBA) there, he revealed his educational program "change." He would use the remaining GI Bill funding to train as a commercial pilot, foregoing the Harvard doctorate.

The VA approved the change.

Dreyfoos took his remaining flight lessons at Westair Flying School at Westchester County Airport near White Plains, New York. This was the same airfield where, as a boy, he had been allowed to rummage through a squadron of abandoned World War II aircraft for electronic parts. "Returning to that airport was like going back to my childhood," he recollects.

Dreyfoos received his pilot's license in 1960. His ratings in 2015 included single-engine land and sea, instrument, multi-engine, commercial, and airline transport pilot (ATP). Since receiving his first license, he has owned six planes and two helicopters, most recently a Cessna Citation Ultra corporate jet and an AStar 350-B3 helicopter. He has logged more than 5,000 hours as single pilot-in-command.

When he found himself unable to instantly recall his IFR clearance details received from air traffic control, Dreyfoos attributed it to his age or Alzheimer's. When his younger pilot friend, Gary Lickle, heard Dreyfoos say this in an interview with CBS, his reaction was: "Any other pilot, including myself, would think occasional lapses were normal. It shows how high Alex's standards are for himself." Other pilot friends agree. By 2015, Dreyfoos let his medical certification lapse. "It was hard to give up," he laments. "I worked hard to buy my first plane. Then, for years, hardly a week passed when I wasn't in a pilot's seat, especially when I had the Citation and the helicopter at the same time. They showed me the beauty of our country in different ways: relatively close-up, from 500 feet above ground level in the helicopter, or above the weather, traveling far more quickly and comfortably at 41,000 feet and almost 500 mph in the Citation."

MIT engineers who founded Digital Equipment Corporation, credited with creating the mini-computer.

"According to Doriot's rules," Dreyfoos explains, "you will always read the *New York Times*. You will always read the *Wall Street Journal*. You will always read the most popular magazine of the day." The purpose is to keep students and future business leaders aware of events affecting business, and to stay in tune with the spirit of the times. There were also Doriot rules for selecting people with whom to work. "Always hire a doctor and an attorney younger than yourself. You will want them to be around when you are finally not around," Dreyfoos laughs. "There are a variety of Doriot rules that some people might see as a bunch of nonsense, but I was grateful to have someone *telling* me something for once, as opposed to having to figure it out for myself."

Don Riehl recalls a few other Doriot rules: "Never put your attorney or investment broker on your board of directors, because their function is as advisor; and always read the obituaries, to learn about those whose path you are following." Riehl adds that Doriot provided these guidelines "to get you started, until you figure out your own." ☞

Dreyfoos at Harvard Business School in 1958.

The front view of the Dreyfoos home, 20 Eagles Bluff, Rye, New York, in the early 1960s.

Donald Riehl in 2003, at Dreyfoos' Adirondacks summer home.

Harvard Business School Professor General George Doriot.

Bernard Shlossman and friend, decades after attending Harvard Business School.

CHAPTER 6

Beginning a Beautiful Friendship

George Mergens and Alex Dreyfoos demonstrating the Pavelle P100 prototype, which they invented while employed by the Pavelle Corporation.

Summer in Technicolor

During the summer of 1957, between his first and second years at Harvard Business School, Dreyfoos worked as a draftsman at Technicolor NY Corporation on 57th Street in Manhattan. The company was a division of the famed Hollywood motion picture enterprise, but this unit mostly processed color film for amateur photographers. Two of the first memorable color motion pictures, *Gone With the Wind* and *The Wizard of Oz* in 1939, had used the Technicolor process. Dreyfoos eagerly absorbed everything he could learn about the Technicolor NY operation.

Dreyfoos worked under the director of engineering there, a man four years his senior named George Mergens. They immediately took a liking to each other. The pair analyzed the quality of Technicolor NY's operations and recognized how paying closer attention to adjustments and processing tolerances would result in better color quality. Dreyfoos enjoyed the work, especially with his new friend, George.

CHANGES FOR KODAK

"Until January 1955," Dreyfoos explains, "consumers purchased Kodak color film with the price of processing included. You got a little bag, and you sent it back for printing. There was almost no color processing for amateurs done outside of Kodak." In 1954 Kodak was facing a federal antitrust lawsuit, so its chairman, Thomas Hargrave, agreed to a consent decree ending Kodak's advance payment processing system. Under the agreement, Eastman Kodak had to drop its fair-trade pricing of color films and license independent processors, who would pay royalties, to use Kodak's color processing patents. The government was essentially charging Kodak with price-fixing under the Miller-Tydings and McGuire acts. "To be fair, the processing of Kodak color film was complicated and difficult," Dreyfoos explains. "Kodak set up its own color laboratories, because it wanted to make sure its color film was properly processed and made its customers happy. Kodak played the consent decree smartly and figured out how to have it both ways. They would comply with the Miller-Tydings rules. Yet they would profit by designing, building, and selling color printers and processing machines, and by teaching their commercial black-and-white print customers how to print color."

The increasing interest in television, meanwhile, had slowed down the economics of the motion picture business and put the motion picture film and processing leader, Technicolor Corporation, in a slump. Compounding this difficulty, black and white "film noir" movies were popular in the 1950s. "Technicolor was hurting, and while I can't back this up," Dreyfoos allows, "my theory is that Technicolor may have in some manner instigated the antitrust suit against Eastman Kodak."

At the same time, Kodak had introduced Eastman Color negative film and color print film that could be processed in modified black and white film processing machines. The major film companies had always done their own black and white processing, so they just started processing their own simpler-to-process color film. Clearly, Technicolor saw they were about to lose professional motion picture processing business to Kodak and that they needed to reposition themselves to gain the best advantage in a changing situation. "The door was open to any photo processing company to tap into the huge amateur customer demand for Kodak color processing," Dreyfoos observes.

Leaving Academia Behind

After graduating from Harvard Business School with an MBA in the spring of 1958, Dreyfoos was anxious to get to work on his ideas to improve color photography that he had been contemplating for years, but the time to become his own boss was not quite right. During the first summer after graduation, he was able to return to Technicolor in New York to learn more about their unique business.

This period added significantly to Dreyfoos' photo processing knowledge and overall credentials. The original Technicolor Corporation had made major contributions to color film technology. The company was built around the inventions of Herbert T. Kalmus, one of the company's 1915 founders and an MIT graduate. Indeed, the "Tech" in Technicolor was said to be a tribute to MIT. The Technicolor process had quickly become the standard for nearly all of the Hollywood studios making color pictures. The company essentially had had a lock on color motion picture film and processing in Hollywood until the 1950s.

Back at Technicolor NY, Dreyfoos also enjoyed reconnecting with George Mergens, but this time was a different experience. Dreyfoos was hired as director of quality control—on the same level as Mergens, the director of engineering. Mergens was happy to see Dreyfoos and showed it with good-natured teasing: "It's good they put you in charge of QC, because you are the world's worst draftsman!"

Mergens had graduated from high school at the Polytechnic Institute of Brooklyn (now Polytechnic Institute of New York University) and apprenticed with his father in aircraft manufacturing at Grumman Aircraft and Republic Aviation, becoming a journeyman tool-and-die maker of the highest skill. When World War II came along, he signed up. "He saw no reason to go to a traditional college," Dreyfoos explains. "He learned languages, he knew math, and he picked up the rest on his own, clearly outshining most anybody who had gone the other route. He was much brighter than I was. But he was not a natural risk-taker."

Herb Stein, a co-worker at Technicolor, later wrote:

We had two first-class engineers on staff. . . . George Mergens and Alex Dreyfoos Jr. were not only outstanding technicians but were blessed with great personalities as well. Their positions with the company were essential since much of the specialized hardware necessary to conduct business was not readily available from vendors. This group had to design and build all required photo equipment by themselves. Pioneers in the world of color photography for sure!

These directors of quality control and engineering gained a reputation as the "Wild Duo." They were out to raise the quality of Technicolor prints, believing that it would lead to more business, but they soon concluded the company needed to fix a whole list of problems in its production line. As Dreyfoos remembers the dilemma, "The company was pulling the strings from 3,000 miles away in Hollywood, with no interest in adding even slightly to costs to achieve that goal. George and I, on the other hand, were motivated to make an excellent product. The result was frustration."

They both decided to leave the company.

Dreyfoos believed Mergens, especially, had a right to his dissatisfaction. He had designed most of the company's mechanical equipment for Pavelle Color before it was purchased by Technicolor in 1956, and knew the company inside out. While Mergens was a master mechanic with sophisticated skills, Dreyfoos felt that Technicolor had discriminated against him because of his lack of a college degree. "They brought in all of these high-powered guys who didn't know what they were talking about."

Unhappy and insulted, Mergens left Technicolor before Dreyfoos, in late 1958. He moved to Winsted Precision Ball Company in Connecticut, a machine works that produced the high-quality balls used in bearings for guidance systems in missiles and satellites. There he could, as he put it, "grind my balls." Joking aside, Mergens truly enjoyed working for the company, because it cared about precision—and, unlike at Technicolor, he could excel in his work.

While still at Technicolor, Dreyfoos continued to think about his idea for a color analyzer. He gave his employer a letter describing a primitive version, but Technicolor passed on the opportunity, showing no interest. Disappointed, Dreyfoos asked for and received from Technicolor the legal rights to his concept. What he learned at Technicolor became one more set of building blocks toward his creation of a new technological approach to color reproduction in photography.

A Growing Family

Dreyfoos also felt the pull of domestic responsibility. On October 24, 1958, he became the father of two with the birth of Robert Whittemore Dreyfoos. After moving his family into the house Joan's father helped them build in Rye, Dreyfoos left Technicolor for IBM (International Business Machines) in early 1959.

As their children got a little older, the family joined White Plains Community Unitarian Church, for its broad religious views. Here Dreyfoos got to know Whitney Young, a decade older, from Kentucky. His mother was the first African American postmistress in the United States and his father, the first black president of a school for blacks. In 1961, after becoming director of the National Urban League based in New York City, Young moved his family to New Rochelle and joined Dreyfoos' church. The activist appreciated this congregation, where members had long been addressing local poverty and racial inequality, founding what became the county's Urban League and other social service organizations. Knowing Young reinforced Dreyfoos' belief that the quality of people was unrelated to their race.

Up the (Hudson) River

IBM hired Dreyfoos as an engineer in the Advanced Systems Development Division, "between the research laboratory and the operating divisions," Dreyfoos says, "just my cup of tea!" While IBM was building a new facility in Armonk, Dreyfoos reported to the temporary space in Ossining, overlooking New York's infamous Sing Sing Correctional Facility on the Hudson River. Despite the accommodations, Dreyfoos' time "up the river" was like a dream come true. "It was a great place to work. I liked the IBM culture, and the research there was second to none." Dreyfoos also eagerly learned about designing transistor circuitry, and received his first patent.

At Dreyfoos' urging, IBM invited George Mergens in for an interview. "They were working on a high-speed mechanical printer that had problems I thought George was uniquely qualified to help solve. They toured him around the shop, and even showed him the printer, which worked off a bicycle chain with the letters on the links. He proposed a couple of ideas right off the bat on how to fix some of the bugs." Ultimately, IBM offered Mergens only a technician's job. They refused to consider him for an engineer position because he lacked a college degree. Dreyfoos advised his friend not to accept the offer. "They would not have treated him with the respect he deserved."

Although Dreyfoos enjoyed the other aspects of working at IBM, he found it difficult to get over his disappointment with the company's inability to see the value in George Mergens. Today Dreyfoos concedes that if IBM *had* made Mergens an engineer, they would likely both have remained "company men" for many years. Dreyfoos and Mergens might never have collaborated on the inventive projects that were to follow.

The Development of Genius

The engineer is the key figure in the material progress of the world. It is his engineering that makes a reality of the potential value of science by translating scientific knowledge into tools, resources, energy and labor to bring them into the service of man. . . . To make contributions of this kind the engineer requires the imagination to visualize the needs of society and to appreciate what is possible . . . to bring his vision to reality.

Sir Eric Ashby
Technology and the Academies
(MacMillan, 1959)

In the first half of the 20th century, lone inventors endowed with the knowledge and tools necessary to harness the fundamental laws of physics brought about dramatic technological changes. Business titans embraced these inventor-scientists, purchasing and controlling patent rights and building great fortunes around a single invention. Eventually, businesses established research laboratories and development departments in order to control the pace of technological change to maximize the profitability of each new invention. By mid-century, the domain of lone inventors had largely given way to corporate research and development, or R&D.

An exception to the corporate R&D model is apparent in the story of engineer Alex Dreyfoos and the Video Color Negative Analyzer, or VCNA.

Dreyfoos aimed to solve a vexing problem that a century of photographic inventiveness had left uncorrected, to wit: Color reproduction could be made more efficient and could produce better quality results more quickly, consequently lowering overall costs. Dreyfoos believed that the key was in predicting how to expose a print with more precision, eliminating the trial-and-error printing method that led to many off-color prints being consigned to the wastebasket.

It was MIT Professor Arthur Hardy who had identified the potential in combining Dreyfoos' dual interests in photography and electronics. What he learned from Hardy led Dreyfoos to visualize how the objective electronic identification of colors could remove the guesswork from color film processing.

Though Arthur Hardy excelled as a professor and author, he had more than the heart of an academic sharing knowledge. He was quoted as often saying, "I've never been interested in projects that wouldn't produce results in my lifetime." Undoubtedly Hardy recognized in Dreyfoos the same goal-oriented drive.

After Dreyfoos accumulated several years of business intelligence, including knowledge of transistor circuitry design, he was prepared to start his own project. All the while, the photo processing industry was heading in a direction that would ultimately leap at the chance to grasp the technology that was brewing in this young engineer's head. He was aware of parallel efforts among the major photographic businesses to create a device to read color negatives. If he was to take the lead, he needed two things, and he needed them fast: a working model of his design, and a partner who spoke his language. The ideal partner would understand his mind, and possess the skills to fabricate mechanical parts, and the drive to work with him through the process of final assembly.

A year before Dreyfoos' summer stint at Technicolor—before Technicolor purchased it—the company had been Pavelle Color, an established photographic laboratory and processing service company.

Latvian-born Leo Pavelle was highly respected in the industry for his understanding of photo finishing. In fact, Pavelle's experience with photo film had started off in the early 1940s with Ansco film and an Ansco print material called "Printon." (During World War II the German-American partnership of Agfa-Ansco dropped the German part of its name and its US interests were taken over by the US government under the Alien Properties Act.)

Leo Pavelle and his brother Si (Simon) had built a color processing plant during World War II for the US Army under a government contract, then purchased it back cheaply after the war. Besides their color processing laboratory in Manhattan, on 57th Street between 10th and 11th Avenues, they now had dealers in 22 major cities, including Hollywood. They were well positioned, with a pickup-and-delivery distribution system primarily built around Ansco's lower quality products.

According to Dreyfoos, the Technicolor offer was one that Pavelle could not refuse. "Technicolor wanted Pavelle Color to get ahead of Kodak in bringing labs who were doing black-and-white processing in drugstores and camera shops into the color business. Kodak's monopoly, prior to the consent decree, limited its profitability. The sale of Pavelle Color to Technicolor made Leo Pavelle wealthy." The new owners immediately prepared to handle Kodak film.

In 1961, after the five-year non-compete clause in his sales agreement with Technicolor expired, Leo Pavelle purchased a small English company, which he renamed The Pavelle Corporation.

About that time, Pavelle telephoned Dreyfoos from his office in the Time-Life Building in Manhattan.

Pavelle offered the young engineer a job leading an effort to build and bring online a new, simpler-than-Kodak, color film processing machine based on a patent held by two men in England. The patent was for color coupler dyes, which would permit the manufacture of a color photographic print paper that could be processed in three minutes instead of the 47 minutes required by Kodak's paper. Leo Pavelle wanted Dreyfoos to design and build a machine to make prints using this new color print paper.

"What will it take to get you to work for me, Dreyfoos?" Pavelle asked. After thinking about it for a moment, Dreyfoos responded, "I will take the job only on the condition that you also hire George Mergens to work on the project with me." Pavelle was agreeable, and soon Dreyfoos found himself at the controls of a small plane rented for the occasion by Pavelle. The two flew to Connecticut and met with Mergens who, after some consideration, accepted the proposition.

Soon the trio was aboard a commercial jetliner headed for England to meet the inventors of the new photographic paper. The offices of Drs. Kurt Jacobson and Gerald White of Photo-Chemical Co. Ltd. were in Epsom, southwest of London. Arriving in Epsom, the Americans exchanged pleasantries with Jacobson and White, who showed them the new photographic paper. Examining and comparing the samples, they concluded that it was better color than Polaroid or Ansco's Printon, but not quite as good as Kodak. Still, there was considerable promise in what they saw. Pavelle directed Dreyfoos and Mergens to get to work on a machine to expose and process prints using the new paper—not unlike the way computer desktop printers do today.

"I designed the exposing system and temperature controls," Dreyfoos recalls. "Three patents were issued for our work. George designed and built a great system for automatically moving paper through the machine. We were written up in *Business Week*. With all of that, Leo took the company public."

Dreyfoos brought in Bernie Shlossman, a classmate from Harvard Business School, to handle marketing. Shlossman spent an "interesting but not so successful year" there before returning to his former advertising agency. The best part of Shlossman's job, he says, was leaving the Manhattan office to spend a day with Dreyfoos and Mergens at the White Plains lab, "watching them invent things." The duo was set up in a former post office, closer to their homes than a daily trek to the big city.

What Jacobson and White never told Pavelle, Dreyfoos, or Mergens (or perhaps they never realized) was that the prints did not last. Dreyfoos was dismayed. "The colors went bad. The whites became yellow. It would never work commercially." As a result of the project's serious defects and ultimate failure, Dreyfoos and Mergens decided to leave the company. Although Pavelle was disappointed, he agreed to sell them, at nominal cost, the tools and test gear they had assembled for the project.

By 1963, all of the elements necessary to permanently change the way color photographs were printed had come together clearly in Dreyfoos' mind. Once his idea was put into practice, color photography would no longer be the inconsistent result of guesswork. He envisioned the photography industry embracing his solution, because it would save time and money and dramatically raise the average quality of non-amateur color photographs. Working with George Mergens, he knew he would succeed. Dreyfoos set the paperwork in motion to create their company, Photo Electronics Corporation. Dreyfoos owned 51 percent of the stock; Mergens, 49 percent. ☜

Cathy Dreyfoos, 1959.

Robert Dreyfoos, c. 1964.

Dreyfoos' IBM identification badge.

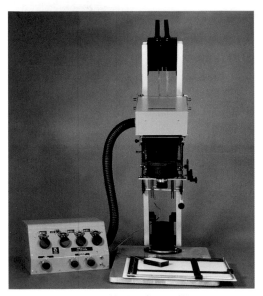

(left to right) Brothers Simon (Si) and Leo Pavelle.

The Pavelle P45, invented by Dreyfoos and Mergens, shown with the lamp housing mounted on a Simmon Omega enlarger.

The lamp housing for the Pavelle P45 color enlarger.

Dreyfoos at the Kodak booth at the 1962 Photo Marketing Association (PMA) convention, holding a brochure for the P100 that Dreyfoos and Mergens developed for Pavelle.

CHAPTER 7

Photo Electronics Corporation

The entrance to PEC's offices in a former church in Byram, Connecticut.

Every once in a while a product comes along that changes the way work is done, that makes such an impact on an industry that time is marked as "before" and "after" that product was introduced. The Video Color Negative Analyzer (VCNA) is one of those products.

Edith Gordon, "Contribution to the Lab"
Photo Lab Management, February 1991

Brilliance in the Basement

Dreyfoos and Mergens moved the tools they had purchased from Pavelle into the basement of Dreyfoos' home in Port Chester, New York. The setup was pleasant enough. They wired the place for sound, listening most of the day to classical music played over WQXR, the *New York Times* station in Manhattan. Dreyfoos remembers one Friday afternoon about two weeks after they moved in, when the music was interrupted: "We were finally getting comfortable, when WQXR reported the assassination of President Kennedy in Dallas. It was such a shock. Like me, everyone alive back then would always remember exactly where they were that day, November 22, 1963." It was already a somber day for Dreyfoos, the 12th anniversary of his father's death in 1951.

In an upstairs office, Joan Dreyfoos kept the books during the period the men operated below. The Dreyfoos children, Cathy and Robert, were in grade school at the time and had a playroom near the office, but they later remembered the basement being strictly off limits.

Though Dreyfoos and Mergens were only ages 31 and 35, they committed themselves to long-term success of the company. With their experience and the new equipment, they were able to secure enough contract work to keep Photo Electronics (PEC) going for its first few years, chiefly from IBM, Pavelle, and Berkey.

IBM had been unable to replace Dreyfoos in-house. They learned about Dreyfoos' new status through his former research partner, Al Staley, who was still employed there. IBM offered Dreyfoos consultant work for more money than he had made on staff.

Computers were monsters then, and the hospitals that IBM was trying to make customers lacked the space to accommodate them. They did, however, have large rooms filled with archival x-rays, from former patients. To free up that space, IBM asked Dreyfoos if he could reduce an x-ray to 35 mm microfilm size, without losing the quality that a radiologist needed for diagnosis. Microfilm was intended for black-and-white without tonal qualities, but Dreyfoos found high-resolution films and modified the process to improve those qualities. IBM was pleased with PEC's results, but before long, their machines shrank and the need faded away. Al Staley managed PEC's IBM contract, and joined Photo Electronics some months later as circuit reliability engineer after that work was complete, enticed with a small part of the ownership in PEC. Dreyfoos credits Staley as a "good detail guy, who had a significant role in increasing system reliability."

While Dreyfoos and Mergens were still on Pavelle's payroll, they had designed a color enlarger that would have competed with the Simmon Chromega enlarger, as well as the P100, a small printer-processor for home use. By now Xerox Corporation had taken an option to purchase Pavelle Corporation. While Xerox was trying to market the P100, they would hire the duo at PEC to act as employees and make presentations of the product to potential customers, including the military.

Berkey Photo, Inc., like Pavelle, was a competitor of Kodak, and manufactured primarily for the professional cameraman. They commissioned Photo Electronics to build two probes in a device called Simtron to go under the Simmon Chromega, one of their major products.

Dreyfoos was grateful for the contract work, but wanted to pursue his idea for a color analyzer. At first Mergens believed the scheme was too complex to build, so Dreyfoos started working on it at night, after his partner had gone home for the day. Finally, Dreyfoos got Mergens interested with a demonstration. Using rudimentary parts, he set up a crude picture of a color negative looking like a positive when viewed using a rotary filter wheel. With that, he talked Mergens into working with him on the analyzer. "Some of the mechanical devices that Mergens made for me were very crude," says Dreyfoos, "sometimes made out of wood rather than aluminum." By now it was the end of 1964, and they were both excited about the prospects for their business.

The Dreyfoos Approach to Color Reproduction

Into the 1960s, the high-quality end of color photographic reproduction relied on the judgment of a human being to facilitate the printing process. This almost always included multiple iterations of prints from a single negative until the photograph had passable colors, a process that wasted not only stacks of paper and gallons of chemicals, but an excessive amount of time. It took 47 minutes of processing to see the latest iteration. Color negatives were orange, with all the colors and tones reversed, and prints took up to an hour just to dry. Because the operator had to decide how many pictures went into the wastebasket before the picture was "good enough," the final product was always a subjective compromise.

When it came to technology, Dreyfoos bristled at that word, "compromise." To him, it meant something less than top quality. Clearly, the solution was a video analyzer that allowed the operator to preview an electronically displayed image *before* printing. Dreyfoos knew that the machine he wanted to create—which he would call the Video Color Negative Analyzer—would have to be seen as the solution to reduce or end this waste. It would be commercially successful because it would pay for itself.

As he engineered his analyzer in his mind, Dreyfoos decided to use an early color television device, the flying spot scanner, to read the colors in photographic negatives. The original mechanical scanner had been patented by American researcher Frank Gray in 1927, and an electronic version a year later by Manfred von Ardenne in Germany. Dreyfoos placed his modified electronic flying spot scanner at the front end of his invention to accurately "read" color negatives before printing. Dreyfoos elaborates:

"In the photo lab, one generally started with the assumption that the negative in front of you might be like the last one, so one would print it with the same enlarger settings and exposure time. An hour later (the time it took to process a color print in the '60s), one could see how right or wrong that assumption had been. Generally, correction was required. While it was easy to determine that the print was, say, too dark and blue, it was very difficult to say it was 12 percent (5 cc's) too blue and 26 percent (10 cc's) too dark. So often, in an iterative process of reducing errors, three, four, or even five prints were made before one could say that the print would probably not look any better lighter, darker, redder (or less red: cyan), greener (or less green: magenta), or bluer (or less blue: yellow).

"The machines that were then being used for drugstore-quality processing to determine exposure—so that your picture of Aunt Millie looked a little bit like Aunt Millie—made certain assumptions, which was better than making no assumptions. Funny, the industry called it a 'subject failure,' but the subject wasn't failing; it was the equipment looking at the subject that was failing.

"The VCNA would present an immediate positive color image view of the color negative on a television screen, allowing the iterative process to take place effortlessly without thinking of 5 cc's or 10 cc's, but just turning the dials until the image looked right. These settings would then be taken to the darkroom, where the analyzer data would be entered and a print exposed." This eye-brain-fingers-turning-the-dial feedback mechanism is described in the study of cybernetics by Norbert Wiener, who had taught at MIT. Dreyfoos considered this and other man-and-machine theories as he designed the VCNA, but adds, "My application was quite simplistic compared to Wiener's complex math on moving targets."

Dreyfoos' design included "feedback circuits" that would allow the machine to correct itself for degradation of the cathode ray tube's (CRT's) phosphorescent screens over time. With his knowledge of transistors, Dreyfoos solved many other difficult problems, especially those caused by heat. His VCNA would be cool-running and would surpass the performance of inventions that used vacuum tubes. He believed it would provide the stability and reliability to better predict the outcome of the printing process. His patents also addressed the distortion of the inherently linear electronic circuitry to match the nonlinear results of the chemical paper process.

All that was missing now was a working model to test his ideas.

A RELIABLE SOLUTION

The first transistors for *applied* uses only appeared in the late 1950s. Dreyfoos' only exposure to them at MIT in the mid-'50s was a paragraph or two in a textbook. Transistors had existed, however, since scientists at Bell Telephone Laboratories in New Jersey found that germanium crystals could be used as simple amplifiers in electrical circuits. Late on December 16, 1947, Walter Brattain and John Bardeen, working under Bell scientist William Shockley, attached electrical contacts to a germanium crystal. They then attached meters to the input and output leads on either side of the crystal. When they applied power and a signal, they observed the output was greater than the input. The crystal had, as was the theory, amplified the input power and signal. The "transconductance" of germanium had been proven and the first practical point-contact "transistor" had been invented.

The advantages of using transistors instead of vacuum tubes quickly became apparent. First, they were smaller, reducing the size of electronic circuits. Second, because they were more efficient as amplifiers than were vacuum tubes, they generated less heat. Simply put, transistors were more reliable than vacuum tubes.

While Brattain, Bardeen, and Shockley built the first practical transistors and improved them to the point of being equal to and better than vacuum tubes, they did not invent transistors. That credit goes to Julius Edgar Lilienfeld, who had developed and patented several devices that would now be referred to as either field effect or point junction transistors. Shockley's original patent claim for the field effect transistor (FET) was completely rejected, and Bardeen's point junction transistor patent had over half its claims dismissed, due to Lilienfeld's prior work.

By the 1950s, scientists, inventors, and engineers like Alex Dreyfoos were replacing vacuum tubes with highly efficient transistors in every possible application. Transistors gave birth to microelectronics. Reducing heat and mass, the transistor's solid-state benefits continue to the present day.

A Functional Prototype

As a parade of trucks delivering parts came and went from his home on a cul-de-sac in Rye, Dreyfoos worried that his neighbors might wonder what was going on in his basement. Perhaps the next knock at the door might be a county code enforcement officer with a lot of questions; his address was not zoned for manufacturing. In order to delay the arrival of an officer as long as possible, Dreyfoos specified that all shipments be made by UPS, which already made frequent deliveries to his neighborhood for stores such as Bonwit Teller and Macy's. "We were able to do a lot of designing with reasonably small parts, but eventually we needed the delivery of large sheets of aluminum," says Dreyfoos. "I knew it was only a matter of time before we would need to relocate."

Building the VCNA was tedious but exhilarating. The duo was now on its way to the mission of inventors. They discussed every component in detail, going back and forth until they agreed on a clear vision of how it worked and how it looked—only then did they plan and fabricate it. The process included calibration, testing, disappointments, more calibrations, more testing, celebrations, and a great multitude of trips to the virtual drawing boards in their minds.

Their combined skills got the job done. As Dreyfoos describes him, "George did not begin with drawings. He visualized what I described. Then with his photographic mind, he would start off with a block of aluminum and nothing else. Only after the whole machine was finished would he make drawings. Most of the design specifications of the VCNA were put on paper after the prototype was finished. Only infrequently would Mergens pull out his ruler and check a measurement. In essence, all of his designs were in his head. It was far more complex for me, requiring calculus and matrix calculations."

In Dreyfoos' head were the function and pattern of every circuit board. From start to finish, he visualized the electronic process over and over to perfect it. He calculated and recalculated the math. He imagined the electronic path from the scanning of the color negative at the front end, through each circuit board, to the analysis data at the other end, the numerical values for the setup of a color processor. The two men were well matched.

As Photo Electronics Corporation took on more work (and local zoning officials eventually caught up with them doing business in a residential area),

Dreyfoos and Mergens decided to leave their basement workshop. Mergens pressed to move to Connecticut, where he and his family lived. He wanted to get out of New York, saying it didn't seem fair that, as a Connecticut resident, he had to pay New York state income tax.

In March 1965, they found a place just over the New York State line in Byram, Connecticut, taking over the Sunday school section of what had been St. Paul's Lutheran Church.

Soon they were settled in and back to work. They had engineered the operating logic of the analyzer from the point of view of the operator. Facing the machine, the analyzer would be a simple and logical device. Working from left to right, the operator placed the color negative to be scanned in the gate at the extreme left of the machine. Next, while viewing the image on the CRT in the center of the machine, the operator turned four knobs, from left to right, for density, then for cyan-red, magenta-green, and last, yellow-blue. One of the three color dials would always remain at zero. At first, the coded processor instructions were written on the negative envelope and delivered to the darkroom. Later the data would be printed on a small receipt-style printer and later still, punched onto a perforated tape at the far right of the machine.

The fabrication process came to a gratifying end. Piece by piece, they had assembled their first VCNA. Not realizing that Underwriters Laboratories would require a metal cabinet for their masterpiece, they enclosed the prototype in a handsome wooden case and stood back, observing it as a thing of beauty, a work of art. Even these artists could not have dreamed where this early machine would lead.

Finally, they could celebrate!

Up until this point, without a working VCNA, only theoretical tests had been possible. While Dreyfoos had calibrated the machine using voltage and illumination measurements, it was time for the "acid test." They had set up a small darkroom to make prints from actual images, first scanning the negative images with the prototype VCNA, then taking the setup data into the darkroom for printing. A problem arose.

Dreyfoos vividly remembers, "I took the readings from the video analyzer and made pictures in the darkroom, and they were terrible! What I discovered was that the Densichron (a type of densitometer used in professional photog-

says Dreyfoos, "but I'm told it was a room full of vacuum tubes—200 or so—with at least one failing every few days. It needed a full-time engineer to keep it adjusted, and it didn't work anyhow," he laughs. His own design had also begun with vacuum tubes. Technicolor had turned down that original design because of those very tubes, which made the machine impractical. Then Dreyfoos went to work at IBM, where they realized the transistor was going to replace everything, and taught its value to their employees.

For Dreyfoos, the light bulb went off. It all came together and made sense.

Kodak descended on Photo Electronics Corporation in Byram. "They were very interested," Dreyfoos says, "but they seemed sure that either I had put trained monkeys inside the box to do the work, or that when they left for the day, I was sneaking in there and recalibrating it. Kodak asked us not to talk with anyone else and paid us to mark time. Actually, that was good, because we made additional improvements that increased the reliability and accuracy of the invention."

Finally, beyond his initial hopes, Kodak told Dreyfoos they would consider, not just recommending, but marketing, the device. First, they wanted him to deliver a machine to Rochester so they could test it themselves. "They absolutely did not believe that it was as stable as it was," he remembers. "They also marveled at how small it was. At that time, the industry was still committed to vacuum tubes but scrambling to embrace transistors. We were one of the few companies outside of the military industrial complex, IBM, and some Japanese radio makers, where transistors were understood and applied. Our analyzer was unique."

Bob Locker at Kodak, who eventually became both friend and liaison, remembers those early days. "Alex and George were really uncanny. They even kept beds in the plant, and if you gave them a problem, they had something working by tomorrow. In the same amount of time, Kodak would have been hard-pressed to cut the paperwork explaining the project!"

As a small company, Photo Electronics Corporation did have the ability to move more quickly than large corporations. It also attributed its success to its knowledge of colorimetry, photographic processing, and transistor design theory. PEC had placed itself in competition with the goliaths of the electronic imaging businesses of the time—CBS, NBC, Technicolor, and Hazeltine—and had won for itself a significant piece of the action.

After all of their work and worry, Dreyfoos and Mergens struck a deal with the biggest name in photography, Eastman Kodak, to market their Video Color Negative Analyzer.

Many people may presume that the man behind this company was named Mr. Eastman Kodak, but it was George Eastman. In 1881 he opened the world headquarters of the Eastman Dry Plate Company at 343 State Street, where they remained, on the left bank of the Genesee River. The word "Kodak" was a meaningless anagram he invented with his mother, the trademark name he registered to give his products a totally unique identification. Dreyfoos remembers learning that Eastman had taken the time to check out the meaning of the word "Kodak" in other languages, to make sure it was universally positive.

Eastman revolutionized photography by producing roll film and selling it in 100-exposure Brownie cameras that were returned to Kodak for processing and printing and reloaded after all of the film was exposed. His market slogan said it all: "You press the button, we do the rest." Pretty soon most every middle-class household in America owned a Kodak and had a family photo album on the coffee table.

By the time Alex Dreyfoos made his deal with Kodak, it had become a major public corporation. The name of the multinational industrial giant had long been synonymous with photography in all parts of the globe. One might wonder what role the VCNA played for Kodak stockholders' fortunes. The device was talked about in Kodak's annual reports without mentioning Photo Electronics Corporation.

The deal did not come easily. Kodak had initially expressed concern about being able to sell the first 15 VCNAs produced by PEC, leading to a "go, no go" agreement that made Dreyfoos and Mergens nervous.

Kodak had already put them through a standstill period, paying them $40,000 to stop working for a few months while they tested the prototype to verify its accuracy and reliability. Kodak's testing lab was located at their Rochester headquarters. Dreyfoos rented a Ford van, loaded up the prototype, and drove it to Rochester. During the ride he encountered a snowstorm, once skidding off the New York State Thruway before reaching the Kodak facilities.

Ultimately, Kodak's engineers were impressed. The remaining hurdle was to see if their customers would buy the machines. Retail priced at $25,000 each, the VCNA was several times more expensive than any Kodak-labeled

VCNA MARKETING

Until the Video Color Negative Analyzer, Kodak had never marketed a device under two names. (See photos, page 145-146) It was listed as the "Kodak VCNA Designed and Built for Eastman Kodak Company by Photo Electronics Corp." In general, it was the Kodak practice with equipment built by other companies to have them labeled singularly as Kodak products.

From a 1968 Kodak VCNA sales brochure:

The KODAK Video Color Negative Analyzer
Heart of a Productive New Method for Evaluating Color Negatives

Faster, more accurate evaluation of Kodak Ektacolor and Kodacolor negatives is now possible—and foolproof production of color prints is closer to reality—thanks to a new Kodak system that lets you analyze a color negative electronically.

Key to the new system's unique capability is the Kodak Video Color Negative Analyzer. Teamed with the Kodak Video Color Negative Translator, it forms a highly specialized electronic evaluating system that helps professional, commercial, and industrial color processing laboratories reduce the time, material, and labor required for the production of quality color prints.

HERE'S HOW
- Simply turn on the VCNA.
- Place any color negative in the gate. Instantly, the negative image is electronically transformed into a positive color picture on the video viewing screen.
- You adjust the density of the picture you see. (The controls allow the operator to get the brightness, or density setting, correct before adjusting the colors.)
- Then adjust the red-cyan, green-magenta, and blue-yellow dials until you are satisfied with the resultant color balance.
- Now, these four easily obtained control settings become the exposure data for your color print. The Color Translator controls are set to match the Analyzer control settings and you're on the way to an acceptable color print the first time with 80 to 85% frequency. Several Kodak VCNA users have reported getting even better results.

THINK ABOUT IT
You've just evaluated a color negative—maybe even a very complicated negative—and controlled the resultant print without the cost, bother or uncertainty of making a test print. Your method is accurate. Fast. And as nearly foolproof as color evaluation can be. Here, at this critical state, where it used to take two or even three tries to get the color print you wanted, you've gotten an acceptable print the first time! In virtually the time it took to move four dials. This is where the Kodak VCNA begins to pay off on your initial investment. And where improved color-print quality begins to shine through!

THE VITAL LINK
This new Kodak system for evaluating color negatives is the critical element in a truly mechanized color processing system. Until now, color evaluation has depended on human judgment alone. Now Kodak offers you the electronic accuracy of the VCNA for maximum speed, quality and efficiency.

Color Lab product sold before that time—most Kodak printers and processors then cost between $2,000 and $3,000.

PEC's owners went to Chicago for the 1967 Photo Marketing Association convention, worried about how sales would go. Dreyfoos, knowing he was risking losing the deal altogether, dug in his heels and told Kodak they would have to buy either all 15 machines or none. At first the Kodak people resisted, insisting that there was no way of knowing whether the machines would sell. Fortunately, the top Kodak vice president, Henry "Hank" Betz, told the others, "We could afford to throw all 15 machines into the Genesee River for a lot less than it would cost us to even consider developing a machine like this."

As the convention was getting underway at the Chicago Hilton, Kodak's Bob Locker took Dreyfoos and Mergens aside. He told them they had obtained orders for all 15 machines in private showings a day or two before the convention started. The prototype never even made it to the convention floor. The Kodak executives went from skepticism about PEC's "go, no go" hurdle to taking orders for their entire stock. For PEC it was a big victory, Dreyfoos recalls. "Overnight, our worries went from selling a few machines, to the requirements of mass production, building a staff, and figuring out how to ship the VCNAs without breaking the glass CRTs." For manufacturing space, they rented the church's former sanctuary in addition to the Sunday school area.

"The VCNA sold like hotcakes," recalls Dreyfoos. "National Geographic wanted one. General Motors wanted one. Ford purchased one. Then all of the big laboratories purchased the machines to stay competitive. We were building them in some quantity for several years."

With a 50/50 revenue split between PEC and Eastman Kodak and orders coming in continuously, Dreyfoos and Mergens kept their Connecticut factory floor busy. The confines of the old church, however, limited their progress. Even after expanding into the former sanctuary, they needed a larger space to improve the workflow and increase their output to keep up with the orders.

Wanted: Productivity with Ambiance

Dreyfoos and Mergens broadened their search for a new location. One place they considered was Puerto Rico, whose government had been advertising a list of incentives in the *New York Times*: "Come on down and build

PHOTOGRAPHIC MILESTONES

Although the principles of image projection were understood by ancient Greeks and Chinese, it took centuries for inventors to bring together their scientific discoveries in optics and chemistry. First, the camera obscura allowed image projection; next, light sensitive chemicals were found to retain images when exposed to light. Here are some more recent highlights, based in part on a timeline by Philip Greenspun of Bard College:

1826 Joseph NIÉPCE, in an eight-hour exposure, takes the first camera photograph.

1829 Louis DAGUERRE discovers that photo plates, treated with mercury vapors, reveal latent images.

1834 (announced in 1840) Henry TALBOT creates the "calotype" or "talbotype" process, using light-sensitive paper to produce a negative from which a positive print is made.

1835 DAGUERRE introduces the world's first commercially successful photographic process, the daguerreotype.

1851 Frederick Scott ARCHER discovers that collodion (guncotton plus ether) adheres to glass plates, creating clear images that can be reproduced.

1856 Hamilton SMITH patents a thin sheet of iron used as a base for a film of light-sensitive chemicals, yielding a positive image Smith calls a "tintype."

1860 James Clerk MAXWELL creates the "additive" color process, using red, blue, and green filters exposing three monochrome images viewed using three photographic "lanterns" projecting a superimposed color composite.

1861 MAXWELL takes the first permanent color photo.

1871 Richard MADDOX introduces his gelatin dry-plate process, facilitating the commercialization of photography.

1873 Herman VOGEL creates orthochromatic photographic plates and uses color-sensitive dyes in processing, with good results except for red.

1877 Eadweard MUYBRIDGE invents a fast camera shutter, allowing still photography of objects in motion.

1888 George EASTMAN popularizes photography by mass manufacturing box cameras and roll film.

1896 Wilhelm ROENTGEN is first to produce an x-ray photograph.

1907 August and Louis LUMIÉRE invent autochrome, a film process that captured all colors; though dark and pastel in appearance, it was nonetheless popular at the time.

PHOTOGRAPHIC MILESTONES

1924 Herbert IVES and other researchers at AT&T's Bell Labs successfully scan photographs and send them by wire, an initial step toward wirephoto, facsimile, and television.

1932 Technicolor introduces its motion picture System 4 using three black-and-white negatives made in a single camera with different filters.

1932 Walt Disney animation is first to use Technicolor's new three-color (vs. two-color) dye transfer system. A five-year exclusive contract was shortened to one year after pressure from other studios.

1935 Leopold Damrosch MANNES and Leopold GODOWSKY, for Eastman Kodak, create Kodachrome, the first multi-layered color film, based on the subtractive theory published in 1869 by Ducas DU HAURON.

1947 Edwin LAND announces the invention of the Polaroid camera and instant photographs.

1967 Alex **DREYFOOS** and George **MERGENS** bring photography and electronics together, receiving patents for their electronic color viewer, the first precision analyzer of color negatives. Their Video Color Negative Analyzer revolutionizes the printing of color stills and motion pictures.

1975 Steven SASSON, at Eastman Kodak, makes the first attempt at building a digital camera, using solid-state Fairchild image sensor chips and a charged coupled device (CCD).

1982 SONY demonstrates its first still video digital camera, the Mavica.

1984 Canon tests its RC-701 still video prototype at the Los Angeles Olympics, using an analog transmitter to send images to Japan for publication in the Yomiuri Shimbun newspaper.

1990 Dycam introduces the first true digital camera, the grayscale Model 1, also sold by Logitech as the Fotoman.

1992 Kodak launches the Photo CD, the first mass-marketed digital image storage method.

1996 Minolta produces the Minolta Dimage V, the first practical digital camera. (Dreyfoos still had his Dimage V in 2015.)

1999 Nikon releases the first digital SLR camera, the D1, capable of 2.74 megapixels.

Mergens continued his struggle to accept the move south, but Dreyfoos was already visualizing the sort of operation the company needed to build in a new plant in Florida. He and Mergens had talked about the layout of the new facility (regardless of its location), but had not gone into detail concerning the business side. Among his first tasks, Dreyfoos needed to secure financing for the new operation and to find a lawyer to represent their growing corporation. One of Doriot's rules came back to him from Harvard Business School: "Always hire a lawyer who is younger than you." So far PEC had only needed a patent attorney, but the stakes were getting higher. At the local library, he consulted the Martindale-Hubbell directory of attorneys to see who was available in Palm Beach County.

It was early 1968, and Dreyfoos was 36. He discovered it was not easy to find an experienced attorney under the age of 36 anywhere around Palm Beach. "There were two listed about my age, and I interviewed both by telephone," he remembers. "One guy really stood out. I liked the way he sounded. His name was Harrison K. Chauncey Jr. So I told him I'd be in Palm Beach in a couple of months and would look him up. Then I went back to thinking about the move and my long list of other things to be worked out."

A couple of weeks later, Dreyfoos was sitting in his office on the Sunday school ground floor level of the Connecticut manufacturing plant, when there was a knock on his window. He turned to see two men looking in.

"Are you Dreyfoos?" the men shouted through the glass.

This knock on the window was not the beginning of their attempt to get into the building. The old church structure was a split-level. There was a sign saying Photo Electronics Corporation, but it was difficult to figure out which door led to the PEC executive offices. The pair had climbed through a window, finding themselves on the production floor in the sanctuary where workers were assembling wiring harnesses for the analyzers. They climbed back out the window, went around to the front of the building, and finally found Dreyfoos.

The two visitors were the Palm Beach lawyer, Harry Chauncey, and his friend George G. Matthews, great-grandson of Henry Flagler, the renowned Florida railroad magnate. Though Matthews lived in Palm Beach, his mother had a summer residence in nearby Rye, New York. Once in Dreyfoos' office, Chauncey announced, "We were in the neighborhood and thought we should stop in and introduce ourselves."

Clearly, Chauncey was interested in the work he and Dreyfoos had discussed on the phone. He made a first impression as the serious type, with piercing eyes and a solidly businesslike demeanor. A small, neat man, with curly, close-cropped dark brown hair and glasses, his dignified appearance concealed the fact that he made friends quickly and was always ready for a good time. Only his pleasant face hinted at the warmth inside.

George Matthews, a friendly bear of a man, had something akin to the air of a Southern gentleman, but hid nothing about his personality. A natural storyteller, Matthews was full of laughs and ready to play. Seizing the opportunity, Dreyfoos pulled Mergens into the group, and all four quickly became friends. Chauncey and Matthews, a powerful sales team, helped convince Mergens that the move to Florida was the right one. To top it off, the pair persuaded the PEC duo to buy homes on Palm Beach, though they might work across the bridge.

The decision to move became final in March 1968. Dreyfoos purchased 10 acres of vacant land in West Palm Beach from Arthur Poisson, a principal at National Capacitor Inc. (NCI). In addition, Dreyfoos secured architectural control of the adjoining properties. Poisson helped him find an architect, John Marion, who introduced him to a local banker, who helped him finance the project. The process quickly connected him to South Florida's business community.

It was Harry Chauncey who introduced Dreyfoos to Lee Spencer of U & Me Transfer, who remembers their first meeting: "Photo Electronics had equipment in the basement of an abandoned church in Connecticut—could I bring it to West Palm Beach? Sure." Spencer also helped arrange for moving the Dreyfoos household from New York and the Mergens household from Connecticut. Indeed, in the nearly 50 years since, every time Dreyfoos has moved home or business, he has turned to his friend Lee Spencer. ☞

Dreyfoos with his children, Robert and Cathy, c. 1961.

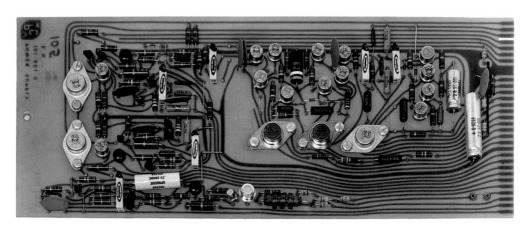

Transistors used on a Dreyfoos-designed printed circuit board in the VCNA.

The former Byram church that housed PEC's offices from 1965 to 1968.

PEC's assembly floor in Byram, in the area that once held church pews, with church windows visible.

Dreyfoos at PEC in Byram in the late 1960s.

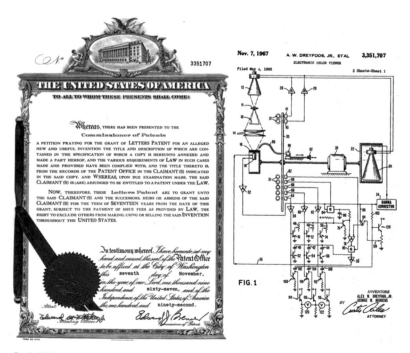

Basic VCNA patent issued in 1967 to Dreyfoos and Mergens for their invention called the "electronic color viewer."

Kodak Video Color Negative Analyzer designed and manufactured by
Photo Electronics Corporation, West Palm Beach, Florida.

The VCNA demonstrated by a Kodak model.

Kodak

VIDEO COLOR NEGATIVE ANALYZER

MODEL 1−K

DESIGNED AND BUILT FOR EASTMAN KODAK COMPANY BY

PHOTO ELECTRONICS CORP., BYRAM, CONN., U.S.A.

T.M. REG. U.S. PAT. OFF.

The nameplate placed on VCNAs marketed by Kodak.

Pages from Kodak's brochure marketing Photo Electronics' VCNA.

Harry Chauncey and his wife, Connie, on the QEII in 1985.

George Matthews celebrating his birthday, 2007.

Lee and Andrea Spencer, at Dreyfoos' home in 1984.

CHAPTER 8

Southern Exposure

(left to right) George Mergens, Dreyfoos, and Renate Hanson, at PEC, 1969.

Acclimation

By December 1968, the new, 20,000-square-foot building for Photo Electronics Corporation was nearing completion in Mangonia Park. The Dreyfooses celebrated Christmas in Rye, then got into the family car and headed for Florida. Alex made it an educational trip for his children over several days, visiting sites such as the Statue of Liberty and Washington, DC, along the way.

Both Dreyfoos and Mergens moved their families into rented homes on Palm Beach. While their wives and kids settled in, the men put their business back in order, which became all consuming. With the husbands' attentions focused solely on Photo Electronics, their wives had to have felt neglected, Dreyfoos reflects. "Every Monday, George and I greeted each other with excitement over moving ahead with all we wanted to achieve." That exciting work, however, did not come without headaches.

Watery Adventures

Immediately upon moving to Florida, Dreyfoos and Mergens had been sponsored by Harry Chauncey for membership in the long-established Sailfish Club of Florida, in Palm Beach, which would result in a network of life-long relationships. The club quickly became their central location for spending the limited time they had for socializing. Here they could relax, enjoy the company of friends, and participate in a variety of fishing events. Dreyfoos also served as second vice president of the club's board, which put him in line to become president; he resigned before that could happen, as it would have conflicted with his other activities.

George Matthews, also a Sailfish Club member, recalls one particular encounter when Dreyfoos had invited him and a few others on his boat for a marlin tournament around Walker's Cay in the Bahamas. They left Palm Beach for West End on Grand Bahama Island before dawn. The trip, which usually took three hours, took six this time. According to Matthews:

> Alex was not used to boating in the Atlantic Ocean. He knew lakes. So he had this pretty small boat, 23 feet, and he used to take it out in the ocean all the time fishing. We were out on the rough ocean with the wind ripping along. Alex was driving, and the boat was coming off the top of the waves going Pow! Bang! The squalls were eight feet. I thought I was going to die.
>
> I figured if I wasn't going to get killed I had better drive the boat. Just short of West End I began to hear all this funny noise coming from the engine. It had been beaten so badly that it had started to pull off the engine mounts and fly out of the boat. We had to stop and fix it. Alex is a very good fixer, and we were back underway soon enough.
>
> I have to tell you what really scared me. While I was driving the boat, I looked back and there were Wade Byrd and Alex. They had grabbed these aluminum lawn chairs and pointed them aft. The waves were enormous. Dreyfoos was sitting there reading Business Week and the Wall Street Journal, oblivious to our imminent death. I told him, "You're about to die and you're sitting there reading a damn newspaper!"
>
> We made it to the tournament, and we brought in a lot of fish. I don't

think Alex and his pals had ever really been big-game fishing before. After that, Alex graduated to a bigger boat.

Alex also used the small boat, *Dolphin Chaser*, to fish with his family on weekends. It carried them out to Lake Okeechobee, into the Cypress Swamp, down the west coast to Key West, and up the east coast. Dreyfoos didn't let its size limit their wanderings.

The Family Spirit

In addition to sharing fun in the sun, the Dreyfoos family made time to address their spiritual needs. Like in New York, they sought out a Universalist church. The 1ˢᵗ Unitarian Universalist Congregation of the Palm Beaches was then located at Florida Avenue and Hibiscus Street, West Palm Beach, a site now in the middle of the CityPlace center. "Their Sunday school was what I would call 'comparative religion'," says Dreyfoos. "My kids really valued it, as did I."

A fire destroyed most of the downtown structure in 1970. Dreyfoos helped to build their new facility in 1987, at 635 Prosperity Farms Road, North Palm Beach. A history of the church reads, "The generosity and hard work of many of our members combined to bring the dream of our new church to fruition. In particular, the vision of Ed Burnham, the fundraising efforts of T. Elbert Clemmons [of IBM], the extraordinary generosity of Alex Dreyfoos, John and Lydia Dodge, Augusta Wells, Harriette Glasner, Ed and Glen Burnham and Elbert and Lanie Clemmons, enabled the church to complete our building program and to fully pay for it."

These donors were also named on a dedication plaque. Elbert Clemmons, also an author, gifted to Dreyfoos his *Great Thoughts of 30 Centuries* (Southeastern Press, 1970). After that, nearly every one of Dreyfoos' Christmas cards included a quotation from his friend's book.

Social activist Harriette Glasner helped to found nine other major organizations or local chapters, among them Planned Parenthood, the American Civil Liberties Union (ACLU), Urban League, Palm Beach County Funeral Society, Center for Family Services, the Florida Council on Human Relations, and Emergency Medical Assistance, Inc. She was one of the few whites to show open support of efforts to desegregate Palm Beach County's schools. Dreyfoos' values were often strongly aligned with Glasner's, and he admired her greatly.

Aerial Adventures

In 1971 Dreyfoos purchased his first airplane. He gave his family a bird's-eye view of nearly every national park in America, and a stop at every island in the Bahamas. His son's Boy Scout troop watched a liftoff at Cape Canaveral from the plane. In his many years of flying, Dreyfoos has had his share of engine mishaps to relate, though not with Boy Scouts on board:

"I was flying N6977L, my Cessna 310, somewhere between Cape Canaveral and Palm Beach County, when all of a sudden a cylinder broke loose. It went right through the engine and the cowling. It looked like World War II! There was black oil all over everything." Dreyfoos was particularly happy to be flying a twin-engine aircraft. "It was the left engine. I shut it down right away. Oil was coming out, but no fuel, and there was no fire. I was about to declare an emergency but changed my mind and just flew back to Palm Beach on the right engine."

Later, there was another incident with the 310:

> We were coming out of Washington, DC, with a full plane. George Mergens was with me, and there were some Kodak guys in the back that we were taking back to Rochester. We ended up in a long line waiting for takeoff and it was pretty cold weather. Idling in the cold, I should have kept the engine RPM up higher than normal to keep the engine warm. Anyhow, everything seemed fine at first.
>
> As we were taking off, George and I both heard an unusual noise and the plane shook for a second. There were no instrument indications that anything was wrong. Since we were flying into better weather, we decided to continue on. Both props were turning, but it was a little hard to tell how much power we were getting from the one engine. Otherwise, the flight was uneventful. We made a successful landing, but as soon as I pulled back the RPM to idle speed, the left engine quit. We had to be towed in from the runway. We couldn't turn in order to taxi without the second engine.

Dreyfoos and Mergens knew that something had happened to the engine with that strange noise at takeoff. They did not want to alarm their passengers and decided not to say anything, but, says Dreyfoos, "when we checked the dipstick to look at the oil, it looked like aluminum paint—oil with finely ground-up aluminum in it. When you are idling at too low an RPM in cold weather, carbon gets deposited on the cylinder head. Then when you take off and apply power, the carbon—instead of blowing off—glows and melts the aluminum piston. So there was a big hole in the piston. That's why there wasn't any compression. We had flown all the way from DC to Rochester grinding up aluminum—grinding up the engine."

"May I Have the Envelope, Please?"

Until the late 1960s, release prints for local television stations and rentals often suffered wide variations in color from scene to scene and from print to print from the same film master print. At the suggestion of Hank Betz at Kodak, Photo Electronics Corporation solved this problem with a motion picture version of the Video Color Negative Analyzer. Where the VCNA held strips of negatives, the motion picture version held long strips of film (reel to reel). For these efforts, the company received a Class III Scientific and Technical Award from the American Academy of Arts & Sciences, which they shared with Eastman Kodak. The citation reads: "For the design and engineering of an improved video color analyzer for motion picture laboratories."

Dreyfoos and Mergens attended the Academy Awards gala in Los Angeles in May 1971 with their respective wives, Joan and Ann. "We received our award during a Texaco commercial," Dreyfoos quips. "Gregory Peck was the president of the academy then. We never expected Peck to hand us the award, but we hired a photographer anyway to get a shot of us going up for the presentation by *Days of Our Lives* daytime TV star Macdonald Carey." Later, still at the awards dinner, Dreyfoos wanted to see if he could get a picture with Peck. "I took my award and went up to Gregory Peck to thank him for being president of the academy. I had the photographer taking pictures of me, holding my award, with Gregory Peck.

"Then the photographer screwed up the film.

"So I do not have any pictures of Gregory Peck there with both me and my award. I do, however, have a picture of Gregory Peck with me when he came to West Palm Beach some years later. What I am doing in that picture is telling him how nice he was to let me have a picture taken with him—and yes, my award—again, because the photographer lost the film the first time."

The Numbers Man

By 1971, Dreyfoos had hired an accountant to handle the Florida operation's increasingly time-consuming bookkeeping requirements. This allowed his wife, Joan, to step out of the job and focus on their children and household. Around the same time, Josh Murray from Price Waterhouse returned to do the annual audit of Photo Electronics. "I understood PEC was looking for a new CFO," Josh remembers, "but I thought they were the proverbial 'one-trick pony' without any real growth potential." After completing the audit, Josh joined Dreyfoos for lunch at This Is It Pub and realized something new was in the wind: "Alex talked with excitement about the possibility of buying the local TV station owned by John D. MacArthur (as Gardens Broadcasting Co.). The business was really different from anything I had ever seen in public accounting. Understanding this changed my view of the company's growth potential."

Dreyfoos knew Josh Murray was the financial officer the company needed. He was in sync with Dreyfoos' managerial style and understood what the company had to do to succeed. Murray became PEC's chief financial officer (CFO) in the spring of 1972, and still held a similar position in 2015.

In PEC, Murray saw a progressive company with an astute leader. "Alex was always the CEO," he asserts. "He focused on facts. He was the best thinker and the best analyzer. He inspired me to look at how to improve the internal exchange of information to enhance the accounting process. He was positive and encouraging to everyone, but he was not a day-to-day manager." Alex also gave people a very long rope, reflects Murray. "He often benefitted from their strengths while overlooking their weaknesses."

Photo Electronics v. Ferrex

The highly successful inventions of Dreyfoos and Mergens, though presumably protected by US patents, were as vulnerable to copycats as those of IBM. When the industry giant encountered patent infringement, it enlisted the services of Fish & Neave in New York, who had defended the inventions of Thomas Edison and Alexander Graham Bell. Though Dreyfoos had left IBM a decade earlier, when he needed similar assistance in 1972, he sought out an introduction to Bill Kerr, the lead litigator at Fish & Neave. Kerr's billing rate reflected his position, but over the next five years, the attorneys on the case—Kerr, partner Al Fey, and Bill Gilbreth—controlled the billings where possible for tiny Photo Electronics. Their VCNA had been "slavishly copied by a company named Ferrex" in California, as Gilbreth explains:

Settlement efforts went nowhere. So we brought suit for patent infringement in the federal District Court in San Francisco. The case was assigned to Chief Judge Robert Peckham, highly regarded but very slow moving.

Back then, the damages issue was deferred until after trial on the liability issues. The liability trial should have taken less than two weeks; it stretched out over two months. Perhaps because he was overwhelmed by the technology, Judge Peckham frequently adjourned the trial to consider other matters. This was frustrating in the extreme.

We proved not only the technical merits of Alex and George's inventions, but also secondary considerations:

1. There was a long-felt need for such a product.

2. Titans of the industry had tried and failed to satisfy that need. PEC's analyzer did satisfy that need, and became an enormous commercial success. (By the time of the 1972 trial, PEC had sold over 500 at a total retail price of over $12 million.)

3. Ferrex had deliberately copied every claimed element of the patented analyzer. They could not even make their analyzer work until they, first, snuck into an invitation-only presentation of the Photo Electronics device and, second, studied the inner workings and operating manual of the device.

Judge Peckham ultimately upheld the patents as valid, infringed, and enforceable. But, in a gross miscarriage of justice, I believe, he sat on the case for three years before doing so, while Ferrex continued to manufacture and sell its infringing devices! His judgment, filed on December 24, 1975, noted: "Never before have I been confronted with such highly technical, scientific evidence as is found in the record of the instant case." Alex, our principal trial witness, had given the judge a tutorial on the technology.

Peckham referred the action to Magistrate Owen Woodruff for the issue of damages, which were usually calculated in terms of a "reasonable royalty." But if it was proven that, but for the infringement, the patent owner would have made every sale made by the infringer, then damages could be awarded in terms of lost profits (almost always, a much higher award).

In the 10-day accounting hearing before Magistrate Woodruff in 1976, we proved this point, and Woodruff did recommend an award based on lost profits. This brought us to the amount of Photo Electronics' lost profits . . . which seemed to trouble the magistrate when he realized that this was close to the dollar amount of Ferrex's gross sales!

But the record supported our numbers, and the magistrate found that Photo Electronics had priced its analyzer in terms of what the device would do for its customers, not what it cost to manufacture. This resulted in a high profit for Photo Electronics, but also in a rapid payback for the purchaser.

Even more important, because PEC had already recovered its direct costs, the lost profits were calculated in terms of Photo Electronics' sales price to Kodak, less only the incremental cost of what it would have cost Photo Electronics to make the number of devices sold by Ferrex. Ultimately the magistrate recommended, and Judge Peckham awarded, $2,934,800 in damages, plus interest and costs.

That's when the case got even more interesting. Pending appeal, Ferrex had stayed an injunction against further infringement by posting a bond. In the meantime, we discovered that (1) over 60 percent of Ferrex was owned by the investment firm of Kidder, Peabody & Co.; (2) its infringing activities had been financed by the estate of a branch of the Rockefeller family; and (3) Ferrex had begun to transfer substantial portions of its assets out of the court's jurisdiction. After we brought these facts to the court's attention, the court of appeals affirmed as to both liability and damages [Photo Electronics Corp. v. England, Trustee in Bankruptcy for Ferrex Corp., 581 F. 2d 772 (9 Cir. 1978.]. Kidder, Peabody, et al. participated in the settlement.

I was left with a decided conflict. The system had failed Alex. It shouldn't have taken so long to try the case. And it certainly shouldn't *have taken the court so long to decide the case! But it was a great pleasure to work with Alex and George, and their wonderful CFO, Josh Murray. Professionally, I was proud of what Al Fey and I were able to achieve for Alex. I tried a lot of cases in my career, and none was more satisfying— or more fun. It has led to a long-standing friendship with one of the truly remarkable men on the planet.*

Josh Murray came to PEC in the first year of this trial and was largely involved in the damages phase. Even more than 40 years later, he thinks of Fey, and especially Gilbreth, as the sharpest lawyers he has ever met. "The magistrate," says Murray, "ruled the testimony of Ferrex's president, Chalmer Jones, as 'inherently unbelievable.' At one point during his cross-examination of Jones, Gilbreth walked over to his steamer trunk full of files and miraculously pulled out a piece of paper from Jones's deposition several years earlier, which totally contradicted what Jones had just said. It was better than *Perry Mason*."

From Ferrex, Dreyfoos learned something: "I learned that patents did not protect me. I never applied for another patent. My motto became, keep quiet and run fast. I'm not going to tell you how I do it, I'm just going to do it." ✎

The original Photo Electronics Corporation building, Mangonia Park, Florida, in 1969.

Dreyfoos in 1969 with Florida Governor Claude Kirk, in office when PEC moved to Palm Beach County.

The inner workings of Photo Electronics:

PEC machine shop in Mangonia Park, Florida, 1969.

PEC's quality control bay, 1976.

PEC's assembly floor during production in the early 1970s.

PEC's machine shop, 1976.

Josh Murray, CFO of Photo Electronics Corporation (PEC), in 1978.

Quite a feat: unanimous participation of the SHITS investment group, with wives, en route to Europe on the *QEII*.

SHITS member Jack Liggett and his wife, Grace, in 1982.

Dr. William "Bill" and B.J. Kemp, in 1971.

PEC's 1968 Christmas party before leaving Byram includes employees who followed the firm to Florida. Row 1, right end: Joe Capozzoli, production manager; Row 2, third from right: JoAnne Dioguardi, production floor supervisor; Row 3, left end: Herb Rutstein, personnel manager (next to George Mergens); fifth from end, barely visible: Al Staley, circuit reliability engineer; Row 3, right end: Al Peloso, operations manager (next to Alex Dreyfoos).

Dreyfoos with Al Staley at PEC, 1969.

Renate Hanson in the 1960s.

Dreyfoos in his and George Mergens' private R&D lab at PEC, 1971.

Kodak's Henry "Hank" Betz, vice president, and Bob Locker, marketing director, with Dreyfoos in Florida.

The Sailfish Club of Florida (Palm Beach) in 1977.

Wade Byrd with large blue marlin aboard Dreyfoos' *Dolphin Chaser* in Walkers Cay, the Bahama Islands.

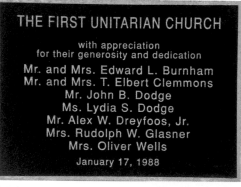

THE FIRST UNITARIAN CHURCH

with appreciation
for their generosity and dedication

Mr. and Mrs. Edward L. Burnham
Mr. and Mrs. T. Elbert Clemmons
Mr. John B. Dodge
Ms. Lydia S. Dodge
Mr. Alex W. Dreyfoos, Jr.
Mrs. Rudolph W. Glasner
Mrs. Oliver Wells

January 17, 1988

1st Unitarian Universalist Congregation of the Palm Beaches, North Palm Beach, Florida, which Dreyfoos helped to build.

Dreyfoos and Mergens accepting an Academy Award from Macdonald Carey in 1971.

Dreyfoos with Gregory Peck, president of the American Academy of Arts & Sciences when Dreyfoos received his 1971 Academy Award, reminiscing years later.

Attorney Bill Gilbreth of Fish & Neave, 1972.

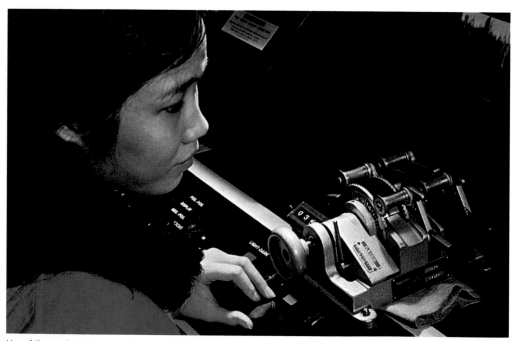

Use of the motion picture version of the VCNA, from the 1971 Kodak Annual Report. The accompanying text reads: "Shown in a motion picture laboratory in Hong Kong is an Eastman video color negative analyzer. The machine electronically reads the motion picture negative and makes possible close quality control of projection prints. More than 90 percent of first-attempt prints made with settings from this device are of salable quality."

Attorney Al Fey of Fish & Neave, 1972.

CHAPTER 9

Mr. Mac

John D. MacArthur (left) and Dreyfoos announcing MacArthur's
sale of Channel 12 to PEC, in 1973.

Fifteen Cents on the Dollar

As recognized by the magistrate in the Ferrex lawsuit, Dreyfoos and Mergens had based the pricing of the video analyzer on its value to the customer, not on what it cost to build. Without a VCNA, photo labs and corporations using a lot of lab services typically wasted a stack of expensive photographic paper before getting their best print. Photo Electronics calculated that labs purchasing a VCNA would pay for the machine in three years, based on the savings they would realize in paper, chemicals, operator time, and reduced costs. "It was a great sales pitch for Kodak," Dreyfoos explains, "and it gave us a good markup."

Always one to look forward, Dreyfoos worried about what to do after all the major photo labs had been equipped with VCNAs and sales slowed down. There were a finite number of laboratories in the country, he reasoned:

"Pretty soon, they'd all have at least one of our VCNAs, and in several years our patents would run out, inviting competition. I wanted to build a fund to do research and development into our next offering." They needed to hold on to as much of their earnings as possible.

The Internal Revenue Service, unfortunately, did not look kindly on corporations it perceived as retaining high earnings to avoid income tax on their stockholders (in this case, Dreyfoos and Mergens). An audit revealed that Photo Electronics Corporation (a C corp) had crossed an important threshold into what government lingo called "excess accumulation of earnings."

The IRS insisted that PEC pay dividends. "We were already paying a corporate tax of 52 percent," says Dreyfoos. "They wanted us to pay out most of the remainder, and then pay Uncle Sam taxes of 70 percent, the top tax rate at that time (the 1970s). So essentially, we'd keep about 15 cents on a dollar. That frosted me."

The IRS auditors gave them two choices: either declare and pay dividends to the stockholders, or spend the "excess" cash on a related business or property. As is his habit, Dreyfoos sought out the opinions of those he respected: friends in banking and finance, and other members of his investment club. He especially spent a lot of time talking with his attorney and friend, Harry Chauncey. In 1972, after a lot of analysis and regular communication with the IRS, Harry told Dreyfoos, "Listen, the only way you're going to beat this thing is to get yourself into debt by buying a company that, to some extent, fits with what you are doing."

What would constitute a good "related" investment for Photo Electronics? A key supplier? The government did not consider real estate speculation to be a satisfactory vehicle. What about an electronics- or photography-related enterprise? How about a television station? Dreyfoos decided to investigate the local ABC affiliate, Channel 12, WEAT-TV. Jim O'Rourke, the station's sales manager, had mentioned to Dick Kreusler, one of Dreyfoos' fellow SHITS members, that it might be for sale, thinking the club might want to consider buying it.

Dreyfoos figured a television station might be a good match for PEC. After all, he had been an amateur ham radio operator. He had built color television systems. Why, the front end of his video analyzer system was even a television camera! (Dreyfoos was certainly responsive to the technology. His former classmate Bernie Shlossman recalls, "Once when Alex came to my home in New Jersey, the TV was on. Before even taking off his coat, Alex had the color adjusted better than it had ever been.")

Dreyfoos decided he needed to meet with WEAT-TV's owner. John D. MacArthur, also known as "Mr. Mac," was one of only two billionaires in America in the 1970s. He lived the last three decades of his life with his wife, Catherine, and two poodles at the Colonnades Beach Hotel, which they owned, in nearby Palm Beach Shores. They occupied a modest hotel apartment with a parking lot view. MacArthur had been busy buying and developing property while planning to eventually sell off everything except his insurance empire, Bankers Life and Casualty Company. In time, MacArthur owned more than 100,000 acres of land in and around Palm Beach and Sarasota, making him Florida's top landowner. Wanting him to own only land and the insurance company when he died, his attorneys urged him to get rid of his "toys," including his broadcasting properties.

Channel 12, founded by James R. and June H. Meacham, had begun operation in West Palm Beach as an ABC network affiliate on January 1, 1955. Media conglomerate RKO General owned both WEAT-TV and WEAT-AM radio from 1955 to 1957, which they purchased for $301,000. They sold both stations for twice that sum to a partnership of Rex Rand (80 percent) and Bertram Lebhar Jr. (20 percent). Lebhar had just arrived in West Palm Beach, after a career in New York managing radio stations and as sportscaster Bert Lee. (Lebhar had, coincidentally, been a year ahead of Dreyfoos at New Rochelle High School, though they were not close friends.) In 1963 MacArthur acquired the two stations for $2.1 million. By 1965, Lebhar owned 49 percent of WEAT; MacArthur, 51 percent. When a loan he made to Lebhar went unpaid, the billionaire ended up with total ownership. By the time Dreyfoos approached him, MacArthur had also added WEAT-FM radio.

Keeping Secrets

Dreyfoos did have a little history with John D. MacArthur prior to 1972. The inventor had been spending a great deal of time in front of schematics and oscilloscopes with a soldering iron in his hand. So when a banker friend asked him to join the board of directors of the YMCA of the Palm Beaches, Dreyfoos accepted the opportunity as a positive diversion. The board seat

negotiated for architectural control of the entire industrial park to prevent warehouse-quality buildings from becoming his neighbors. Then the State of Florida entered a period of *not* wanting to attract new businesses, frustrating Poisson because warehouses were the only thing he could sell there anymore. Dreyfoos gave up his control in exchange for the 10 acres between PEC and Australian Avenue. Although he had no immediate intention of developing it—and 40 years later, it is still mostly woods—Dreyfoos kept his options open, and in the meantime had control of the appearance from the street.

This was just the kind of forward thinking that impressed John D. MacArthur. If anyone could appreciate Dreyfoos' strategy in owning double the property than he needed, it was the county's largest owner of vacant land.

After a tour of the technical facilities, the two men got down to business in Dreyfoos' office.

"What's this all about?" demanded MacArthur impatiently.

"Well, I learned through my investment group that you might be willing to sell your TV station. Is it for sale?"

"Maybe."

"Well, what would it cost?"

"Five million dollars."

"Mr. MacArthur, you must be kidding. The TV station is losing money." The radio stations were making quite good money.

"That's for the three stations: AM, FM, and TV."

Dreyfoos politely told MacArthur, "The FCC wouldn't allow that. You have to sell the radio properties separately from the TV station."

"Oh, that doesn't apply to me," said MacArthur, waving the question away with a sweep of his hand. The meeting was over, but MacArthur agreed to speak with Dreyfoos again. The next meeting took place at the Colonnades—not in the coffee shop, but in a small office MacArthur kept in the hotel. A short, balding man in his early 50s joined them, the highly respected attorney Leonard H. Marks. (Marks had worked for the FCC until 1946. His private firm, Cohn & Marks, was one of Washington's premier communications law firms.) Correcting MacArthur on the FCC ownership rules, Marks said Dreyfoos did, indeed, have his facts straight. At that time, while someone could start a TV, an AM, and an FM station, they had to sell the TV station separately from the radio stations to dilute the concentration of media. This clearly gave pause to MacArthur.

"Well, which do you want? Radio or TV?" he demanded.

"I'm interested in the TV station. I know it's losing money, but I believe I can keep it afloat with my electronics business until we learn how to turn it around." Dreyfoos explained why he saw the TV station as a good match for his business and defended what he knew about television broadcasting: that he was a ham radio operator and PEC's main product involved a color television camera.

Dreyfoos analyzed the TV/radio station purchase as he would a Harvard Business School case study, seeking out all the potential problems and solutions. With data Josh Murray provided on Photo Electronics Corporation, Dreyfoos did some difficult number crunching and "what if" calculations of what it would take to break even and to become profitable. Jim O'Rourke from Channel 12 provided financial information about the station, which Dreyfoos built on with his own research. There were no personal computers or Microsoft Excel. He used a General Electric time-share computer system to run a series of hypothetical scenarios, balancing all of the factors he could imagine. (See sidebar, page 186.) Dreyfoos was able to analyze commercial and program rates, statistics on local commerce, population breakdown, income levels, and buying habits. West Palm Beach was a small but growing community in the early 1970s. Although it was then in the 92nd A.D.I. (Area of Dominant Influence) market, Dreyfoos saw an upward trend. [The term A.D.I. was replaced by Nielsen Media Research's D.M.A. (Designated Market Area) after Arbitron stopped providing TV ratings in 1993. Nielsen acquired Arbitron, now a radio ratings company, in 2013.]

From what he could determine, MacArthur was paying little or no attention to the station and operated it through a management committee, which Dreyfoos avows, "really doesn't work. It was just one of MacArthur's toys." When his analysis was done, Dreyfoos was certain that the TV station alone was the best arrangement. Accepting that MacArthur wanted to unload all three properties, he reasoned that he could find a buyer for the financially successful radio stations.

Dreyfoos made progress in understanding MacArthur's negotiating style. "It was important not to arrive with unrealistic expectations, and you had to be a good listener," he says. "Mr. Mac told you how to deal with him. When we first met, he told me, 'Just because I've got more chips than you, doesn't mean I'm not going to play poker just as hard as you.'"

Finally, Dreyfoos offered MacArthur $4.8 million for all three stations. He presented his offer to the Federal Communications Commission and was quickly rejected, as expected. He moved on to his backup plan, creating two separate proposals that together would give MacArthur $4.8 million. The AM station, WEAT, was a successful country music station. The FM station had just recently gone on-the-air with "Easy Listening" music. FM band reception had just been added to car radios, and WEAT could be heard on Interstate 95 from Orlando to Miami, making it a real powerhouse. Clearly, the radio stations had value, says Dreyfoos. "I presented the radio package to my investment group (SHITS) at $1.2 million and we made MacArthur an offer, which he never bothered to answer. (MacArthur eventually sold the radio stations to sportscaster Curt Gowdy for $1.5 million in 1974.")

Dreyfoos' offer to MacArthur was for $3.6 million for WEAT-TV, with $1 million down and a note for the other $2.6 million.

Nothing happened.

Finally, after weeks of waiting, there was a call from MacArthur. "Dreyfoos, are you still interested in that TV station?"

"Yes, Mr. Mac, I am."

"Well, come on over. Let's talk about it."

On several occasions in late 1972, Dreyfoos drove over to the Colonnades Beach Hotel at lunchtime. "At first, I figured Mr. Mac and I would have lunch and talk about the contract." However, each time he arrived, there would be a table full of people around MacArthur—and not just anybody. "Guys like Paul Harvey (the "rest of the story" radio commentator from Chicago) were there. Bob Hope showed up once. There was always a lot of chitchat, bragging, and jokes, but never a business discussion." Pretty soon, Molly the waitress would bring Mr. Mac's personal "MacArthur" brand of scotch on the rocks and take drink orders for everyone else. The lunches extended into dinners. To Dreyfoos, all of this was just more waiting. He could not make sense of MacArthur's new behavior. Was he slowing everything down as a negotiating tactic?

Though Dreyfoos could not let on to MacArthur, he felt a constant sense of urgency during these "games," as the IRS continued to pressure Photo Electronics to either invest in another business, or accept additional tax liability.

Dreyfoos began to insist on leaving when dinnertime arrived. "I had kids and a wife waiting at home, but I'd try to be polite. I'd stand up. Mr. Mac would say, 'No, no, no! Stay for one more drink.' There had been zero discussion about the deal, nothing. Eventually I'd get up again. Mr. Mac would stand and put his arm around me, then he'd walk me towards my car. Then he'd say something like, 'Clean up the language on page 16, paragraph four of the contract.' When I'd examine the document later, the change would involve something really minor, just boilerplate."

MacArthur seemed to enjoy introducing Dreyfoos to his celebrity guests and friends and seemed sincerely interested in his accomplishments. In conversation he would often bring up the fact that Dreyfoos was an inventor and that he piloted his own airplane. MacArthur took particular pleasure in mentioning Dreyfoos' Academy Award for creating a motion picture version of the Video Color Negative Analyzer. Dreyfoos eventually concluded that MacArthur simply enjoyed his company. He seemed pleased to share time with a young man smart enough to get big money together to buy his TV station. He treated Dreyfoos like a son, but this son was getting impatient.

The situation was getting complicated, though, and had Dreyfoos worried. "I was heartbroken that I might miss the deal, but also worried about having adequate cash flow if the deal was consummated." Most of all, he was concerned that none of the local banks could finance a deal this big.

Dreyfoos' friend Thomas R. Pledger also learned MacArthur's TV and radio properties were for sale. His Kiwanis chapter held its meetings at MacArthur's Colonnades Hotel, after which Pledger would frequently chat with the billionaire. Pledger, who would later become CEO of Dycom Industries, was then president of Burnup & Sims, Inc., which he had helped bring into cable television. He found the idea of owning a TV station intriguing.

Neither Dreyfoos nor Pledger knew that the other was interested in buying Channel 12. Dreyfoos only learned much later that Pledger (with a silent partner from Georgia) had made an offer to MacArthur. It was for less money ($3.1 million), but all cash, which MacArthur preferred.

Then came a phone call from Louis Feil, known as MacArthur's "hatchet man." Every morning at about 5 or 5:30 a.m., MacArthur started his day with a cup of coffee and a call to Louis Feil, a vice president in his company, Bankers Life. They discussed what looked good for purchase, how various deals were going, and who was in trouble and in need of a loan.

Dreyfoos had met Feil at one of MacArthur's lunches and was surprised when the man immediately blasted away at him, declaring, "Your credit's no good! This will be a cash deal or nothing." Pledger's all-cash offer had evidently turned the tide.

"Well that could be true, Mr. Feil," Dreyfoos responded calmly, "but it's better today than it was a year ago when we first started negotiating." MacArthur had originally suggested to Dreyfoos 10 percent down and in-house financing, and Photo Electronics had only grown since then. Dreyfoos was dumbfounded about this switch. Plus, though there was nothing wrong with PEC's credit, Feil must have known it was unlikely that a local bank would lend him that much money. This behavior was also a departure from MacArthur's dark reputation as someone who would happily agree to accept payments over time, then foreclose and seize the property when a payment was missed on a minor technicality. Feil would hear nothing of Dreyfoos' plea for more discussion: "If you want to make the deal, it must be all cash. You can have two weeks—10 business days—to make it happen."

How could Dreyfoos meet such a deadline? Lacking a local bank with the financial strength and courage to make such a deal, he decided to try a different path. "My relationship with Bank of New York was very good. Since moving to Florida, I had continued to pay all of our Florida bills through them. My contact initially expressed skepticism, saying there was no way they could respond in two weeks, but he suggested I transmit to him whatever information I had. When they saw my computer projections for the station, they got excited—this from guys who never got excited about anything." Bank of New York agreed to provide the money, and Dreyfoos is convinced it was, once again, the computer projections that made it work. Relieved, and feeling powerful, he called Louis Feil.

"Mr. Feil, I have the cash. When do you want to close?"

At first there was total silence. Then Feil snorted, "Where'd you get the money?"

Dreyfoos wanted to reply, "It's none of your business." Instead, he said, "From Bank of New York."

"Give me the name of your bank officer. I'll have to call you back." Soon a less gruff, almost pleasant Feil returned his call. They agreed on a time and place for the closing.

It had taken one day short of a year to conclude the deal, a difficult year for Dreyfoos, but now a triumph. His wife, Joan, and George Mergens were both against the purchase. "All they could see was that the station was not making any money, and I was taking on a huge debt. I had to pull rank on George a second time," he says regretfully, "in deciding to go forward." His financial projections convinced him that he could meet his payments and even record some profit. Adding to that the projected growth of the Palm Beach market, Dreyfoos was certain he would have a moneymaker, and that everyone involved would eventually benefit.

On April 5, 1973, the principals in the TV station transaction held a news conference to let the media and public (Tom Pledger included) know what they had done. The stage for the announcement was the Colonnades Beach Hotel. Facing the audience were John D. MacArthur, Alex Dreyfoos, and George Mergens. All three wore neckties and jackets. Dreyfoos remarked later that it was the first time he had seen MacArthur really dressed up, sure that it was Eleanor Larson, head of the WEAT's management committee, who made him look presentable.

As they got started, MacArthur was smoking a cigarette, with a cup of coffee and an ashtray beside him. All of their measured words to the media expressed their satisfaction and happiness with the deal they had made. Polite statements were made about maintaining and improving the station's responsiveness to community interests and to serving the public in times of emergency. Pressed by reporters for more about his plans for future investment in Florida, MacArthur admitted that he would be liquidating his considerable holdings around Palm Beach County "in an orderly fashion," adding that the TV station was his first such sale.

The headline in the *Palm Beach Daily News* (known as the "Shiny Sheet") the following day read, "MacArthur to Sell State Holdings," with a subheading, "PB Resident to Purchase Channel 12. (Both Dreyfoos and Mergens lived on the Island). No one, even Dreyfoos, could realize how this event set him

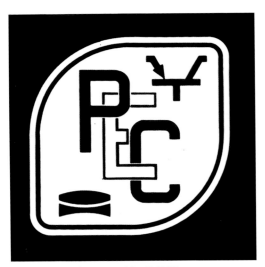

The PEC logo before ownership of WPEC.

John D. MacArthur sketched by LeRoy Neiman in 1977 at the American Academy of Achievement annual awards in Orlando, Florida, where both received Golden Plates. Gayle Pallesen, a friend to both Dreyfoos and MacArthur, negotiated purchase of the original after Dreyfoos admired a copy the artist had made for her.

(left to right) John D. MacArthur, Dreyfoos, and Mergens holding a press conference to announce the sale of Channel 12 from MacArthur to PEC in 1973.

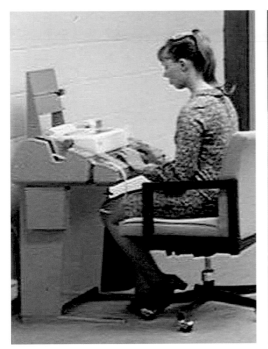

The ASR 33 teletype modem at Dreyfoos' PEC offices in 1969.

Llwyd Ecclestone's *Volcano*.

Dreyfoos' trophy lamp showing his name as navigator three times.

Dreyfoos (left) receiving from Harry Chauncey the first-place trophy in the Sailfish Club Memorial Day Tournament, won with Llwyd Ecclestone's *Bikini* on loan for the summer, 1972.

Llwyd Ecclestone (right) lets Jordan's King Hussein take the helm of *Bikini* in 1972, while Dreyfoos filled the role of navigator.

Llwyd Ecclestone at the helm of his *Bikini*, with Bob Dodd, taken by Dreyfoos while in navigator role, 1970s.

CHAPTER 10

Broadcasting and Other Business

The WPEC studio and helicopter, c. 1985.

Getting Signals Straight

Since a broadcast television license is a public trust, the federal government, in the Federal Communications Commission, had approved the fitness of Dreyfoos and PEC Communications, Inc. to hold the license. Such approval had come through before the closing, in November. Dreyfoos had also asked for and received from the FCC a change of Channel 12's call letters to WPEC, to reflect the new ownership. Although he waited until this change was official to physically move the station, he began running things as of the December 1 closing.

MacArthur told Dreyfoos he could offer a job to any employee except two. Eleanor Larson and the sales manager, George Jaspert, would both be staying on with him. Dreyfoos hired MacArthur's assistant engineer, George Danner, who he credits for having placed the station's FM antenna close to the I-95 corridor to reach far to the north and south. He promptly promoted Danner to chief engineer.

"Danner had his own way of doing business," says Dreyfoos. "When you approached him with something that needed to be fixed, he would come back at you with his technical assessment of the problem and then all of the reasons why it would take too long to repair and why he couldn't fix it right away. Then half an hour later, whatever it was would be fixed." All of this "TV station behavior" left Dreyfoos flummoxed.

Dreyfoos kept the news department together but needed a news director to manage the operation. After a time, he hired New Orleans native Jules d'Hemecourt, who had filled the role at two other stations. The *Palm Beach Daily News* quoted Dreyfoos regarding the hire: "I wanted to get away from ambulance chasing . . . to try to influence the community in some way. . . . Jules has a very interesting educational background. He is a doctor of laws (Juris Doctor), an attorney . . . and was very much attracted to doing this." D'Hemecourt also held a master's degree in Mass Media from Columbia University.

For his $3.6 million, Dreyfoos got a TV station license and all of the equipment needed to run the Channel 12 studios and transmitters. MacArthur did not sell him the building and trailers that housed the gear and staff, so Photo Electronics had to vacate all of the TV equipment from MacArthur's property on South Congress Avenue, West Palm Beach, leaving the AM and FM radio equipment behind. "Mr. Mac had run the TV and radio stations as one integrated operation," Dreyfoos explains. "The first thing we had to do was pull them apart. It didn't come apart easily, and there were a number of people wearing hats in both operations."

Moving was a big chore. The vintage television studio and production equipment were big and bulky; as always, Dreyfoos trusted it to his friends at U & Me Transfer and Storage. "On the technical end," Dreyfoos remembers, "George Mergens and George Danner orchestrated the move and quickly hacked everything back together, squeezing it into our PEC manufacturing facility in Mangonia Park. We signed off on January 26, 1974, moved the equipment overnight, and signed on again the next morning, January 27, at the new location."

Breaking Down Barriers

Having come from the North and a very social service-minded church, Dreyfoos was not accustomed to racial intolerance. He found South Florida, he says, to be "very prejudiced, both religiously and racially, which bugged me right from the beginning." South Florida was not as severely discriminatory as the Deep South, in part because of so many Northerners in residence. But still, Dreyfoos remembers that there were public restrooms for the "colored" when he arrived in 1967. In *Brown v. Board of Education*, the US Supreme Court had ordered the desegregation of public schools in 1954, but Palm Beach County did not obey until 1971. The first several years of Dreyfoos' presence in the area, Palm Beach County was in transition.

Dreyfoos was right in the midst of the happenings. He is among the 20 individuals whose three years of conversations led to incorporation of the Urban League of Palm Beach County, Inc. and national recognition a year later, in 1974. This was also the year that the Economic Council was born, which assisted the Urban League in many ways. Other Urban League founders included Dreyfoos' friends Harriette Glasner, William T. Dwyer from the Economic Council, and Charlie Lovett Ellington, the head of the school district's north area special education office and a descendant of local black pioneers. The founders helped build the first, small facility, then their permanent quarters through community efforts. WPEC also went on-the-air in 1974, where Dreyfoos was able to add support to the Urban League with TV coverage.

The first two staff members of the Urban League were the president, Percy Lee, and his secretary, Charlie Ellington, who then worked with the programs. A decade later, Dreyfoos invited Ellington, who actively supported the black community through various organizations, to put together a public service show on WPEC. In 1985 and 1986, she and Dr. Clarence Reynolds hosted the talk show *Insight* on Sunday mornings. When Dreyfoos built the Kravis Center, he invited Ellington to serve on its board. He calls her "a wonderful citizen."

One of the first ways that Dreyfoos used his television station as a tool was to hire an African American, AnEta Sewell. After studying speech and drama at Fisk, Sewell had earned a master's degree from Kent State, where she did a public affairs show and fell in love with broadcasting. In 1973, back in Baton Rouge, she was hired as newsroom assistant by Jules d'Hemecourt, then news director at the local ABC affiliate. D'Hemecourt soon left the station for Channel 12 in West Palm Beach, but invited her to join him in August 1974. "We didn't have a lot of diversity in this area," she recalls, "but Alex Dreyfoos wanted to show he believed in diversity; he wanted an African American face on his TV. So, Jules thought of me. He had a law degree, and I think he was fascinated by my education." Very soon, Sewell was doing public service announcements on *Datebook*.

"I was the first African American in television in the Palm Beaches and Treasure Coast," she says. "On one of my first assignments as a reporter, to The Breakers, a woman asked me to get her coffee. People hadn't seen someone that looked like me on their TV sets. I really thank Alex Dreyfoos for giving me that opportunity."

"AnEta started as a reporter and eventually became our early evening anchor," says Dreyfoos. "We then had her do her own program. She really represented the black community." Dreyfoos gave Sewell a half-hour Sunday show, *AnEta's World*, in 1975, saying, 'Bring in anyone you want.' Sewell preferred "regular folks" who wouldn't otherwise have a public voice, but she also invited familiar faces, like West Palm Beach Mayor Eva Mack, and Percy Lee and Vernon Jordan from the local and national Urban League. Her most controversial guest was the Florida head of the Ku Klux Klan.

Sewell continued the show until she left WPEC in 1982 to care for her mother. She returned in 1990 and stayed until 2000, after Dreyfoos had sold the station.

Adjusting the Channel

At the time PEC purchased Channel 12, color television was still new. NBC and CBS had been broadcasting in color for many years, but ABC had been last to switch to full color programming, in September 1962, with the first episode of the animated series, *The Jetsons*. First in the network ratings was NBC. Coming in second was CBS, considered the leading network for news. ABC was in last place. After 11 p.m., ABC affiliates would air reruns— typically, old movies or a syndicated TV series—or just sign off-the-air.

Art Stark had semi-retired to Palm Beach a year earlier with an impressive resume. He had produced and performed with USO shows during World War II, produced Johnny Carson's daytime quiz show *Who Do You*

Trust? and moved with Carson to *The Tonight Show*. When Stark heard that Dreyfoos was buying Channel 12, he called to offer his help.

"We needed to buy some movies," says Dreyfoos. "Some of my friends and I got together and started making a list." Those friends included Bernie Shlossman and Len Brown, who were both in advertising. "We thought we were experts," says Shlossman. "Based on the ratings, our judgment was terrible." Stark told Dreyfoos that their tastes were too sophisticated. "He declared that we did not know anything about our audience," says Dreyfoos. "Well, he was right. I eventually realized that if there was a film or program I liked, our audience probably would hate it." Dreyfoos brought Stark out of early retirement to be the station's program manager.

Community Television

Dreyfoos maintained that the TV station purchase had been a grand idea, and in terms of making money, had the potential to match or eclipse the Photo Electronics manufacturing model. He also calculated that TV revenue would replace the cash flow created by the VCNA when its demand began to wane.

Beyond economics, Dreyfoos knew the station would be a powerful tool to advance the positive growth of Palm Beach County. Beginning seven months prior to the sale closing, news stories repeated the drumroll that community involvement would be a "major commitment":

- Dreyfoos and Mergens (PEC) were "anxious to become more involved with the community, and feel that the purchase of a TV station . . . will provide the ideal vehicle." (*Palm Beach Daily News*)

- Dreyfoos planned to take an "activist role" in the community and to follow a "moderate editorial policy." He said: "People need to take a stand, to be willing to speak out about what they believe. I've seen too many situations develop in a vacuum. No one did anything and the outcome was not good. . . . I'm interested in trying to stir the imagination of the people in the county. We should seek out imaginative approaches to problems on the local level. We should help people see the advantages of applying these approaches countrywide. I've gotten a lot out of the community and I've been active in it personally. Still, I thought it was time the company started giving back, too. That's why we purchased a television station instead of an automobile agency or construction company. This is where the company is capable of making a contribution." (*The Palm Beach Post*)

- Dreyfoos: "I think that a television station can influence the community by which groups it solicits for public service announcements [PSAs]. Even now [under policies of former management] the station has a policy that lets almost any group get its message to the community." (*The Palm Beach Post*)

Rochelle Jones of the *Palm Beach Post* concluded, "Dreyfoos leaves the impression that the purchase meant more to him than the chance to acquire a laboratory for his business."

The FCC set a quota for PSAs, which WPEC consistently exceeded. The sales manager set the station's commercial advertising rates almost every day, on an options-style market. If all of the advertising spots sold out, the rate had been set too low. Ideally, a few spots were left unsold, indicating a good rate. It was an ongoing effort toward a delicate balance. The station used the unsold ad inventory for either promotions or public service announcements. Though it served a good purpose, the station lost revenue if that airtime was in demand by advertisers.

Like in other small television markets across the country, it was WPEC's news department that drew the most local revenue to the station. WPEC booked advertising from West Palm Beach area businesses, which was clustered mostly around the local early evening news program. In the early years, this was a 15-minute show that aired after the 15 minutes of national news produced by the ABC network.

From the start, getting along with the news people was a challenge for Dreyfoos, and consolidation of his two companies under one roof turned out to be less than ideal. The news department was hesitant to trust any PEC employee—the TV employees called them "PECK-ees"—and that included Dreyfoos, he says. "Whenever the news people saw me—the owner—coming, they changed their behavior. I wanted an open relationship with them, but it was always tough. They had a natural tendency to be distrustful of management—it was part of their culture—but they did a good job of assembling the local news with the limited equipment they had then. Everything was shot on 16 mm film cameras for several years, handheld but very bulky to carry. Later we switched to ENG (electronic news gathering) gear. They did have a film processor and a small film editing table."

There were times when local business owners would ask Dreyfoos for a favor, he remembers. "Frequently, I would get a call from somebody who was opening a new business, like a car dealership, and would ask for news coverage. I would tell them they'd be better off calling the news people directly. If I walked into the newsroom and told them to go down and cover the opening, no matter how I sugar-coated it, you can be sure the film would break, or the processor would get screwed up." Dreyfoos laments that the news people often thought he had ulterior motives in getting business events covered as news stories.

Dreyfoos' efforts were probably more appreciated than he may have realized. Former sportscaster Dan Oliver and his wife, Susan Mann, both enjoyed working at WPEC during the Dreyfoos years. "Alex delivered our paychecks himself to get to know everyone," says Oliver, "and took Polaroids of new employees to help him learn their names. We also appreciated that Alex gave us what we needed to do our jobs well. There was no cutting corners."

Initially, Dreyfoos decided he would be part of the "hands-on" management of the station, even announcing so to the press. "I made some dumb mistakes because, coming from manufacturing, I thought you could do things logically." Only later did he learn that the nature of a commercial television station is different from anything he had known, rarely coming close to an operation that could be called "logical."

Technicalities

Dreyfoos also had hopes to improve television's technical quality. Rochelle Jones of the *Palm Beach Post* wrote that Dreyfoos wanted to use WPEC to experiment with some new approaches to color correction. Dreyfoos cited the problems with color shifts that occurred when stations switched from a network program to run a local program or commercial: "We should also be able to add additional information at the local station so the color will be automatically corrected before the pictures are transmitted to the public. If just one station could do this, it would have a big impact on the industry."

Another problem that concerned Dreyfoos involved the non-synchronous switches that took place in accessing, or departing from, a network program signal, which arrived in those days over a coaxial cable system owned by AT&T Long Lines. The difference in the electronic timing of the local TV signal versus the network signal caused the entire picture to break up momentarily. This switching problem was solved with the advent of the "time base corrector," or TBC, introduced at the 1973 National Association of Broadcasters convention by Consolidated Video Systems.

Although the scientist in Dreyfoos took an active role in creating such technology, his interest started to move away from the fine points of television's technological medium, and towards the message.

Spinning the Wheel of Fortune

"Wheel! Of! Fortune!" the audience screams. Over theme music and rousing applause, the announcer intones, "From Hollywood! It's the Wheel of Fortune, America's most popular game show!"

Early on, Dreyfoos made a conscious decision to gather all the knowledge he needed to manage WPEC properly: "I had decided that between George and myself, we would run the station. What kept coming back at me all the time was the fact that television was a marketing game, not a technology game."

To gather more information about how to succeed at this new game—and to escape from the office for a while—Dreyfoos attended TV industry events. He went to ABC affiliate meetings, and conventions of the National Association of Television Program Executives (NATPE) and the industry's leading group, the National Association of Broadcasters (NAB).

The 1974 NATPE convention was held in Atlanta, and WPEC was there to look over the offerings. Among the fare was a new game show by Merv Griffin Productions. The program, introduced for the 1975 TV season, was a Las Vegas-themed version of the word game "Hangman" called *Wheel of Fortune*, hosted by Chuck Woolery.

WPEC secured a contract and ran the program in the so-called "family hour" slot, 7:30 to 8:00 p.m. "We purchased *Wheel of Fortune* the very first year that it came out," Dreyfoos points out. "Nobody knew whether it was going to be good or not. We just saw the pilot and purchased it. It turned out to be a top hit."

A Man in Demand

While he would not fully realize it until later, Dreyfoos' life changed when the first headline reported the TV station purchase. He had been a relatively private person before the announcement. Thereafter, he became a public figure, part of a small fraternity of media owners/operators—some of the most powerful people in the nation. People who wanted to use television to promote their agendas locally often sought an association with Dreyfoos.

Dreyfoos' visibility and standing in the community rose rapidly. "I was invited to join the board of the new Flagler National Bank," he recalls. "After some consideration, I resigned from the board of the First American Bank, which held the mortgage on the PEC building, and joined Flagler." Named after American tycoon Henry Flagler, in 1974 it became the first national bank to be chartered in West Palm Beach in 38 years. Flagler Bank had been established by major Palm Beach County insiders, including insurance men William C. Clark and Richard S. Johnson, developer William G. Lassiter Jr., architect R. Carroll Peacock, attorneys Ward A. Wagner Sr. and Phillip D. O'Connell Sr., and contractor John Murphy.

Also in 1974, Tom Pledger and retired Florsheim Shoe executive Joseph "J.B." Stancliffe assembled a team to manage their start-up Economic Council of Palm Beach County. The mission of the new non-profit, non-governmental, non-partisan organization was "to create an environment to help business prosper." They invited Dreyfoos to join them. "A lot of changes were taking place at that time in Palm Beach County," he recalls. "This group—pillars of the business community—had until that time been running the show, but they recognized it was time to make changes, which included bringing in new people." The Economic Council was a big-picture group, looking at properly managing growth. It was a perfect platform for Dreyfoos to get to know the influential business and professional people in the region, and the government officials with whom they had to work.

Pledger observes how one thing fed off another: "Involvement with organizations like the Economic Council and the Florida Council of 100 also helped Alex with the Kravis Center." (In 1980 Gov. Bob Graham appointed Dreyfoos to the Florida Council of 100, a group of key business people invited to affect public policy.) Pledger, himself a Kravis Center Life Trustee, says, "I admire Alex's ability to work with different factions: the wealthy, the working class, male and female. He relates to all people, takes their input, analyzes it, and, most of the time, makes the right decisions."

George T. Elmore of Hardrives, Inc. was also a founder of the Economic Council. Before this group became official, Elmore belonged to a "non-group" of about 25 businesses that met every four to six weeks to promote community relations. "The bigwigs did not typically attend," Elmore notes, "but the P.R. people did. Judy Goodman was the representative from WPEC, and I first got to know Alex through Judy. [Although she was Judy Axel until she married in August 1981, Judy is always referred to as Judy Goodman herein.] Later, on the Economic Council, we would be sitting in a meeting, and Alex would take out a scrap of paper and start scribbling to work out a problem. He's just so smart."

Dreyfoos has often been told that people "blossom" under him. After serving a term as chair of the Economic Council, he convinced Elmore to do the same. "He didn't believe he was qualified," says Dreyfoos, "but did a fine job, and went on to lead other organizations."

Over the years, Dreyfoos would also use these skills on the boards of national corporations. For seven years (until reaching the age for mandatory retirement) he served on the board of FPL Group, Inc. (NYSE: NEE, which became NextEra Energy, Inc.), the largest rate-regulated electric utility in Florida. He was also a member of the board of Kuhlman Corporation (NYSE: KUH), until BorgWarner Inc. acquired it in 1999.

But in the '70s, because of Flagler Bank and the Economic Council, Dreyfoos saw himself able to take a role in guiding the development of Palm Beach County through organized community groups. When would he find the time? WPEC ran at a constant boil. There were always long lists of issues—technical operations, news personnel, technical personnel, sales, accounting, traffic—every one of them needing immediate attention. The small problems simultaneously slowed down decision-making on big-picture items. In addition, Dreyfoos' constant attention to station matters often put the electronics division on the back burner, ultimately derailing its next product line. It was a lot to juggle. In 1975, Dreyfoos realized he needed to step back from hands-on management of WPEC.

Finding a moment to analyze the situation without interruption was difficult enough, but finding the right person to take over as general manager was critical. Dreyfoos only had to look as far as the sales department for Chuck Conrad. Originally a MacArthur hire, the mustachioed Conrad was good at juggling a long list of projects and duties. While Dreyfoos recalls that he did not have the best management skills for a top position, Conrad excelled at sales, and it was sales that the station most needed. Including Conrad, there would be four general managers at WPEC during the 23 years of Dreyfoos' ownership.

The Social Side of Success

Although Dreyfoos' business life flourished, his personal life took dips and turns. He and Joan had not been happy for some time, but it was important to him for a divorce to have the least possible impact on their children. After their son, Robert, received his driver's license in the fall of 1974, Dreyfoos purchased him a car so he would have mobility when, for example, he wanted to see his father. Their daughter, Cathy, came home from college and enjoyed Christmas break with the family, then happily returned to her friends. Dreyfoos took an apartment, and Joan purchased a smaller home for her and the children.

Three years after the divorce, *Forbes* magazine did a cover story on Dreyfoos that showed him apparently enjoying life "Under the Banyan Tree": "All of the things I love are down here—swimming, fishing, sailing." As owner of a local TV station, Dreyfoos commented, "Now people seek me out. I could be at three different social functions every night." One of Palm Beach's movers and shakers in the mid-'70s, the entrepreneur was at the peak of fitness, youthful, and wildly successful in business.

Palm Beach is host to many captains of industry. What set Dreyfoos apart was how he parlayed commercial success with community involvement. He typically greeted people with a warm smile and a handshake. Acquaintances described him as "soft-spoken" or "easy-going," more a listener than a talker, but when it came to his business ventures and his visions for the future of Palm Beach County, he was passionate and single-minded.

Forbes described Dreyfoos as "intense [and] self-absorbed. . . . He has two college-age children. Now there's his business life ('90% of what I do'), scuba diving, gourmet eating ('I eat out three nights a week'), and dating." When he first became single, his friends' wives had set up a few dates, not understanding why he didn't do it on his own. After he divorced Joan in 1975, he had proposed to Renate, but she could not see herself in the spotlight that surrounded Dreyfoos. Privately, he longed for Renate, who he believed to be the true love of his life. In her absence, for one of Palm Beach's desirable, eligible bachelors, frequent female companionship took little effort.

Forbes described Dreyfoos' home as that of the quintessential single male: "He lives alone in three sparsely furnished rooms of a $300,000 house built in 1940. It needs a new coat of paint. Only a luscious shroud of orange, avocado and grapefruit trees and a huge old banyan tree that umbrellas the circular drive save the single-level structure from looking ill kept."

The property received an upgrade [and a renumbering, from 381 North Lake Way to 380] after daughter Cathy asked to hold her wedding to Michael Carter at her father's home. In the spring of 1978, Dreyfoos had the house substantially rebuilt from a design by Carroll Peacock. The work was finished by Cathy's wedding day, though barely, possibly in part because Dreyfoos had sent wedding invitations to the contractors. Peacock & Lewis had referred Dreyfoos to interior designer Susan Smith, known as Spectrum Design, who recalls, "An hour before the wedding, we were installing the electrical in the master bedroom headboard." After that, Smith started new jobs by asking her clients to schedule a party at the deadline. Over more than 30 years, Dreyfoos called on Smith when he acquired new homes, boats, airplanes, and offices. Says Smith, "Alex has had a chance to work with whoever he wanted, but he's been so loyal. You give him your best, because he makes you feel good about what you do."

On the Cutting Edge

By its very nature, the environment of WPEC was high pressure and deadline oriented. Dreyfoos and Mergens were more comfortable in their laboratory, confronting challenges at their own pace, and the Wild Duo never stopped wanting to improve the photographic process. From the beginning of photography, this process had been controlled entirely by chemists. Except for photographic lights and a few cameras with built-in light meters, photography strictly involved the capture of images through the interaction between light and chemicals that resulted in a negative. A second step—processing—repeated this light-chemical interaction and resulted in a positive print or transparency.

Photographic chemistry emerged slowly from black and white to color, and in the 1970s, competing approaches to color image capture and processing still had not been standardized. Even the best color prints included compromises, never presenting "true" color replications. As always, the idea of a technological compromise frustrated Alex Dreyfoos.

For years Dreyfoos had taken photographs using 35 mm Kodachrome slide film for its higher resolution and saturated colors. Nonetheless, he was consistently disappointed with the reproduction and printing processes available for slides. For the best print results, he needed expensive inter-negatives, and still the results never matched the rich color and sharp focus of the original projected onto a large screen. After considering the possible ways to engineer a machine that would simplify and improve production of high-resolution prints from 35 mm slides, Dreyfoos and Mergens set to work and made it a reality: the LaserColor Printer.

The LaserColor Printer received positive press from *Popular Photography* (see sidebar, page 209) and from the *New York Times*, which showered it with praise such as "astounding," "wondrous," "confounding," "revolutionary," and "positively futuristic." "These were no ordinary prints." Despite the rave reviews, selling LaserColor to the photo industry proved difficult. Delays in increasing the working life of the machine's argon lasers prevented its full rollout as a new PEC product. "The laser we needed for the blue and green color beams had an MTBF (mean time between failure) of only a few hundred hours," Dreyfoos explains. "They were very expensive, and the laser makers said that in another year or two they'd be up to 10,000 hours of reliability. They never got there."

Dreyfoos and Mergens spent hours discussing what they should do with their LaserColor product. For a short time, they experimented with a mail order slide-to-print service, branded LaserColor and LaserColor Art. LaserColor Art allowed customers to alter the colors of their originals for creative results. "At the suggestion of Jim Shepherd, the lab manager, we offered a limited special, direct retail business, priced at $13.25 per slide print versus about $200 for a dye transfer print. We saw it as a loss-leader," Dreyfoos explains. "It was also a way to get the machine out where the public and commercial photography businesses could see it. That was our real motivation, for people to see the high quality pictures. We really wanted to work with professional photographers, never retail sales." Dealing directly with the public was a new experience for the company, and one they did not care to prolong.

PEC set up a toll-free number for accepting orders nationwide and opened a New York sales office, on Vanderbilt Avenue, where photographers could bring in their slides by appointment. Dreyfoos and Mergens, along with LaserColor engineers Donald Land, Charles Bray, and James Shepherd, created a LaserColor "Previewer" that allowed photographers to see what the system could do in terms of LaserColor Art. The preview settings were sent with the original slide to PEC in Florida for processing by the LaserColor Printer.

Soon Dreyfoos and Mergens realized that dealing with the public took a lot more time than they had expected, and a return on their investment was nowhere in sight. For most people, there was no sense of urgency to have this work done. They could just wait for the next special, and never pay full price. It promoted the wrong habit.

Between the expense and unreliability of lasers, marketing problems, and the fact that film was on its way out, the project slowly faded away. Before too long, other innovations such as digital cameras, slide scanners, the personal computer, and inkjet printers largely solved the problem of attaining good quality prints.

Sailfish Marina

Between WPEC and Photo Electronics, Dreyfoos needed a break from the hectic pace of the business world, and fishing was one way he could really relax. He consulted with his CFO, Josh Murray, about whether he could buy a sportfishing boat and put it up for charter to provide a tax advantage. In 1977 Dreyfoos traded up from *Dolphin Chaser* to a 1963 Rybovich that he named *Prime Time*.

Josh Murray expanded on the original idea dramatically. "Originally I looked for a small motel on Lake Worth," says Murray. "With Harry Chauncey's paralegal, I poured over plat maps and aerials, and Harry sent out letters of interest without identifying his client. One came back with a number written on it, a good number." Two of the property's owners were real estate developer Lou Perini Jr. and automobile dealership giant Roger Dean.

COVER STORY

"LaserColor: Future Trend for Photography?"
Popular Photography magazine, May 1979

Just as we have seen a vast application of space-age electronics in the design and engineering of our picture-taking equipment, so has that same science been actively applied in printmaking. What could be one of the most interesting breakthroughs in printing has taken place in Florida where PEC Laboratories, Inc. has developed a process of creating an inter-negative from slides using a laser readout technique.

Basically, the process works like this: A slide is cleaned and sorted into its emulsion group (Kodachrome, Ektachrome, etc.) and placed into a Laser-Color printer. In a 20-second process, three laser beams focused red, green, and blue (the primary colors in optics) scan the slide. Photo sensors record this and, in turn, three more laser beams are electronically focused on 70 mm Vericolor II film to create an inter-negative.

Why create an inter-negative electronically instead of optically? PEC technical people say traditional problems of dye absorptions and mismatched H&D curves (Hurter & Driffield, measurement of the relation between density and exposure) are solved. The result is a much-improved inter-negative that will provide more of the subtleties of color, detail and resolution. As a result, you can obtain prints from 35 mm and 2 ¼-inch format chromes coming close to dye transfer quality at a fraction of the cost.

The property was situated two blocks west of John D. MacArthur's Colonnades Hotel, in the town of Palm Beach Shores on Singer Island. The marina had evolved from a dock built in the late 1940s and known first as Roy's Dock, for its builder. Since the 1960s, the property had been called "Bill's Marina," after long-time owner Bill Bachstedt. Motor or sail into Palm Beach Inlet from the ocean, turn right, and it was the first marina on the right. It had one dock with slips for 30 vessels.

Murray convinced Dreyfoos that this would be a good investment, a place to dock his boat and to charter it when he wasn't out fishing. There were also vacant lots adjacent to the marina, mostly covered with Australian pines, where captains and their crews would park their cars and drink beer after a day at sea. Murray proposed that Dreyfoos should buy the vacant lots for future expansion.

Another large dock, just south of Bill's, was called the "Sailfish Center," with an owner who wanted out of the business. Dreyfoos combined all of the properties to create The Sailfish Marina and Resort. The total purchase cost PEC about $1.5 million and was completed in the spring of 1979.

One of the properties that became the Sailfish Marina came with riparian rights. This Eastern US system of water law is complex, and contains controversial limitations in Florida. They are "not of a proprietary nature," for example, and "are rights inuring the owner of the riparian land but are not owned by him or her" (F.S. 253.141). Because in Florida the state owns the water bottom, but no one owns the water—a state resource—the holder of riparian rights (a riparian) is unlike classic property ownership. Many court cases arise when old riparians have to adjust to new riparians. So, when one of the properties that became the Sailfish Marina came with riparian rights, the state was happy to trade them for an underwater lease.

In 1986, Dreyfoos applied for a permit to build a third T-dock at the marina. The state sent an inspector and a scuba diver to look at the area where Dreyfoos wanted to build, as dock building was not allowed where seagrass beds were present. A neighbor of the marina, John Hook, related to Josh Murray what he had observed of the state's visit. According to Hook, the diver came up out of the water and called to the inspector that it was clear below; no seagrass was present. The inspector replied, "Look again, until you find it." Hook also repeated the incident in writing to state officials. Shortly after, Dreyfoos received his permit.

Before Dreyfoos upgraded to *Prime Time*, he helped start the Gold Cup at the Sailfish Club in 1972, where 25 boats and 50 anglers each competed for points independently. Dreyfoos proved himself repeatedly in the tournament. Another tournament had been hosted there since 1963, the Invitational Masters Angling Sailfish Tournament. One of the founders was John Rybovich Jr., president of Rybovich and Sons Boat Works, the highly respected local company started by his parents. From the first year, the catch-and-release "Masters," focused on individual angling ability, received accolades. (*Sports Illustrated* wrote: "If there must be contest fishing, let it be modeled on this.") In 1978, the year after Dreyfoos purchased his Rybovich *Prime Time*, both he and his boat were finally invited to compete in the Masters. He kidded John

Rybovich, "I wasn't good enough as a fisherman. Now you've invited me only because of my boat!"

Tastevin

Through his love of yachting, Dreyfoos got to know Jim Kimberly, the Kleenex heir, who sponsored him for membership in the New York Yacht Club. Kimberly also invited Dreyfoos to join the Palm Beach chapter, which he had founded, of the Confrérie des Chevaliers du Tastevin (Brotherhood of the Knights of the Wine-Tasting Cup). Since 1934 the order (then all-male) has been promoting the Burgundy region of France, especially its wines and cuisine. Dreyfoos has enjoyed this "fine very-sensitive-nose wine tasting group," though he claims to have a poor sense of smell.

Growing Pains

Judy Goodman had joined Photo Electronics Corporation in December 1975, but by 1977 was working exclusively at WPEC. "I was production manager, public service manager—whatever Alex wanted to call me. I did lots of different things," Goodman remembers. The station's business rapidly picked up speed in the mid-1970s and needed to secure new syndicated shows, an important revenue source. Dreyfoos stayed away from making such decisions, not trusting his judgment on content, so Goodman assisted Program Director Art Stark in choosing the early programming for the station. At 58, Stark was older than most of the staff and described as "slick"; no one could ignore his impressive network-TV credentials. Goodman, an extremely bright person with a commanding presence, had no such background, but had a clear vision of her goals and the station's needs. Eventually, her success in programming would lead her to head up WPEC's on-the-air community outreach efforts.

A few months after Goodman's arrival, Dreyfoos decided to replace WPEC's general manager, Chuck Conrad, with Gary Dean, a smart, ambitious salesman already on staff who got along well with the sales department.

Palm Beach TV News: Star Wars

In 1979, rivalry was heating up in the nation's 80th populous television market. The *Miami Herald* noted on September 2: "Competition between

WPTV (Channel 5) and WPEC (Channel 12) is measured by Live-Eye trucks, action mini-cams, color weather radar, and an anchor man's finesse as he chit-chats with his weather girl."

Dreyfoos prepared WPEC for the 1980s with the latest weather radar and a Bell Jet Ranger news helicopter, registration number N212TV. A new building was scheduled for completion by the fall of 1982 to provide new studios, offices, and technical facilities with state-of-the-art television equipment.

This sort of competition was more common in the largest markets, but, as the *Herald* observed, "In Palm Beach, the powers behind two TV news staffs don't let that number 80 ranking make them lethargic. Here—particularly in money spent on promotional blitzes at ratings time, and in on-the-air personalities traded like baseball cards—it's Big City even if the market might not require it."

WPEC General Manager Gary Dean told the paper, "I have to admire [Channel] Five for wanting to be a leader. I, too, want to be a leader. What that means is that both stations are spending beyond what the market dictates. . . . I find it exciting that we're acting like a Top 30 market."

Although competition between the stations had been escalating since Dreyfoos purchased his station in 1973, it was difficult to point to a specific area of spending (such as promotions, the news department, color radar, or a helicopter) to attribute to either station's competitive success. The *Herald* concluded that it was "debatable whether consistently high quality TV journalism is the immediate result when big money is pumped into any market." The paper let Dean have the last word on the matter: "Everyone is so damned concerned about the cosmetics that there's no concern for the news."

During this competition, in October 1980, WPEC hired Laurel Sauer as news anchor for its 6:00 p.m. and 11:00 p.m. news reports. Born and raised in Houston, Texas, Sauer came directly from WALA in Mobile, Alabama, where she had been an anchor for two years. Before that, she had worked in the news department of WJHG in Panama City, Florida. Gary Dean, meanwhile, was replaced. In Cincinnati, Ohio, a "head-hunter" employment agency discovered Robert C. Wiegand, a far more experienced TV station general manager.

Right on schedule, in October 1982, the new WPEC building was dedicated, with Florida Governor Bob Graham and a list of local notables in attendance. Smartly designed by Carroll Peacock, the building was functional and spacious, and shamelessly represented the station's powerful stature in the community. Peacock, who eventually designed three projects for Dreyfoos, says, "Of all the people I've worked with, there are only a few that really stand out as luminaries. It was a pleasure to work with Alex."

Wide-Angle Lens on the World

Thanks to the success of Photo Electronics Corporation, Dreyfoos could have qualified for membership in the prestigious Young Presidents' Organization (YPO) before he turned 40 in 1972. This international education and travel organization included people who (1) were president of a company with at least 40 employees, and (2) had made more than a million dollars in sales before age 40. Dreyfoos, not appreciating the value of YPO, did not bother to apply and join until 1975, which he regrets. The requirements allowed, until age 43, for an applicant to prove that he would have qualified before turning 40. Dreyfoos met this deadline, but missed out on the value of YPO for those several years.

Dreyfoos enjoyed photographing exotic locations with the select group until 1982, when he turned 50. That's the age when YPO requires qualified members to graduate to the World Presidents' Organization (WPO), where idea exchange continues to enhance lives, enrich families, and improve communities. "The idea behind being forced out at age 50 is to keep the organization vibrant," Dreyfoos explains. "They also found that executive focus tends to shift by then, from internal focus and learning to a more worldly focus. While all YPOers in good standing at age 50 are eligible to join WPO, there is also a related group, Chief Executives Organization (CEO), which selects members from YPO/WPO who have demonstrated community or organizational leadership." Dreyfoos qualified for membership in CEO, sponsored by his friend Stan Rumbough, with the support of Llwyd Ecclestone, in the mid-'80s. The customized trips and conferences only got better.

Although, as a photographer, Dreyfoos possibly appreciated traveling with YPO/WPO/CEO more than many other members, one of the key components of membership was education, through conferences and classes. Speakers included Ronald Reagan (before he was president), Henry Kissinger, and Deepak

Chopra. Members could purchase recordings of such talks, which Dreyfoos made available to his staff. In 1989, Dreyfoos dined with Jehan Sadat, the widow of the assassinated former Egyptian president, Anwar Sadat, and met the current president, Hosni Mubarak.

At times, the YPOers walked in on history in the making.

Dreyfoos was unexpectedly present in Zagreb, Yugoslavia, in 1980, when the coffin of then-President Josip Broz Tito, the last of the World War II Allied leaders, toured the country before his funeral. While several thousand rain-drenched people gathered outside, Dreyfoos, in his hotel room, was told to close his window shutters. Instead, he opened both shutter and window and took several historic pictures. He quickly packed the roll of film away and loaded a new roll before the knock came at the door. The officials were quite pleased to confiscate the (empty) roll of film from his camera.

In July 1991, Gavriil Kh. Popov, then mayor of Moscow, addressed Dreyfoos' WPO group in Madrid, Spain. The Russian extended an invitation to some of the Americans, including Dreyfoos and his friend Tom Pledger, which they were pleased to accept: celebrate New Year's Eve in beautiful apartments within the Kremlin.

Dreyfoos' group arrived in Moscow just after Christmas 1991, the day that Russian President Boris Yeltsin had ordered the dissolution of the Soviet Union. A communiqué went out to Russian embassies around the world: "On New Year's Eve, the hammer-and-sickle flag of revolutionary red that has flown for 74 years over the Kremlin, the medieval brick fortress on the Moscow River, will be lowered, marking the formal end to the Soviet Union." The Commonwealth of Independent States (CIS) alliance, replacing the USSR, also took effect on December 31, 1991.

In the midst of these historic changes, the WPOers, though aware of the events, enjoyed the hospitality of their Russian hosts. The spectacle at the Kremlin on New Year's Eve included a military band and fireworks. At dinner, Pledger recalls a bottle of vodka sat between each two people. They were matched with members of the Russian government who were knowledgeable in their fields, and dined in their homes, which Pledger recalls were not at all elaborate. Mayor Popov—indeed, the Russian people—had great hopes for their future, and for the usefulness that these Americans might be.

Tying a Second Knot

When Dreyfoos decided to marry again after about five years of bachelorhood, it was in a large part to enjoy fully the benefits of his membership in YPO. Dreyfoos would eventually visit about three-fourths of the countries of the world, many of them with YPO, but "traveling as a bachelor was really a downer," he recalls, and Renate was still beyond his reach. The organization also, in those days, took a dim view of its members traveling without wives. He started courting Barbara Murphy Williams, who worked in community relations for First National Bank in Palm Beach, and then as assistant manager of the exclusive Colony Hotel in Palm Beach. "Barbara was a very nice, easy-going woman," says Dreyfoos, "and a good traveling companion."

Dreyfoos and Williams married quietly in April 1981. What the ceremony lacked in a family presence was more than made up for on the honeymoon, according to Dreyfoos' daughter, Cathy: "We all went with them. When Dad said he and Barbara wanted to take everybody on his boat, I told him, I have this old college friend who's coming in from New York. So it was my husband, Mike, and me; my friend Trish; my brother, Robert, and his first wife, Martine; Dad, and Barbara." Sadly for all involved, the marriage came to an end five years later.

New and Improved Models

Photo Electronics enjoyed a highly lucrative partnership, with Kodak marketing PEC's video analyzer. The VCNA allowed an operator in a photo lab to preview an accurate representation of what a print would look like from a negative, and then adjust the brightness and color prior to making the print. As technology advanced through the 1960s and '70s, Photo Electronics had updated the machine to perform with increased accuracy. There were four models in all, counting the internal test model used to prove to Kodak the viability of the product.

When Dreyfoos and Mergens invented the VCNA, there had been only one type of film and photographic paper in use. A primary impetus for some updates was that new types of films came along, says Dreyfoos. "By the 1980s, Kodak had variations, and along came Fuji Color and Agfa Color. Though Kodak wanted us to cater only to their films, laboratories wanted to handle them all." For Kodak to be successful in the professional photographic market, it was also important that their systems worked well for all materials that were being used.

Each model included a single light bulb, which Dreyfoos explains was key to the success of the device—the machine's internal standard of stabilization. "It was dimmed well below its rated operating voltage so that it appeared yellow in color temperature, giving it a life of several years. We ran that bulb off a very precise power supply. I don't remember ever replacing one."

Despite the modifications to support multiple films and papers, a laundry list from Kodak drove the effort to design a new machine in the early 1980s. The way the analog circuitry worked, there were certain things that could not be done. Moving into the digital realm seemed like a logical progression, even if at the time it was a big stretch in technology.

The staff by then included Dreyfoos' son, Robert, who had graduated from Worcester Polytechnic Institute with a Bachelor of Science degree in Electrical Engineering. Rob had worked at PEC for four summers, but most recently for Pratt & Whitney Aircraft in nearby Jupiter, processing instrumentation data from testing of their jet engines. Pratt offered Robert a position upon his graduation, and Dreyfoos quickly matched the offer. "We were going to go from analog to digital, and I wanted my son involved. I grew up in an analog world, but what Robert had learned in school was focused on the digital world. I felt I *could* become expert in that new world, but it was enough for me to know the general concepts, as I wanted to pay attention to other things. I could tell Robert what I needed, how I thought we might do it, and let him be the expert on digital matters. Anyone who had a question could go to Robert."

The timing was right for both of them, his son recalls. "This design work was right in my expertise at the time. It was also a great opportunity for Dad and me to work together doing things that both of us greatly enjoyed. Dad had an opportunity to teach the apprentice and pass along his great wealth of knowledge in photo science, electronics, and general engineering. I believe this was something very important to him and drove much of what he did during that time. I also met my wife, Julie Stevenson, at PEC; we were married in 1987."

The successor to the VCNA was named the Professional Video Analyzing Computer (PVAC). PEC went hybrid, with a digital image-processing engine to support a wide variety of photographic film/paper combinations. The input (film reader) and output (display) parts were analog, while the manipulation that was done to make the system accurately analog the photographic process was done via digital technology. All of the controls on the machine were also digital. It used a Trinitron color tube and followed the same operating principle as the VCNA. In the VCNA, transistors switched and amplified electronic signals. In the PVAC, however, integrated circuits (hundreds of thousands of transistors) accomplished a comparable job cheaper and better.

As with the VCNA, there were multiple models of the PVAC, each one enhancing some aspect of the machine. Examples include: (1) adding a PC (IBM XT generation) computer; (2) additional data-handling functionality using an Atari-like data cartridge; (3) changing from a 5¼-inch single floppy disk drive to dual 3½-inch disk drives; and (4) replacing the film reader for a solid-state, broadcast-quality camera.

While Rob was leading the digital division, his father and George Mergens were eliminating the final bugs in the LaserColor printer. Along with management of the Sailfish Marina and WPEC, Dreyfoos worked constantly. His public profile continued to rise, primarily due to his ownership of the television station and involvement in the emerging plans for an exciting addition to the Palm Beaches.

Intrigue in the Greater Miami TV Market

By the mid-1980s, Dreyfoos had placed trusted employees in key positions of all his operations. At WPEC, he, Mergens, and the station team had eliminated the MacArthur committee style of management and created their own organization. While Dreyfoos never found the same enjoyment managing TV staff as he did with Photo Electronics employees, he established *his* management style, the success of which was proven by increasing revenues and an expanding portfolio of businesses. He once described it to the press as "rational."

In 1984, signaling the start of broadcast television consolidation, the Federal Communications Commission raised its limit on TV station ownership. This action, and the 1983 death of Mitchell Wolfson Sr., founder of the Miami-based theater chain Wometco, set in motion a series of events that caused a major shakeup in the Miami broadcast television market with ripples throughout South Florida.

An intriguing rumor had long circulated that Wolfson had written a secret plan to run Wometco after his death. No plan was found, resulting in a successful takeover in 1984 by the investment firm of Kohlberg Kravis Roberts & Company. (This Kravis was Henry, a son of Raymond F. Kravis.) The $1 billion deal was the largest corporate buyout ever. KKR began to sell off Wometco's assets, including TV stations.

All of this would soon play into Dreyfoos' plans for his business activities in South Florida. There was excitement in many arenas in the Palm Beaches during this period, and he had placed himself right in the thick of it. ⟐

AnEta Sewell of WPEC, the area's first African American TV reporter and anchor, in the 1970s.

Dreyfoos scuba diving at Walkers Cay in the Bahamas, 1987.

Dreyfoos at his home, 380 North Lake Way, Palm Beach, during a photo shoot by *Palm Beach Life* magazine, 1980.

(left to right) Architect R. Carroll Peacock, designer Susan S. Smith, and Dreyfoos, at Cathy Dreyfoos' wedding in 1978.

Dreyfoos dancing with his daughter, Cathy Dreyfoos Carter, on her 1978 wedding day.

Aron "A.J." and second wife, Irma Jacobson, at 1978 wedding rehearsal for granddaughter Cathy.

Aerial of PEC in the late 1970s, with LaserColor Lab addition and TV tower.

PEC's LaserColor printer prototype.

Marketing the LaserColor Art process.

The original photo of a Toronto sailboat race (top) shown with LaserColor Art applied (center and bottom), a process invented at PEC in the 1970s.

Bill's Marina (top) and the Sailfish Center (bottom) in 1977, properties Dreyfoos purchased to create Sailfish Marina and Resort.

Dreyfoos' 51-foot Rybovich, *Prime Time*, taken from his helicopter.

Dreyfoos and his catch of the day, a pair of blue marlin, in the US Virgin Islands in 1978.

Dreyfoos with his 680-lb. catch, a blue fin tuna in Bimini, 1980.

Dreyfoos during 1979 lobster season in Bimini, the Bahama Islands, in front of his first Cessna 421, the B model.

Dreyfoos (left) and Jim Kimberly, his sponsor into and founder of the Palm Beach chapter of the Confrérie des Chevaliers du Tastevin (Brotherhood of the Knights of the Wine-Tasting Cup).

Dreyfoos (right) at a Tastevin dinner with Curt Gowdy, former sportscaster who bought radio station WEAT from John D. MacArthur in 1974.

THE BUSINESS PEOPLE MAGAZINE

WINNING!
PALM BEACH COUNTY

Alex Dreyfoos, Jr. and his electric success

Plus: Architect Carroll Peacock helps design the foundation for West Palm Beach's future.

Dreyfoos on the cover of *Winning* magazine (1985) with his first helicopter, also used by WPEC.

Anchors Reg Miller and Laurel Sauer at WPEC's new news desk, 1982.

Dreyfoos showing Florida Governor Bob Graham around the new WPEC building, 1982.

The reception area of the new WPEC building, 1982.

Dreyfoos' office in the new WPEC building, 1982.

The WPEC conference room, 1985.

Dreyfoos' photograph of "Three Wise Monkeys," a Japanese pictorial proverb, taken in Japan in 1982, and hung over the news director's office door at WPEC.

(left to right) Dreyfoos, former Palm Beach Mayor Lesly Smith, and Stan Rumbough in the 1990s.

Barbara Murphy Williams, before she became Dreyfoos' second wife in 1981.

Dreyfoos with his son, Robert, on Robert's receiving his electrical engineering degree from Worcester Polytechnic Institute, 1980.

Dreyfoos (center) with his son, Robert (left), and George Mergens with the PVAC (left) and VCNA (right).

CHAPTER 11

Water for the Cultural Desert

Kravis Center CEO Judy Mitchell with Dreyfoos, 2004.

Palm Beach Culture 101

Creative engineers were always in demand at Photo Electronics. "I tried to raid Route 128," says Dreyfoos, "the circular highway around Boston where most of the high-tech companies are because of the MIT connection. When people came down to interview at PEC and I thought I might offer them a position, I would invite them to stay for the weekend to get a feel for the area. They would inevitably ask, 'What is there to do here, beyond enjoying the sun and surf?'"

It bothered Dreyfoos that his community was perceived as being a cultural desert when there was in fact the Norton Art Gallery, the Four Arts Society, a playhouse, an orchestra, and ballet and opera companies. *He* knew there was cultural activity in Palm Beach County, but apparently it was unlikely anyone would discover it on his or her own during a weekend visit.

What was clearly needed was a regularly published public calendar of events. It was Dreyfoos' perception of this need—without thought of a new performance venue—that motivated him to found a cultural council.

In 1978, Dreyfoos used his ownership of WPEC to air a public service announcement, inviting anyone interested in starting a cultural council to attend a meeting at the WPEC studios. The response: more people than could fit in the large room. The resulting non-profit was called Palm Beach County Council of the Arts (now the Cultural Council of Palm Beach County), a coalition of 45 of the 80 arts groups then in the county. Dreyfoos provided seed money to cover the first three years of the council's operating expenses. Along with a calendar of events, the council published its objectives, which eventually included a performing arts center.

Unfortunately, as George Elmore remembers, "For most anything in the arts, we still had to go to the 'leaky teepee' (West Palm Beach Auditorium), where there may have been mud wrestling or a tractor pull the week before," with its lingering odor. *The Palm Beach Post* quoted Jimmy Buffett as calling it "the scummiest place in the country." Before the auditorium opened in 1967, Civic Music and Civic Opera of the Palm Beaches had sponsored events at the former Palm Beach High School Auditorium—on the site of what would become the Dreyfoos School of the Arts decades later.

The coming of serious cultural events to the auditorium is credited to impresario Clyde Fyfe, who since 1972 had taken on the role of local arts leader. Fyfe founded the Regional Arts Foundation in 1975, though his actual vocation remained "cook slash steward" on the 78-foot yacht of Ford Motor Co. executive Benson Ford. Through Regional Arts, Fyfe "created the audience for the Kravis Center," says Will Ray, former president/CEO of the Cultural Council. Dreyfoos agrees: "Fyfe and others have tugged, wheedled, and sometimes kicked South Florida's arts out of their amateurishness and isolation, out of their status as society hobbies and high-school-kid diversions." Regional Arts was underwritten by Leonard Davis and his wife, Sophie. Davis, founder of Colonial Penn Group, Inc., had helped establish the American Association of Retired Persons (AARP); the couple also made possible the performing arts center at the City College of New York.

Another group, Fine Arts Festival, Inc., led by Mary Stuart Howes of Palm Beach, had been pursuing the idea of an arts center to replace the West

Palm Beach Auditorium. With the added efforts of Ralph Boyes, then manager of the auditorium, the City Commission told this group in January 1974 that they could develop a center on three vacant acres adjacent to the auditorium (which the city owned), *if* they could raise groundbreaking funds within five years. Howes had raised about $60,000 at the time. The project was endorsed by the Auditorium Advisory Committee of West Palm Beach; Civic Opera of the Palm Beaches, Inc.; Ballet Arts of Palm Beach, Inc.; and Palm Beach Symphonette.

Fine Arts Festival commissioned a feasibility study from C. W. Shaver Company, which was completed in two phases in 1974 and 1975. Phase I identified only 15 arts organizations in Palm Beach County. Phase II concluded: "Additional expenditures on this project should be made with the understanding that the risk of not succeeding is considerable." In the consultants' informed opinion, the community was not ready for a multimillion-dollar arts center.

Three years passed.

"The Appropriate Body"

On May 3, 1978, many of the same parties explored the question again: Is Palm Beach County ready for a performing arts center? This time the setting was a small but public forum held in Palm Beach County Commission chambers, sponsored by WHRS Fine Arts Radio (a National Public Radio member station and predecessor to WXEL). This time the conclusion was 100 percent positive, not surprisingly, considering the panel: Mary Howes, Clyde Fyfe, Rodney McCallum (then manager of the auditorium), Everett Aspinwall (owner, WPBR Radio), Dr. Edward M. Eissey (then president-elect of Palm Beach Junior College), and County Commissioner Dennis Koehler. Eissey initiated a lively discussion on the benefits of building a center on PBJC property that would remain under PBJC management. All of this was made public in the local press.

Just weeks after this forum, the Council of the Arts held its first meeting, with a good turnout. A month later, the council was registered as a not-for-profit corporation. It was organized by Judy Goodman at WPEC, one of the first people with whom Dreyfoos discussed his ideas for making Palm Beach a cultural center. Goodman agreed to take on the additional role of executive director of the council, working from the TV station, and soon identified the right people to serve on the council's board. Dreyfoos agreed to chair the board for just the first year, immediately naming John R. Smith, a fellow Economic Council member, as his successor.

The council immediately drew the media's eye. Charles Calhoun of the *Palm Beach Post-Times* was present when the nominated board was elected *en bloc* that December. "If future meetings are as entertaining," he wrote, "they ought to start selling tickets." A January 4 *Post* editorial, without mentioning the council, called for a "cultural revolution" and for the County Commission "to put the subject high on the public agenda." Dreyfoos took the opportunity to respond publicly that he already had the support of the commission, who had declared the council as "the appropriate body to do the type of necessary homework" for a performing arts center. That winter, Goodman recalls, "a resolution of the Palm Beach County Commission appointed the council as the official agency on arts matters. Dennis Koehler was the one soldiering it through and was very instrumental in early efforts, as were County Administrator John Sansbury and his assistant, Louise Grant." Goodman started the "homework" by distributing a questionnaire to local arts groups to help in making recommendations on a center's size and location, and went on to execute a "massive research project."

About this time, Fine Arts Festival ran out of time with the West Palm Beach City Commission and received a two-year extension. The *Palm Beach Daily News* reported that the location for the proposed center was undetermined, while describing the three acres adjacent to the auditorium as "earmarked by Fine Arts Festival and the Palm Beach County Council of the Arts, Inc." Mary Howes told the press, "This idea of both groups working together is only in the beginning stages; nothing is definite." Her attorney, Bob Salisbury, had kicked off the marriage of the two organizations a month earlier by giving the council the reports from Shaver. Eventually, says Goodman, "Howes asked us to take over her project, as she'd taken it as far as she could at the auditorium site." Her supporters migrated as well: "Fyfe assessed users' input; McCallum looked at other auditorium managers' experiences— that kind of thing—and Mike Hyman looked into tax-increment financing to do the center downtown."

The name Palm Beach County *Center* for the Arts, Inc. was reserved for

60 days on November 6, 1979, though it would not be used until the summer of 1983. In the meantime, the project existed as the Center for the Arts Committee *of* the Palm Beach County Council of the Arts. Dreyfoos served as chairman of the committee, Robert M. Montgomery as vice chair, Merrill L. Bank as secretary-treasurer, and John J. Brogan and Leonard Davis as members at large. Goodman was project coordinator. Her research produced, in August 1979, a 62-page "road map" that indicated strong local desire to build a performing arts center. "Once the legwork was done," she says, "we moved into the fundraising sphere. That's where Alex really took off."

The Founders Committee for the center included prestigious business leaders: E. Llwyd Ecclestone, builder-developer; William C. Clark, Flagler National Bank; James Y. Arnold Jr., former builder and representative to the Fine Arts Council of Florida; Daniel J. Mahoney, publisher of Palm Beach Newspapers Inc.; Thomas R. Pledger, chair of Rubin Construction and member of the Economic Council; Marshall M. Criser Jr., Palm Beach attorney and chair of the Florida Council of 100; and Frank W. McAbee Jr., Pratt & Whitney. Strong bonds were forged in the name of progress.

Location Location Location—Act I

In early 1980, Dreyfoos asked the City of West Palm Beach about building a performing arts center in Currie Park, on the western shore of Lake Worth. At about the same time, he was able to get the attention of renowned architect I. M. Pei. When Pei—also an MIT alumnus—showed up in Palm Beach with MIT President Jerry Wiesner to raise money for what would become the MIT Media Lab (see subsection "Massachusetts Institute of Technology," page 347), Dreyfoos seized the opportunity. Taking the architect for a ride on his boat, *Prime Time*, he cruised up the shoreline of the Intracoastal Waterway, just where Currie Park juts into the water, and asked Pei:

"Wouldn't the performing arts center look great there?"

Pei agreed excitedly, "Like the Sydney Opera House!"

"Will you design it for me?"

"I'd love to."

The council, through its committee for a center, moved the idea forward.

Dreyfoos asked Clyde Fyfe if he could say a few words to the audience at the closing performance of the 1980 ballet season—at the usual venue, the West Palm Beach Auditorium. A reporter from the *Palm Beach Post* happened to be covering the event and reported in her Sunday review: "After the second intermission, the stir of the normal excitement in the air heightened. Alec [*sic*] Dreyfoos . . . announced the long-awaited plans for a performing arts center. His opening remarks drew an extended round of applause and some cheers. When he announced architect I. M. Pei's acceptance to design the project on a portion of the 18-acre Currie Park . . . he was met with a gasp and applause. He announced the names of the Founders Committee who will assist in fundraising for the $25 million project. Repeated applause interrupted his announcement. Dreyfoos called on the community to come forth and support the project financially. 'It will only become a reality with substantial private support,' he said."

Most of the audience did not appear to Dreyfoos to be especially affluent, but he told the *Post*, "It doesn't matter how small or large the donation." If those who applauded were unlikely as major donors, they were also noticeably enthusiastic for change. Music critic Thelma Newman wrote, "Audiences came to the auditorium—but how they complained. The protests were loud and vocal, and who could blame them?"

Dreyfoos also found a way to approach Leonard Davis about building a center privately: "Leonard politely said, 'You have a great dream, but you can't do it privately. The county's not ready. If I ever think you can, I'll be with you.'"

When Dreyfoos, armed with an extensive proposal completed by Goodman with consultants Kimley-Horn & Associates, asked the city if he could build the center at Currie Park, "On first reading, they said yes. Then some people from the community spoke up, saying, 'Don't take our parks away,' which drew a lot of news coverage."

A second public hearing on the fate of the Currie Park location was held on November 11, 1980, when a capacity crowd included a number of opponents. Dreyfoos spoke of the new arts center as having the potential to become "the cultural center of the Southeast." To derisive laughter from opponents, Dreyfoos defended his choice by invoking the name of the famous architect: "I. M. Pei fell in love with Currie Park." Although speakers for and against the location were reported to have been about even, the board rejected the proposal. Dreyfoos decided not to fight the city on the Currie Park location after all, realizing that traffic could have been a significant problem.

The *Post* started its lead editorial two days later: "Alex Dreyfoos says he hasn't given up the idea of a performing arts center for this area despite the West Palm Beach Planning Board's rejection of Currie Park as a site. We hope he continues to provide leadership for the project and that the cultural community rallies around him for a second effort. . . . The important thing is to keep this dream alive."

The same day, Thelma Newman vented in her column. "I am mad—furious—at the shortsightedness of this community. . . . [B]y procrastinating again, we are back to square one. . . . A performing arts center is more than bricks and mortar. It can be the difference between existence and living. We may never again have this chance of a lifetime."

A few days after the proposal's defeat, Dreyfoos told the *Post*, "Palm Beach County is promoting itself as a haven for businesses to escape the cold. Why not do the same for artists? They don't like the snow either."

Privately, Dreyfoos believed he could convince Pei to continue with the project, but after more than a year went by, Pei initiated a call.

"Alex, how are you doing on raising the money?"

"I've sure got a long way to go."

"Well, Dallas has their money together, and they've asked me whether I would design their performance center. You'll remember I said that I was only going to design one performing arts center. I would respectfully ask if I could get off the hook with you."

Sadly, Dreyfoos released Pei from his commitment.

Location Location Location—Act II

At the end of 1980, the West Palm Beach Civitan Club honored Dreyfoos for his community efforts as its Outstanding Citizen of the Year in Palm Beach County. The acknowledgment fueled his resolve to make the performing arts center a reality; when media attention waned, he brought it back to life. Dreyfoos' friend Llwyd Ecclestone, president of the National Investment Company, told the *Post*, "Alex marches to his own drummer. He does exactly what he wants to do. He makes up his mind, sets his program, and follows through. He's willing to take a chance. You could say he is typical of the free enterprise system."

As time went on, Dreyfoos remained confident a location for the arts center would be identified. The Palm Beach County Council of the Arts conducted a survey that concluded the most likely site would be in West Palm Beach or Lake Worth. South County residents complained that it should be more accessible to them. "The thing is not going to end up in the Glades," Dreyfoos assured the *Miami Herald*.

In 1982, the council mounted two county referendums. The first ran in the September primary, to create a "bed tax" to fund the arts and promote tourism. "The hoteliers were running ads against it," recalls Dreyfoos. He approached Stayton D. Addison, president of Flagler Systems Inc., owner of The Breakers, with a deal: "I'm willing to take one-third and let you take two-thirds, because I think you'll use it responsibly." And that's how it played out: 30 percent was designated for arts programming. The *Palm Beach Post* called for the Council of the Arts to administer that share, citing their "well-established record of coordinating, evaluating and promoting artistic endeavors."

"We got it on the first try," says Will Ray, the council's executive director at the time. "Goodman (then board chair of the council) was a master strategist. We knew what to play up and play down. It was our first major accomplishment." As of 2015, the tax raised nearly $65 million.

In April 1982, the Florida Legislature had passed a bill allowing counties to levy an additional one-cent sales tax, for one year only, towards building or improving facilities. Though originally aimed toward sports venues in Broward and Dade counties, Rep. Jim Watt (R-West Palm Beach), helped extend the idea to arts centers. "It's a one-shot item, and I think this county desperately needs a theater for the performing arts," said Watt. Dreyfoos convinced the County Commission to put the referendum on the November ballot: "After all, all they'd be doing is letting the people decide."

With the bed tax vote behind them, the Council started campaigning the next day for similar success with the sales tax, estimated to raise about $52 million. "This is the time for the people who have been saying all along they want a performing arts center to exercise their option," announced Judy Goodman, then council chair. "No more bellyaching."

Goodman and Dreyfoos made an effective team. "I can't tell you," she says, "how many times Alex had to appear before some public tribunal with the usual adversaries claiming this project would be elitist or somehow take away from the poor and downtrodden. He was always very clear that a community must serve many needs and, frankly, he was a great salesman because he was sincere, committed, and focused."

One audience that Dreyfoos found supportive was the board of Flagler National Bank. Dreyfoos appealed to his fellow board members to make as large a donation as they could, he says, about $50,000. "We then determined the ratio of that amount to the bank's deposits. It was a high percentage of the deposits, but the deposits were a small part of the county. Then we went around to all the local banks and said, 'Listen, get involved with the community. Little Flagler Bank has given x dollars per dollar of deposits to this center. You should do the same.' It worked! Barnett Bank gave us a quarter of a million just following this little formula."

Despite all efforts, the second county referendum failed to pass a penny sales tax to build an arts center. Dreyfoos was not surprised—he'd seen it fail in other counties—but felt they had to give it a try. Dreyfoos chose to see the glass half full: "More than 30 percent of the voters voted *for* it, which means roughly two-thirds of those necessary to pass it [half] voted for it."

He took this outlook to Sen. Harry A. Johnston, in 1984 the incoming president of the Florida Senate, who happened to be from West Palm Beach: "Find us a good chunk of what we would've gotten if the tax had passed—say, $10 million." Sen. Johnston was concerned about accusations of favoritism to his home county, but he found the money. Its structure ensured another $10 million from the Board of County Commissioners over two years. The arts group promised to raise another $10 million in private funds. A detailed preliminary construction estimate in August 1983 of $25 million, adjusted for inflation, set their sights at $30 million construction costs plus $5 million endowment for operating expenses.

The state funds came attached to a big string, as part of a $185 million Public Education Capital Outlay (PECO) bill, but Dreyfoos resigned himself to the partial victory in the name of progress.

The plan moved ahead based on building the center at Palm Beach Junior College in Lake Worth, south of West Palm Beach, where Dr. Edward M. Eissey was the current president. Eissey had wanted the performing arts center on college property back in 1978, when he was president-elect. During a tour in Dreyfoos' helicopter, the two men picked out a 10.3-acre site on

Lake Osborne in county-owned John Prince Park, adjacent to the college campus. Eissey convinced the County Commission to deed the land to the college for a performing arts center through a complex public hearing process, after fair warning through the press. There was no public hint of connection to the Council of the Arts, except a brief reference to "the most serious effort [for a center], when one group proposed Currie Park."

Although Eissey would not confirm it, the *Post* named his "biggest ally in the project" as Sen. Johnston, a known champion of education and, thus, of other endeavors by Eissey. The senator had undoubtedly been hearing about this project for a long time, while wearing other hats as attorney for Clyde Fyfe and co-trustee of the family foundation of Thomas Chastain, who was on Dreyfoos' team. He and his fellow legislators worked on the large PECO bill until June, when Gov. Bob Graham vetoed it without any warning. Although he said at the time he "had no objections to the money being spent on the fine arts center," that $10 million was a small part of the defeated bill. Johnston called for a two-day special session in hopes of salvaging the entire $185 million. Indeed, the *Miami News* reported that at the start of the session on December 7, "to the chants of 'do it, do it' on the chamber floor, House members overrode the governor's veto . . . by a stunning 114 to 1 vote."

Dreyfoos and his council got busy planning the building-to-be.

With the goal of a world-class venue with optimal acoustics, in February 1984, Dreyfoos' group had hired Artec Consultants Inc. of New York. Starting that July, Artec had led them on a whirlwind tour of 12 arts centers in the US and Canada. For their $30 million budget, they were encouraged to model Pikes Peak Center in Colorado Springs, which had opened in 1982.

In April 1985, they formed a Performance Advisory Committee made up of eight cultural leaders from the community, to offer their input: Dr. Wilfred Bain (chair), Mark Malkovich III, David Gray, Marie Hale, Paul McRae, Mark Azzolina, Clyde Fyfe, and ex-officio member Will Ray.

The Million-Dollar Pledge

As they'd been paid to do, C. W. Shaver Co., the fundraising consultants hired by the Performing Arts Center board, offered their advice, welcome or not: Don't expect anyone to commit more money than your chairman, Alex Dreyfoos, does.

This was in the spring of 1985. Dreyfoos explains, "George Mergens and I were still wrestling with turning the TV station around financially, reorganizing its debt structure and all. Leonard Davis came to me and said, 'I think the consultants are right. Just take the plunge, Alex. Don't worry about it.' Our pledges were payable in five years, and we had made sure they were legally enforceable. Leonard assured me, if at the end of five years I couldn't come up with the million, he would cover it.

"George and I agreed to make the million-dollar pledge as a company gift. Just as predicted, there was never another gift above a million dollars, except for Leonard Davis himself, who made a second million-dollar gift in the name of a friend who had died." Dreyfoos later said that he'd been trying to set an example for other businesses to follow: "I hoped it would start a stampede." It didn't have quite the desired effect, but in September 1985, gifts totaled $4 million.

The Galoshes Moment

Dreyfoos noticed his most difficult fundraising task was with some of the winter residents, or "snowbirds": "I would get comments like, 'Why would I want to give to a puny little center when I've got Lincoln Center or Kennedy or Boston Symphony Hall or what-have-you?' I confess I developed a rather flippant response: 'So you wouldn't have to wear your galoshes.' Then I realized what these people were saying was, they were used to the best, the top quality. It hit me that we might add significantly to the scope of the project, such that people would say, 'Okay, in the summertime, I go to Boston Symphony Hall, and in the wintertime I come to the Palm Beach County Center for the Arts.' Someplace there is a newspaper editorial that says, 'Dreyfoos can't raise $30 million, but thinks he can raise 50.' But the simple fact is, it was easier to raise 50, and that's really why we set out to do this quality."

What's in a Name?

It became clear that $30 million would not suffice to build the world-class arts center that he envisioned, his supporters now expected, and construction costs dictated. The project required more than the additional $10 million in private donations they had first calculated. During the fundraising process, when Dreyfoos was pursuing a stronger connection with the top philanthropists in Palm Beach County, he received a call from Merrill Bank, the center's secretary-treasurer and a fellow member of the Young Presidents' Organization.

"Alex, I'd like to help you fundraise for the center."

"That's very nice, Merrill, I could use the help."

"No, you don't understand."

"Well, I don't know what I don't understand, but no one else has called to offer to help raise funds, so thank you."

"I'm going to be president of the Palm Beach Country Club next year. I think I can help you raise a lot of money from that position."

"That's terrific."

"No, you don't understand," Bank repeated. "You know the club is predominantly Jewish, but you may not know that we emphasize our members' philanthropy. Each year, a member has a pet project that everyone else supports. I've noticed that one member, Ray Kravis, is always quick to write a check for everyone else's projects, but he's never brought forth one of his own." An oilman and philanthropist from Oklahoma, Raymond F. Kravis and his wife, Bessie, had enjoyed decades as winter residents of Palm Beach. "I'd like us to build the center in Ray's name," continued Bank, "to thank him for everything he's done. I know people in the club who would like to help you do that." Bank insisted that Dreyfoos had to sell Kravis on the idea, which he did at a lunch that included Leonard Davis.

Dreyfoos had reservations. "We had commitments from the state and county for what was then known as the Palm Beach County Center for the Arts. How could I rationalize changing the name?" Davis suggested the goal to name it should be $5 million (he and Bank had already pledged $1 million each), and guaranteed that he would pay the difference if the club members did not come through. Dreyfoos asked for and received permission from the County Commission.

The feat proved as propitious as advertised. When Kravis learned that $3 million had been given in *his* name by a group of his friends, the oilman was astounded: "I am truly touched by this wonderful honor." On December 19, 1985, Dreyfoos, "glowing like a 6-year-old with a new bike" announced the donations as anonymous; Kravis did let slip Leonard Davis' name before his wife "shushed" him. The next morning, *Palm Beach Post* Editor Tom Kelly spoke for many: "Merry Christmas, Palm Beach County." That first $3 million quickly grew to $7 million. It went a long way in convincing additional contributors that the dream of an arts center was to be a reality, now christened the Raymond F. Kravis Center for the Performing Arts.

Most of this early generosity came from the Jewish community, and Dreyfoos says he didn't pay much attention to that at first. "Then all of a sudden it was like [claps hands], we hit a brick wall, no money coming in at all." In March 1986, Dreyfoos approached former industrialist John Brogan, "a Catholic, pretty well known, and a good fundraiser. I convinced John to not only get involved with a contribution [of $100,000], but to co-chair our capital campaign with Merrill Bank, who was Jewish. All of a sudden, I got maybe four times that in more money out of the [Palm Beach Country] Club. Then it sort of died again. Then I got Stan Rumbough, a good WASP-y socialite name . . . and some more money came in."

Dreyfoos also paid a visit to his former employer, IBM, who then had a major facility in Boca Raton. "I'm sure it was a fraternal kind of, 'Oh, he used to work at the Advanced Systems Development Division, great! Here's a quarter-of-a-million dollars'—whether they knew me personally or not, there was that camaraderie." That seemed to trigger another couple of million dollars from the community. He finally figured it out: "I realized, I don't have to ask any Jewish person for money. All I have to do is raise non-Jewish money, and it will come. The Jewish community doesn't want this to be viewed as a totally Jewish project, which I thought was great. Leonard [Davis] eventually 'fessed up to that being a fact."

Because Dreyfoos appreciated that he needed diversity among his donors, he approached Marshall E. "Doc" Rinker (Rinker Materials) about underwriting the theater with a million dollars. After much haggling, Rinker agreed, but only if he could pay it over 10 years instead of the usual five years required. Other donors were upset by this deal, saying they, too, would have given more if granted that same flexibility.

Kravis Center officials publicized the many commemorative (naming) opportunities of the fundraising campaign, named "Landmark" to reflect their confidence in the long-term significance of the building. Tom Chastain became secretary-treasurer. Soon after, they named Tom Pledger chair of the campaign's Corporate Committee, and Bill Clark chair of the Banking Division. The following year, with $15 million in private gifts or pledges, a second campaign office opened in Boca Raton to connect with South County donors, run by co-chairs George Elmore (Hardrives) and Bernard Starkoff (CRC Press).

While Dreyfoos would have liked to reconnect with I. M. Pei to share the news that funding was coming together, he knew the celebrated architect had moved on to another arts center. A list of nearly 70 other firms was considered, which shrank to seven and then to three. On June 30, 1986, the final selection was made by a seven-member joint committee of the Palm Beach County Center for the Arts and Palm Beach Junior College, and approved by the college's Board of Trustees.

Their choice was Eberhard Zeidler, an acclaimed German-born architect, of Zeidler Roberts Partnership in Canada. Zeidler presented excellent credentials, including the designs of Ontario Place in Toronto; the Walter Mackenzie Health Sciences Centre in Edmonton, Alberta; the Yerba Buena Gardens in San Francisco; Queen's Quay Terminal in Toronto; MediaPark in Cologne, Germany; and Canada Pier in Vancouver, British Columbia. For Dreyfoos, the choice was clear from Zeidler's first visit: "He carried a small notebook filled with sketches he had made of every performing arts center he had seen throughout Europe, though he had never designed one. He had all these ideas to draw from, to create a vision for the future. As for the other architects we were considering, I felt they were going to give us a cookie-cutter design of what they'd done before."

The matter of an architect for the Kravis Center was finally settled. It should have been a time for celebration, but just three weeks earlier, the unthinkable had happened. ☞

West Palm Beach City Auditorium, known as "the leaky teepee."

Judy (then Axel) Goodman, 1978.

The first Kravis Center board of directors: (left to right, front) Leonard Davis, Dreyfoos, Merrill Bank; (rear) Robert Montgomery, John Brogan, Tom Chastain, c. 1980.

Dreyfoos (left) in the 1980s with Florida Senate President Harry Johnston.

Dreyfoos (left) with Bessie and Raymond Kravis.

Donor Marshall E. "Doc" Rinker and his wife, Ruby, at Kravis Center's Opening Night.

Dreyfoos with Eberhard H. Zeidler, architect for the Kravis Center.

CHAPTER 12

Fade to Darkness

Still together after 29 years, Dreyfoos and Mergens in early 1986.

Loss

The Lake Trail in Palm Beach, which dates back to pioneer days before Henry Flagler's transformational arrival on the island, runs about six miles north and south along Lake Worth. In modern times, it's a path removed from auto traffic and used regularly by runners, walkers, in-line skaters, and cyclists. In June 1986, however, the Town closed part of the trail for repaving and re-routed it along the narrow side streets lined with tall hedges.

George Mergens routinely rode his bike on the trail with fellow SHITS member Jack Liggett, who lived nearby, but on June 11, a gloriously sunny day, Liggett called to bow out due to a schedule conflict. As Mergens rode alone along the alternate route, the housekeeper for a local family left the driveway of her employer's home near North County Road and Kawama Lane. She struck Mergens with her car. He was rushed across the bridge to

249

Good Samaritan Hospital, just two miles away in West Palm Beach.

Dreyfoos was with his fellow board members of Flagler National Bank at the time. "My SHITS friend Bill Kemp, formerly chief of staff at Good Samaritan, hunted me down to hurry to the hospital. After I arrived, Bill told me George was in grave condition, and I fainted."

Mergens was soon airlifted to Jackson Memorial Hospital in Miami, and Dreyfoos made the drive to see his friend every day. Judy Goodman recalls, "Alex had fear in his voice. He seemed on the verge of breaking." Dreyfoos was not with Mergens on Sunday, July 6, three weeks after the accident, when he succumbed to pneumonia. "George let himself die," Dreyfoos accepts sadly. "He knew he'd be a paraplegic if he lived." George Mergens was 57 years old.

Publicly, Dreyfoos was stoic about Mergens, telling the *Palm Beach Post*, "He was a friend to everyone in the company, universally loved by everyone who came in touch with him—he was always open and friendly." "Because no one worked directly *for* George," Dreyfoos says, "everyone felt comfortable in going to him. He worked *with* everyone, wherever his help was needed."

Connie Graham, Dreyfoos' assistant since 1982, says, "Only twice in 30 years have I seen Mr. D. get emotional. This was the first time."

Judy Goodman describes Dreyfoos as a different man after Mergens' death. "His personality changed. Alex worshipped the ground George walked on. When George was killed, Alex went into a tailspin and deep depression."

Dreyfoos' sister, Evelyn, had never seen her brother so sad: "George Mergens was like a brother to Alex, in addition to being a best friend and brilliant fellow. If ever Alex's heart was broken, it was when George died."

Dreyfoos will always remember the impact of the loss: "It was just tragic. Everything that had once been at such a constant fast pace seemed to stop. George and I had finished each other's sentences. I would have an idea about doing something, and George would suggest a way we might do it by making this or that. When I lost him, I lost the motivation to pursue ideas."

A Nasty Situation

It was also clear to attorney Harry Chauncey that Mergens' death had been a major blow to Dreyfoos. Chauncey had been named legal representative of Photo Electronics Corporation to deal with the ramifications of Mergens' death

GEORGE W. MERGENS 1928-1986

George Mergens was born in Manitowoc, Wisconsin, on August 17, 1928, where he grew up with three brothers and a sister: Edward, Robert, William, and Mary. After graduating in 1946 from Polytechnic Institute of Brooklyn (now Polytechnic Institute of New York University), George apprenticed with their father, who was a tool-and-die maker for the big-name aircraft manufacturing companies Grumman and Republic.

Mergens worked for Pavelle Color Corporation and Technicolor NY Corporation, where he and Dreyfoos first met. A few months before Dreyfoos left Technicolor, Mergens resigned to take a job at Winsted Precision Ball Company in Connecticut. Dreyfoos and Mergens founded Photo Electronics Corporation in 1963.

Mergens and his wife, Ann, had two children, Mary and Paul.

Dreyfoos has described Mergens' mastery of mechanical skills as "remarkable," adding, "His ability to visualize a functional concept and then turn it into an actual operating part was truly amazing, considering his level of formal education. He had learned so much on his own."

as it related to co-ownership of their businesses. At her husband's funeral, Mergens' widow, Ann, approached Chauncey. "You're named, but you've got to resign. You've got a conflict," Chauncey remembers her saying. "Ann was already angry with Alex and planning something. Why, I could never figure out." Still, Chauncey resigned as legal representative.

Dreyfoos acknowledges that Ann Mergens seemed to dislike him: "It was just a shame. Somehow she felt that I owed her more. I think she got some bad advice." Ann eventually took legal action against Dreyfoos. As Chauncey relates it, Dreyfoos' friends and associates advised him to countersue her for "specious, ill-founded lawsuits." Dreyfoos told Chauncey, "Leave it. Enough is enough."

Ann Mergens was reluctant to pursue liability issues regarding the bicycle-automobile accident, but Dreyfoos pressed her to let his attorney and friend Robert Montgomery handle the case, which he agreed to do for a nominal fee. Like Dreyfoos, Montgomery realized there was great value in the creativity and productivity that was lost with Mergens' death. A year later, a three-member arbitration panel awarded the Mergens estate $13 million, directly benefiting Ann Mergens. (See sidebar, page 252.)

"Now here she was, with plenty of cash in hand," Dreyfoos recalls of Ann Mergens. "There was no reason for her to sell her stock in the company, but somehow she got this idea that I ought to buy her out. I told her I didn't have the cash to buy her out at that time, and it would be crazy to put the company in debt."

"You've got money," he pointed out. "The time will come when I sell the company, and you will get the full percentage that George had." Although Dreyfoos had contributed additional capital and acquired additional shares as needed during the early years, after that period the percentage ownership had remained unchanged.

Dreyfoos believes someone convinced Ann Mergens to act against him. "Eventually we got our accountants to a value and her accountants to a value,

---

THE SETTLEMENT

"Inventor's Estate Awarded $13 Million"
Sun Sentinel, March 12, 1987 [excerpts]:

The estate of inventor, local television-station owner and civic activist George Mergens was awarded $13 million on Wednesday, possibly the largest out-of-court settlement ever in Florida. . . .

Mergens' estate was awarded $8,160,000 for loss of potential wealth, $2,860,000 for loss of support and $2 million for mental anguish, according to attorney Robert Montgomery. . . .

At the time of his death, Mergens was working on an invention "that would have revolutionized color photography," Montgomery said. Montgomery was pleased with the verdict, returned by a three-member arbitration jury after three days of consideration, but said he was still saddened by Mergens' death. "I have kind of mixed feelings," Montgomery said. "His death was such a loss. This was very painful to go through. He was a wonderful man. But I think justice has been done."

Mergens, a low-key partner at the television station, was vice president of the Boys Club of Palm Beach County and chairman of the Palm Beach County Better Business Bureau at the time of his death. . . .

Both Mergens' insurer, United States Fire Insurance Company, and the driver's insurer, North River Insurance Company, will have to compensate the estate.

and then split the difference." Her insistence on this timing resulted in a settlement that was far less than what Ann Mergens would have received had she waited for Dreyfoos to decide when to sell. "It was a nasty situation," he says in summary.

Reflections

In due course, after Mergens' death, Dreyfoos made himself review the events, good and bad, that had brought him to this point. With George at his side, he had invented a device that dramatically improved color photographic processing, and a second, award-winning version. This success had so enriched the company that they had needed to invest in another business to avoid losing hard-earned savings to the IRS. So they had purchased a television station, elevating their public recognition to a level they had never anticipated. Renate, the woman he deeply loved, had turned away emotionally, though she would remain with the company for several more years. (She, too, felt the loss of George greatly, after working with him for 17 years, and would also lose her father later that year.) Now his best friend—the man who had helped him turn his inventions into physical and economic reality—had died. Alex Dreyfoos felt very much alone.

What would he do next? He remembers his feelings at the time: "I had no business owning a television station. I knew nothing about marketing. It was Eastman Kodak that successfully marketed our products worldwide. My rationale for buying a TV station had been misguided." Nonetheless, with a team of talented individuals, it was a success.

Of all the projects Dreyfoos had going before Mergens died, he was most passionate about establishing a performing arts center for the greater Palm Beach community. First, he had to take care of the business at hand. Without Mergens, Dreyfoos now bore full responsibility for a TV station, an advanced photographic technology company, a photographic laboratory, and a marina. But, he says, "It wasn't fun without George."

Tying a Third Knot

Dreyfoos' marriage to Barbara was officially over in August 1986. With no hope of being with Renate, that December he married Carolyn Buckley of Palm Beach, who had an adult son, Gregory Meyer, from a previous marriage. Carolyn's social connections would contribute to the success of fundraising galas and other activities leading up to the opening of the Kravis Center for the Performing Arts.

The couple purchased a large Palm Beach home at 14 South Lake Trail on the Intracoastal Waterway. The house had been designed by Marion Sims Wyeth, designer of the Florida Governor's Mansion, and built by (James Y.) Arnold Construction in 1969 for Helen Fraser and her husband, Andrew, who died soon after. Mary H. Woolworth Donahue, who had married the dime-store heir, purchased it from Helen Fraser's estate in 1984.

After completing repairs and renovations to the property, Dreyfoos says, Carolyn worked with renowned interior decorator Robert Metzger of New York, furnishing the house mostly with French antiques. "We had a carpet in this huge room in the center of the house that was probably more valuable than all the rest of the room's furnishings combined. The Great Room, as we called it, featured a Steinway grand piano, elegant seating, and a media room off to the side." Though it was more than he had in mind, he concedes it was a real showplace for guests.

Although once again he had married for the wrong reasons, recognizing there would be issues, Dreyfoos was determined to work at this marriage. He remained committed to the relationship for its duration of 13 years.

George Mergens in 1983, celebrating 20 years of Photo Electronics Corporation and 10 years of WPEC.

continued, "but they're like friends in our living room. They've been replaced by less knowledgeable, less experienced reporters. They say they're going for a younger image. Would they also have fired Walter Cronkite?"

Before very long, Laurel Sauer found other employment at WPEC's chief competitor, WPTV, and co-anchored their top-rated 6 p.m. and 11 p.m. newscasts with Jim Sackett. A few years later, the pair was named "one of South Florida's most successful anchor teams." After 20 years at Channel 5, Sauer took a break from television in September 2008.

Dreyfoos took over temporarily as general manager of WPEC in July with Bob Wiegand's departure, which the official press release called the beginning of a "phased retirement." The station hired a headhunter to find a new GM, who narrowed down the search by fall. Among the candidates was 45-year-old William B. Peterson, born in Pittsburgh, married with two children, and employed by CBS affiliate WTKR in Norfolk, Virginia. Peterson's parents lived in Winter Haven, Florida, and his brother Robert was an executive with the Art Institute of Fort Lauderdale. Quickly sold on Peterson's personality and experience, Dreyfoos invited him to move closer to his Florida family as WPEC's general manager.

Continuing Intrigue

The CBS Television Network had lusted after its affiliate WTVJ, Miami's top TV broadcaster, since Kohlberg Kravis Roberts & Company (KKR) put it on the market in 1984. Perhaps overconfident in thinking KKR would not sell the station to a competitor network, CBS bid low. KKR then extended the offer to NBC and ABC. NBC had been looking for its own station in the growing Miami market, and the FCC's new, less restrictive ownership laws may have encouraged them to make the deal.

These were the first substantial changes since the 1940s. TV station ownership was now limited to (1) 12 stations nationally, and (2) stations with a combined reach of 25 percent of the national audience. "Most importantly," Dreyfoos points out, "the percentage was locked in at the percentage that you were broadcasting to when you purchased a station—a good reason for a buyer to look for a growth market. This turned television stations into more attractive investments—certainly in Miami."

KKR and NBC's corporate parent, General Electric, closed on their contract in 1987, and that September WTVJ became Florida's first net-work-owned and -operated station.

Now CBS had a real problem. Their obvious move would have been to affiliate with NBC's former Miami station, but it had opted to join the quickly growing new Fox network. CBS scrambled to keep their programming on-the-air in Miami, eventually buying WCIX in Homestead in 1987. Located south of Miami and more than 60 miles south of Fort Lauderdale, this solution only partially filled the void in CBS coverage. In the meantime, NBC was busy stripping Miami's WTVJ of all vestiges of its previous CBS affiliation, dropping the lower-rated CBS shows. Contractually, the station was a CBS affiliate for another year, until December 31, 1988. Nobody in the CBS or NBC corporate offices could have been happy about this arrangement.

CBS saw a solution to its South Florida coverage problem in Dreyfoos' ABC affiliate in West Palm Beach. Viewers in the Palm Beaches had long been pointing outdoor antennas at Miami to pick up CBS programming. Even though WTVJ was outside the West Palm Beach market, it took a large share of WPEC's potential audience.

"After refusing us for a decade, all of a sudden WPEC became important to CBS," recalls Dreyfoos. "Our signal was strong in Fort Lauderdale, even though we didn't get ratings credits for it in the West Palm Beach market. CBS offered us a sweetheart deal. They made us an affiliate as of January 1, 1989, and paid us a million dollars to promote the new relationship. Network compensation was based on market size. They added a premium for Fort Lauderdale—which was assigned to the Miami market—as if it had been part of our market. Afterward I said, 'They bought me fair and square, and threw in a satellite truck to boot!'" Although ABC was less than pleased to lose WPEC, they picked up the brand new WPBF-Channel 25, which also went on-the-air the first day of 1989.

A week after WPEC's switch to CBS, Dreyfoos was thrilled to make public more good news, the hiring of General Manager Bill Peterson, and he remained thrilled. "From the day Bill walked in, I no longer had to run Channel 12. Peterson made it possible for me to turn my attention to the performing arts center." This single focus was exactly what Dreyfoos wanted and needed to break the spell of inertia that had set in after Mergens died. ◁══

Views from the front (east side) and lakefront (on the Intracoastal Waterway) of 14 South Lake Trail, Palm Beach, where Dreyfoos lived from the late 1980s to 2000.

Coupon with logo of Emerald Valley Water Company.

Mike Graham (senior buyer in PEC's Purchasing Department) with an Emerald Valley Water Company delivery truck.

H. Wayne Huizenga and his wife, Marti, flying Dreyfoos and others from Egypt to Israel in 1989.

The popular weekly event, "Sunset at the Sailfish Marina."

A 1987 aerial of the built-out PEC campus, including LaserColor Labs, expansion for manufacturing, and WPEC station.

WPEC news anchors Steve Wolford and Chandra Bill.

CHAPTER 14

More Than a Glimmer

The Kravis Center after completion of Phase II, including the Cohen Pavilion, 2005.

The Path of Progress

"Glimmer Becomes a Glow as Arts Council Turns 10," read the June 20, 1988, *Palm Beach Post* story by Chris Dummit. Playing directly into Dreyfoos' longstanding arguments for building a performing arts center, Dummit quoted Palm Beach Council of the Arts strategist Judy Goodman, citing the progress made over the group's decade of existence. Goodman noted that in 1978, acceptance of the idea of a performing arts center had been low; business people were suspicious of supporting it. Council Executive Director Will Ray acknowledged that competition for arts funding was intense, but predicted a change in the community's view of the arts during the next decade.

Rising Estimates

Because the center was to be constructed in collaboration with, and on the main campus of, Palm Beach Junior College, Dreyfoos and newly hired

Managing Director Paul Beard kept PBJC President Ed Eissey informed about their fundraising progress. (Beard served the Palm Beach Council of the Arts and Kravis Center for the Performing Arts between 1985 and 1993. He went on to be an executive with Bass Performance Hall in Fort Worth, Texas, and then vice president and chief operating officer of the Smith Center for the Performing Arts in Las Vegas.)

By the summer of 1987, the estimate to build the Kravis Center had risen to $42 million. Such figures were not grabbed from the air or manipulated by contractors; Donnell Consultants Inc. of Tampa had been retained as independent cost consultant. The stage needed 10 more feet of width, Dreyfoos and other backers argued, in order to accommodate operatic performances. They also wanted to add a small pipe organ. The Council of the Arts was pleased with its decisions aimed at building a center that accommodated the widest range of performances. President Eissey viewed the additions as problematic.

Eissey argued that government rules did not allow approval of any plan unless the money to pay for it was already in hand. He also complained that the new estimate was unrealistic, and wanted to keep it a secret. He sent a memo to the community college trustees:

> *I would like to request that the budget figure of $42 million not be discussed at the board meeting, simply because of the press being in attendance. This is an inflated working figure. We would not want the newspapers to tell the public that the $30 million project is now a $42 million project. There is no need to cause a major media controversy.*

Undeterred by what he considered a minor disagreement with the college, Dreyfoos remained confident that he and his fellow supporters could raise the additional money to cover any increases. The project's leaders pushed ahead.

You Get What You Pay For

After architect Eberhard Zeidler was hired in July 1986, he came up with two designs for the Kravis Center in the form of art renderings. The board rejected the first one as too futuristic, but embraced the second, with twin towers inspired by The Breakers in Palm Beach. Shortly after the board approved Zeidler's drawings, it commissioned a model to be constructed: $\frac{1}{16}$-inch scale exterior and $\frac{1}{8}$-inch scale interior.

Zeidler joined Dreyfoos and Paul Beard in making presentations to supporters and to the college. They started with a press conference to present the newly designed center. The scale model itself was saved for a gala the next day, but they had Zeidler's renderings, 30-inch-by-40-inch photographs, a site plan, floor plans, and a video at their disposal. The most excitement, as well as confusion, was caused by 6-foot-by-9-foot photomurals created from the scale models using Dreyfoos' own LaserColor processing. "At first people thought they were seeing a completed building," says Dreyfoos. "I believe it was a huge impetus in moving things ahead." Private donations at this time were reported as $17 million. As fundraising progressed, Dreyfoos continued to see a variety of reactions from audiences because the murals were so realistic.

The scale model was displayed at the gala for 590 guests who represented, as the *Post* observed, "every cultural organization in the county and every corner of the community. It was a rare blending of interests [that] took Alex Dreyfoos' brand of relentless determination." Feedback on Zeidler's design was mostly positive. Clyde Fyfe said simply: "I like everything about it." *Miami Herald* architectural critic Beth Dunlop wrote,

> *Palm Beach County's new performing arts center will be a European-inspired building designed by a Canadian architect for a location that is quintessentially American. These disparate worlds will converge to produce a performing arts center of considerable beauty. . . . The Kravis Center will seem of our era yet somehow timeless, and that will be a major architectural achievement.*

Ron Schwab, whose firm, Schwab & Twitty Architects, was retained as local troubleshooter, called Zeidler's design "so far ahead of its time it's unbelievable." On a visit during construction, Zeidler himself said, "This building in the end will be the expression of your emotions and the symbol of your community."

Donnell adjusted its construction-only estimate in February 1988 to $48 million, where it remained through the cycle of bidding the project. Dreyfoos acknowledged, "The project is pricey. . . . We raised our sights."

The original space of 140,000 square feet, judged inadequate, was now to be 200,500 square feet, adding to public areas such as the lobby, backstage, and storage areas under the audience chamber. Paul Beard explained that the cause was quality-minded decisions: "I think there will be a tremendous pay-off. . . . We're trying to make up in ingenuity what we lack in dollars." Construction industry increases also had their effect, in steel, electrical, structural, and performance equipment. To aid the community in understanding, Beard reviewed the building's evolution: How the center's officials had visited other performance centers and had tried to relate to Pikes Peak Center, known for its exceptional acoustics, particularly for symphony orchestras. The Kravis Center had many more planned uses, so its cost had expanded with the list. Artec, who had created those exceptional acoustics in Colorado, worked with Zeidler as acoustical designer. Dreyfoos later reflected, "The $30 million center would have been very much like a public elementary school—concrete block, steel staircase, pipe railing. The Colorado Springs building has almost no lobby space. It's functional but unattractive."

In reaction to the rising cost estimates, Dreyfoos and his board decided to write a contract for as much of the construction as was funded by pledges and gifts. This meant that their plan was missing a few things, such as a driveway from the road to the theater's main door, sound systems, signage, chandeliers, and seating inside the theater. Under what they called a "flexible bidding schedule," the items not funded would be bid later, as the money was raised to pay for them.

That December, the board voted to accept the lowest bid for the initial hard cost construction of Zeidler's design, $45 million, from Alabama-based Blount Construction Company. However, because the building would be owned by a state institution—the college—President Eissey said he could not accept any bid until all building funds were in hand.

Dreyfoos convinced Mike Strickland, president of Barnett Bank and a fellow member of the Economic Council, to assemble a consortium of banks to cover the gap. The group offered a $17 million construction loan, which the county backed with industrial development revenue bonds, to be repaid with private funds raised by the center's officials. It was still debt, so the college trustees still refused to sign the deal.

Groundbreaking No. I

Despite the absence of a construction contract, on the morning of January 12, 1989, several hundred people had attended a groundbreaking ceremony for the Raymond F. Kravis Center for the Performing Arts in Lake Worth, on the campus then known as Palm Beach Community College.

Later that evening, a gala event benefiting the center was held at The Breakers, organized by Dreyfoos' wife, Carolyn. The *Palm Beach Post* rated the benefit "extraordinary—even by Palm Beach standards," and described the evening's "pre-dinner opera concert and vignettes representing the arts tucked into shadow boxes in each corner of The Breakers ballroom. Centered in the midst of the action was the architect's model of the center."

Among the 560 guests were Ray and Bessie Kravis and their sons, Henry and George. Dreyfoos used the occasion to announce the campaign's seventh contribution of a million dollars, given by Blanche and A. L. Levine of Palm Beach and New York. Dreyfoos introduced the couple, also patrons of Carnegie Hall and Lincoln Center in New York, and noted that gifts from the private sector now exceeded $20 million. Though construction estimates kept rising, Dreyfoos seemed unconcerned. "The people attending (the gala)," he assured the *Post*, "are committed to the construction and support of a world-class performing arts center in Palm Beach County."

Location Location Location—Act III

Midway through March 1989, Palm Beach Community College had yet to sign the construction contract presented by Dreyfoos and his board some five months earlier, since all the building funds were still not in hand. "I am very frustrated," Dreyfoos told the *Post*. "Either we build it at the college, give people their money back, or put the theater someplace else." He believed that changing the location of the arts center would be a "headache." He said the theater might have to be redesigned for a new site and, he asked rhetorically, "How do you walk away from $10 million?"—the promised funding for the center from the State of Florida.

The *Post* also reported on Dreyfoos' discussions with West Palm Beach city leaders and officials from Downtown/Uptown, described as a "redevelopment project involving 77 acres of blighted downtown property." Real estate magnate Henry Rolfs Sr. and his associate David Paladino had been buying up parcels quietly to avoid prices from spiking.

Gary Lickle, who later joined the Kravis Center board, holds a vivid memory of this location at the time. "That part of town was 'crack town.' I was coming from the airport in a taxi on a rainy night, seeing the entrance to West Palm Beach and Palm Beach as a tourist would. The taxi came over the hill at Okeechobee Boulevard, and there was a man lying in the middle of the street near a mini-market. A group of people stood nearby, as if he wasn't there."

West Palm Beach City Manager Ron Schutta made it known, "If something happens, I'm sure the city would welcome the opportunity of having it here. . . . We're certainly here to help."

On March 19, the *Palm Beach Post* published an editorial by Executive Editor Edward Sears:

> *A determined group of right-thinking people is rushing to pull the Kravis Center for the Performing Arts from its bureaucratic tar pit at Palm Beach Community College and move it back to West Palm Beach. It is the latest of many rescue missions by those who have cherished a dream for 10 years and can see beyond the smoking controversy over bricks and mortar.*

Sears went on to ask if the community college was the right location for the center, answering his own question with a resounding "No." Under the heading, "A Second Chance," he added:

> *With things at a standstill, offers of help came from two unexpected areas last week. The West Palm Beach Commission, the body that time forgot, suddenly woke up and realized that it had a second chance to get the center. Several commissioners, including Mayor Pat Pepper Schwab, started making telephone calls. So did local businessmen and civic leaders. Even the county got interested, privately passing the word that the county's $10 million was portable.*

Sears wrote that the "best news" was that the Downtown/Uptown developers were willing to "give 5.2 acres of property just off Okeechobee Boulevard to the center," situated on the highest point in West Palm Beach. The editorial concluded that "Mr. Dreyfoos and his board" should consider their options carefully as they "may find it's too good a deal to pass up." The downtown location just happened to border the former Twin Lakes High School, which the county planned to turn into a performing arts high school. Three days later, in another editorial, the *Post* clarified its position:

> *The Kravis Center for the Performing Arts will surely be a jewel when it is finally built, but it was not intended to adorn any particular political jurisdiction. It should be built where it will best serve the people of this region as a showcase for the performing arts.*

The paper also called for an end to the battle over the location:

> *[T]he trustees of Palm Beach Community College would be unwise to engage in a legal or political contest to keep it on the PBCC campus merely to enhance the prestige of that good institution. It was first intended to be built in downtown West Palm Beach, a proper metropolitan setting that will assume important new dimensions with the projected developments of the next few years. Ten years ago no location seemed feasible or affordable in downtown West Palm Beach. . . . [Now] a combination of circumstances make a downtown location seem not only possible but almost mandatory.*
>
> *Ultimately the sensitive question of a new site will be left, properly, to the Kravis Center board and its chairman, Alex Dreyfoos, who are responsible for bringing the performing-arts center dream this close to reality. They deserve the community's support no matter what their decision, but people whose only interest is in a center that best serves its original purpose will be pulling for the downtown site.*

With considerable worry over a range of issues—possible damage to their fundraising efforts, traffic congestion, lost state funding, a possible three-year delay, and the dilapidated condition of the proposed site—Dreyfoos and his board gave themselves two weeks to make a decision.

"I don't want us to be in the position of flipping a coin," Dreyfoos said, urging his board to "play the devil's advocate" in weighing all available options. In West Palm Beach, he pointed out, the center would be the owner of the property, instead of the college as called for under the initial contract.

Contractor-developer Shannon Ginn, part of the architect selection committee years earlier, was chair of the Council of the Arts in 1989: "Things couldn't get done right with so much politicking going on. There were problems keeping the project independent, private, in the hands of Alex and the board. Things were falling apart."

Ray Kravis, the theater's namesake, cast his vote, saying the new location was "more convenient" and "There'll be more people to go to the theater. . . . I'm leaning toward downtown."

The close date for the board's decision prompted a panic at City Hall. At a workshop of city commissioners, Mayor Schwab addressed potential patrons: "Not to embarrass anyone, but to be blunt, we need to close this $4 million gap. And we need to do it in two weeks."

At the end of a week, the *Post* reported commitments of only $115,000.

The proposed downtown site for the center already held historic, if not artistic, significance. On this field of grass, locals were treated to the luminous talents of Lou Gehrig, Babe Ruth, Joe DiMaggio, Jackie Robinson, and Mickey Mantle. In the city's pioneer days, everything west of here had been pretty much swamp. In 1924 Municipal Athletic Field was built, and renamed Wright Field in 1927 for West Palm Beach City Manager George Wright. It served not only local teams, but as spring training ground for the St. Louis Browns from 1928 to 1936, and for the Philadelphia-Kansas City Athletics (A's) from 1946 to 1962. Connie Mack (born Cornelius Harvey McGillicuddy Sr.) owned and managed the A's, and in 1952 the field was renamed again for him. Forty years later, his grandson, US Senator Connie Mack III, attended the Gala Opening of the Kravis Center.

A plaque on the grounds of the Kravis Center marks home plate.

"No Comment"

Discussion of moving the new performing arts center's location to West Palm Beach broke the recalcitrance at Palm Beach Community College. President Ed Eissey called on Lake Worth Mayor Ronald E. Exline to "do something" to counter the talk of this change. In response, Exline called a meeting of the mayors of 16 towns south of West Palm Beach to secure their support for keeping the arts center at PBCC.

Dreyfoos responded to the college action by telling the *Post* that he would stay in his "information-gathering mode" while waiting to hear whether West Palm Beach's "grand gesture" would become a reality. He wanted assurances that West Palm officials would clean up the area around the proposed site. Dreyfoos and other board members welcomed the idea of not having to deal with all of the regulations required for taking state money. So far the city had pledged $5 million in revenue-bond proceeds, and assistance in a private fundraising effort.

At the start of May 1989, the decision whether to move the Kravis Center to West Palm Beach was only a few days away. PBCC had just enough time to come up with Plan B. The *Palm Beach Post* headline quoted Eissey: "If Kravis Goes Downtown, PBCC May Build Its Own." The college's president told county commissioners that a number of Kravis Center donors had agreed to divert their pledge to the college, so long as the county kept its promise to contribute $10 million toward the theater construction. Eissey refused to identify which donors and what amount of money he was talking about.

West Palm Beach officials said Eissey was "bluffing." One county commissioner said Eissey was "blowing smoke." Another said Eissey's actions were "tearing the community apart." Dreyfoos, the *Post* noted, was "not available for comment."

Decision day . . . finally?

May 5, 1989, was set as the date when the Kravis board would, once and for all, decide where the performing arts center would be built. Vice Chair Robert M. Montgomery Jr. made it known he was pulling for the college site, though he was prepared to lose his case. The next day, Montgomery joined his board in a cohesive front, announcing their unanimous agreement to build the Raymond F. Kravis Center for the Performing Arts in downtown West Palm Beach. The announcement meant that the building would not be owned by the community college but by the Kravis Center non-profit, which Dreyfoos viewed as very positive.

The center's board agreed to provide PBCC with a presence in downtown West Palm Beach in the form of an arts program, thus preserving what remained of the $10 million state grant. It was immediately clear that legislators from other parts of Florida could object to the use of state money in this manner.

"Not so fast!" proclaimed supporters of the college location. They argued that the $10 million from the state had to go to the college and not to the Kravis Center package. State Representative Ray Liberti of West Palm Beach declared, "Somebody's going to have to do some fancy explaining."

On May 22, another news conference was held to address the decision and to do that "fancy explaining." Robert Montgomery was in an awkward position. Although he had a role on the Kravis board, he was also president of the college's foundation, and thus head of the school's fundraising program. Montgomery spoke positively about the issue, offering a qualified declaration that although he had bowed to the majority view of the Kravis board, he still wanted to see the center built at PBCC. "But I don't want it badly enough to throw the baby out with the bath water," he told the *Post*.

Eissey threatened to start a competing board in a move to pull some donations away from the Kravis Center to PBCC. State House delegates predicted that, even if the college succeeded in keeping the grant, which was due to expire on June 30, 1989, it still might not be extended by the legislature, and it could end up cut into small pieces and doled out across the entire state of Florida.

Still without final settlement, and with grant money hanging in the balance, a celebrity jumped into the fray. Actor Burt Reynolds, an alumnus of the community college and a good friend of Eissey's, announced that he would either (1) give his Jupiter Theatre (now Maltz Jupiter Theatre) to the school to turn into a performing arts educational theater, or (2) work with them to build a "theater education center" at either the college or his dinner theater. In that way, the college could stay in control of what was left of the $10 million state grant (about $8.7 million after design costs). About Reynolds, Ed Eissey told the press, "He loves the college so much," and confirmed that the school was "looking at alternatives" for use of the state money at the college. PBCC was clearly backing away from its partnership with the Kravis Center.

"Tempers were flaring," reported the *Post*, when Montgomery offered to donate half a million dollars to the Reynolds proposal. Montgomery then called Eissey and told him to stop his efforts to secure the state grant or he would "pull the plug on his Reynolds donation."

The story remained front-page news on an almost daily basis for some time, the *Post* and others reporting less than cordial behavior among some of those involved. One day at Palm Beach International Airport, Eissey and Kravis Center attorney Jon Moyle exchanged heated unpleasantries as the two passed one another going to and from Tallahassee, where the ultimate decisions on the $10 million state grant would ultimately rest. In the span of one week, the paper spoke of the "$10 million rift"; county legislators "yell[ing] at each other"; and Rep. Lois Frankel declaring that "the whole community is upset, everyone is trying to manipulate the situation, and as a legislator I don't know what to do." In "Round 2," they wrote, "Rep. Frank Messersmith was so mad at Sen. Eleanor Weinstock that he said you couldn't print what he felt like saying."

On the last day of May, Palm Beach Community College trustees formally severed ties with the Kravis Center in an "anti-climactic dissolution—sealed with a simple parliamentary procedure." Negotiations for the term of this separation went on throughout the summer.

The issue of $8.7 million was still on the table for legislators to settle, and things did not improve come June. The *Post* described legislators as "bloodied by infighting over an arts grant" and one of them, Rep. T. K. Wetherell (D-Daytona), called it "the biggest mess I've ever seen."

Developing from the Negative

Throughout the confusion, Dreyfoos, as Kravis Center board chair, worked overtime to calm the hot rhetoric and to focus all the players on a positive outcome. As communications director, Frank Keel tackled most of the media demands. Dreyfoos chose his battles. In early June, Dreyfoos called for the $8.7 million to go to the Kravis Center. "If the PBCC isn't involved, another educational institution should have the opportunity to join with the Kravis Center to keep the state money." He also publicly committed to cutting the cost of the center: "This has got to be a project somewhere in the $50 million range."

Dreyfoos turned to Shannon Ginn with a challenge: "I'd like you to chair the building committee. I should have had you involved all along." The college, in conflict with Ginn on another project, had insisted on keeping him out of the picture, but they no longer had a say. "The bids are $12 million over budget," said Dreyfoos, "and we need to be in the ground in September." He needed to have the project redesigned to accommodate the existing plans on the new site, and negotiate with contractors to bring the cost within

NOT YOUR AVERAGE BUILDER

Winton Blount Jr. (1921-2002) had founded his construction company with his brother in 1946, but he also pursued other paths. He held prominent positions in presidential campaigns, and was president of the US Chamber of Commerce. As US Postmaster General, in 1971 Blount oversaw the transition of the US Post Office Department from a Cabinet-level department of the federal government to an independent agency. To commemorate the event, his profile was depicted alongside that of Benjamin Franklin on a silver proof coin. After making an unsuccessful run for the US Senate, Blount returned to the presidency of what had grown into the very diversified Blount International, Inc.

In the early 1980s, Winton Blount sold parts of the business and acquired new ones. Like the Dreyfooses, he and his wife were patrons of the arts; they donated 250 acres for the Blount Cultural Park in Montgomery, Alabama. They gave $21.5 million to build the Alabama Shakespeare Festival there, said to be the largest private donation to an American theatre at that time. In 1988, the Montgomery Museum of Fine Arts also moved into a new building in the park.

The following year, Dreyfoos brought his contingent to consider Blount's work. Though Blount had also built the Louisiana Superdome in New Orleans, and the complex at Cape Canaveral that had launched Apollo 11, these cultural buildings were important for the group to see. That September, Dreyfoos signed the contract for Blount to build the Kravis Center.

The year after Blount completed construction of the Kravis Center in 1992, they left the construction business and turned entirely to manufacturing. Lehman Brothers took it public in 1999. Winton Blount has been memorialized with a liberal arts honors program at the University of Alabama, where scholars reside in the Blount Living Learning Center. An endowment from the Blount estate funded the Winton M. Blount Center for Postal Studies and the Winton M. Blount Research Chair at the Smithsonian National Postal Museum.

budget—all in 90 days. Ginn says he was "flabbergasted and honored—but scared." He accepted the challenge, and met it. In early September, Dreyfoos signed a $51 million agreement with Blount Construction, who PBCC had refused to contract with since December. This, after Dreyfoos personally flew a team to Montgomery, Alabama, to view other centers built by Blount.

Coming Into Focus

Because Shannon Ginn had joined the project early on, he realized the great loss Dreyfoos had experienced when George Mergens had died three years prior. "Alex was surely full of regrets that George wasn't with him step by step through this process." Ginn felt an increased sense of responsibility as building chair, in the belief that Mergens may have filled this position had he lived. Ginn hired, for the Kravis Center, a project manager to assist him during the construction. Jim Mitchell, like Ginn, had received his training at University of Florida's School of Building Construction.

"All during the process," Ginn explains, "Alex would nudge me when I needed it, in a way that I never felt nudged. He was like a mother hen, gathering everyone around him and making each feel his or her job was critical to the success of the mission, and that you were the most important person to be doing what you're doing. That's the ultimate sign of a true leader."

In Ginn's view, everyone pulled together. "There were a lot of egos involved, but Alex got people to check them at the door. There was a lot of cooperation by a lot of smart people, and we accomplished the goals through the summer. In that process, and in fundraising and selecting people and courting big donors, Alex had a way that made you think that he was right, and this other idea that it would never happen was wrong."

Ginn is one of many who have used the word "visionary" to describe Dreyfoos. "His vision for a performing arts center goes back a long way. Sometimes, over the years, people would say Palm Beach is not ready for it. Alex never had a doubt. Vision is the mother of invention, and Alex is an inventor. He makes happen what he sees as necessary.

"Even after it was done, I would hear that he said nice things—and only nice things—about me to other people. That was one of the biggest rewards of working with him." Dreyfoos has good reason to speak highly of Ginn. "I take my hat off to him. To complete a $50 million building without a single lawsuit, that just doesn't happen."

When the dust settled, the plan called for a January 1992 opening of the performing arts center. Leading up to the signing, the county had recommitted its $10 million to go to the Kravis Center, and City of West Palm Beach officials had donated $5 million.

Mayor Schwab said that back in November 1980, when Currie Park was turned down, she had been very disappointed about West Palm Beach losing the center, though she was then an onlooker, a long way from being able to make a difference. In a 1998 interview she recalled, when she "floated the idea" of its current location to the City Commission, "I could drive past that [current] site and see it there." Pepper (divorced from Ron Schwab) died of Lou Gehrig's Disease (ALS) in 2003, at the age of 58. Will Ray, Cultural Council CEO, expressed the appreciation shared by Dreyfoos and many others: "The Kravis Center was the catalyst for CityPlace and the [Palm Beach County] convention center, and she extended the invitation. No elected officials in my time until then had shown that kind of leadership. She had style and she had beauty and she had charm. She had connections and she had softness all at the same time."

The second groundbreaking occurred on schedule in late September 1989 without fanfare. Ginn told the *Post* a ceremony "would seem kind of ludicrous," since one had already been held at the previously proposed college site.

Media attention accentuated the positive. *Post* opinion writer Clarke Ash predicted that placement of the center, now frequently called the "crown jewel of West Palm Beach, would generate the kind of prosperity for the city that has always seemed just out of reach."

Also in the fall of 1989, Leonard Davis suggested to Dreyfoos that it was time for the Kravis Center to have an executive director, preferably one who was also a showman. The board hired Arnold Breman, from the Richard B. Baumgardner Center for the Performing Arts in Clearwater, Florida. Breman accepted the position on the condition that he could bring his assistant, Judith Shepherd. They brought her in as director of development, succeeding Dreyfoos himself in that role.

Breman proved to be more of a showman than the board liked. Much worse, though, was the realization that without Judy Shepherd, he was unable to carry out many of his responsibilities. Breman seemed put off by dealing with numbers, and by the corporate types that peopled the Kravis board. In 1992, Dreyfoos fired Breman and put Shepherd in place as CEO.

Dreyfoos stepped up his efforts to complete the funding package. During construction, Dreyfoos held regular "Cocktails for Culture" events. Visitors had drinks while Dreyfoos gave a talk and led them on a tour of construction areas as permitted. This effort brought in gifts of all sizes. Later Robert Montgomery came up with the "Please Be Seated" campaign. This brainchild allowed a donor without deep pockets to participate by contributing $10,000 for a theater seat, which would receive a plaque bearing his or her name, and could even be paid over five years. A gift of $5,000 was also payable over five years, and gained a listing on a "Wall of Honor."

By the time the three-year construction phase ended, the tab would reach $58 million.

By the 1992 grand opening, however, the center would be debt-free.

As the fundraising progressed, Llwyd Ecclestone asked Dreyfoos why he had not asked him to contribute, believing the answer would be that he had not wanted to ask his friends. Instead Dreyfoos said, "Because you are not prepared to give what you should. You need to fall in love with it." Ecclestone did give, and on opening night, he was so delighted with the center, he told his friend, "Alex, I should've given you more!" So Dreyfoos walked him over to a WPEC reporter who was providing live coverage of the event, and announced Ecclestone was making a gift. His total giving is in the one-half to one million dollar range.

At one point Dreyfoos publicly acknowledged that though a lot of people had donated money, "some have donated time that just cannot be measured in any kind of dollars." He needed and appreciated both.

Getting it Right

As a scientist with unending curiosity, Dreyfoos took a direct interest in all aspects of the design and construction of the Kravis Center, and understood some of them better than most people would, such as acoustics. What makes music sound right? Dreyfoos educates:

> When the sound from a violin is reflected off a wall, it becomes rounder, less sharp. There is a wonderful tone when the delay—as it travels to the wall—and the intensity are just right, not too loud or too quick. That optimum characteristic varies for different people and for different kinds of performances.
>
> In the past, good acoustics were either accidental or they tried to duplicate what had worked elsewhere. Our timing in designing the Kravis Center was good, and our acoustician, Russell Johnson, founder of Artec, was an acoustic genius. He understood computer synthesis of music. Most of his halls sound better than Lincoln Center.
>
> Before computers, acoustics were arranged by placing microphones

around a space, shooting a pistol with blanks, and recording the sound. We did the same thing by building a model, where we had to duplicate the materials to be used on the walls and ceiling. We created an electronic version to record the sounds.

Behind the mesh ceiling of the Kravis Center are hidden chambers with doors that can be adjusted, or "tuned," for different kinds of performances. Also, there are movable fabric-covered fiberglass panels that fold into pockets and can be brought out to cover the hard plaster walls. The acoustic panels absorb while the plaster reflects, so again, by moving the panels, they can adjust the sound.

The Kravis Center's chief operations officer, Jim Mitchell, adds: "Some performances require soft, or dead, acoustics, where all the sound is directional from speakers. Others need sharp, or alive, sound that reflects off the walls."

Dreyfoos' team of architect, contractor, and others sought out ways to be extraordinary. When they learned that it typically took three or four days to switch shows in a performing arts center, they asked why? "The roadblocks," Dreyfoos recalls, "were the number of docks and elevators in the theater. So we doubled the quantity of truck docks and elevators, added an elevator in the stage to move scenery, and another one to raise the orchestra. That cut the transition time and increased the number of days the hall could be productive."

The completed Kravis Center included three venues in 1992: the 2,193-seat Alexander W. Dreyfoos, Jr. Concert Hall, the 305-seat Marshall E. Rinker, Sr. Playhouse, and the outdoor Michael and Andrew Gosman Amphitheatre with the capacity to hold 1,400 people. Although many people insisted early on that the entire center should be named for Dreyfoos, he knew he could not raise money for a building named for himself. The Board, unbeknownst to Dreyfoos, decided shortly before the Kravis Center opening to name the main concert hall in honor of his efforts.

An Extended Grand Opening

As the end of summer 1992 drew near, anticipation grew throughout Palm Beach County for the opening of the new Raymond F. Kravis Center for the Performing Arts. Several "openings" for a variety of groups started in late September. The *Miami Herald* pointed out that Palm Beach County was a "geographic contradiction" in that it was home to poor migrant communities alongside "The Donald, the Pulitzers and the Kennedys." Yet when the Kravis Center opened its doors, the *Herald* acknowledged, it welcomed people "living at the county's extremes."

Management had not waited, either, until those doors were officially open, to offer a friendly handshake. During the construction period, free events entertained large crowds on the grounds: Ricky Skaggs performed a concert for the construction workers and their families. Children and parents filled the lawn for a modernized production of Shakespeare's *The Taming of the Shrew*. Les Ballets Africains from Guinea, Africa, headlined a show for more than 1,200 guests.

Leading up to the Gala Grand Opening, the Kravis Center presented the African-American Community Chorus, an exceptional assemblage of singers from churches across Palm Beach County, who performed a program of Gershwin and gospel with the Florida Philharmonic Orchestra. The concert took place on the largest stage in Florida.

Phase II

During his fundraising, Dreyfoos tried to obtain a gift from developer and philanthropist Julian Cohen, a fellow board member at the Community Foundation of Palm Beach and Martin Counties. Dreyfoos knew that Cohen had given, among other cultural donations, $13 million to Boston Symphony Hall, and served on its board. Cohen would listen politely to Dreyfoos, however, without committing. Then one day Cohen approached Dreyfoos on his own.

"We had a problem at Boston Symphony Hall," he explained. "We had no lobby, no amenities at all. So I purchased the building next door and gave it to them, and it became their space for exclusive use of their donors." Cohen then offered Dreyfoos a million dollars to help add space to the Kravis Center for the same purpose. At first the board did not want to accept the gift. They were still raising the funds for the original design, and the additional building would require additional fundraising. "Finally they accepted Cohen's gift and concept," says Dreyfoos, "and we built the Eunice and Julian Cohen Pavilion, a $1.4 million building that included a small restaurant but that turned out not to do anything well."

Part of the original plan was the Founders' Room, a gathering space on the lobby level. Initially it allowed access by donors at the $50,000-and-up level. As fundraising progressed, it became clear the size of the room was inadequate, even after raising the requirement to $75,000 and then to $100,000.

The board looked for space for a larger Founders' Room; it had to be in the main building to allow for timely movement to and from the theater. It turned out that the only other space there was on the second floor, but it was being used for the administrative area. If displaced by the Founders' Room, where would the offices go? As a solution was sought for these problems, the need for more education space also became apparent.

Dreyfoos came up with an idea for Phase II that was at first fairly unpopular amongst the board, since it would require significant fundraising. Nonetheless, the Encore Campaign—including additional gifts from the Cohens and other major original donors—made possible multiple changes that proved very successful.

The first Cohen Pavilion was torn down. The original space for the Founders' Room became a lovely amenity room where sponsors and dignitaries could "meet and greet" performers after a show. This space was renamed the Ellen and Robert M. Jaffe Windsor Room. The Carl and Ruth Shapiro Founders' Room was relocated and greatly expanded in the former administrative area on the second floor, thanks in part to a gift that Carl and Ruth Shapiro made contingent on this use. The new Founders' Room was so inviting that other people increased their generosity to qualify for entrée.

Another unpopular aspect to Phase II was proceeding with construction while still raising funds. The board had avoided debt thus far and didn't want to incur it then. The center obtained a 30-year bond issue to cover the gap, which has continued to benefit the center through years of low interest rates.

A new Eunice and Julian Cohen Pavilion, completed in 2003, contains the Elmore Family Business Center for the Arts and much more, such as the Roberta & Stephen R. Weiner Banquet Center, housing the Herbert and Elaine Gimelstob Ballroom, which has seated as many as 700 people but can also be divided into six smaller spaces; J. Ira and Nicki Harris Pre-function Hall; and the Picower Foundation Arts Education Center, which includes the 291-seat Helen K. Persson Hall, the 200-seat Khoury

Family Dance Rehearsal Hall, music rehearsal spaces, classrooms, and a recording studio.

Many very substantial gifts came from people who chose not to be acknowledged by any kind of naming opportunity, such as Richard M. DeVos Sr., co-founder of Amway and owner of the Orlando Magic basketball team. Construction of the entire campus ultimately cost close to $100 million, more than 80 percent of which was covered by gifts from corporations and private citizens. The Kravis Center rewarded all donors by maintaining the high standards it promised. As of June 30, 2015, in the category of venues with fewer than 10,000 seats, Dreyfoos Hall ticket sales ranked No. 6 worldwide, No. 4 in the nation, and No. 1 in Florida among the "Top 100 Theatre Venues" tracked by *Pollstar* magazine.

Musical Memorial

When 2014 arrived and a pipe organ had yet to fill the space left for it in the initial plans for the Kravis Center, Dreyfoos took action to fulfill a dream. In October of that year, the Kravis Center Board approved the use of a portion of an unrestricted gift from Dreyfoos to build a world-class organ in Dreyfoos Hall.

Since the Kravis Center was designed, technology had advanced to the point that a custom-made electronic virtual pipe organ was obtainable with the quality of a world-class pipe organ, by incorporating a massively parallel processing (MPP) digital computer. Dreyfoos explains, "It is understandable how traditional pipe organ enthusiasts are unimpressed by this technology, given that when electric organs were introduced as early as the 1930s, they used simple electronic oscillators that bore very little resemblance in tone to a fine organ pipe. While circuitry has improved, it is only within the last few years that comparable pipe organ quality has been achieved—indeed, extraordinarily high quality.

The overwhelming proof of the pudding for Dreyfoos was the story of Trinity Wall Street Church, located just 200 yards from the former World Trade Center. Dust and grime irreparably damaged Trinity's fine Aeolian Skinner pipe organ during the 9/11 attacks. As a temporary replacement, in 2003 the church installed the best quality high-tech solution available, a massively parallel system. When the *New York Times* asked Trinity's director of music, "Might the instrument prove satisfactory enough that the church would simply adopt it as a permanent fixture?" he replied, "There will be pipes again at Trinity. Everyone is committed to that."

In the following years, however, many organ critics commented on the excellence of this supposedly temporary instrument, and gave it such high ratings that a committee of experts determined that the quality could not be matched by returning to a traditional pipe organ. "Apparently budgets were not a factor," says Dreyfoos. "One of the problems with pipe organs is that they require considerable maintenance to sustain their outstanding quality. Given that decision by experts at Trinity, I had no qualms in recommending an MPP organ for the Kravis Center."

At a concert performed by Cameron Carpenter, the main impetus behind this new system, Dreyfoos will dedicate the George W. Mergens Memorial Organ to his former partner and friend. "I am glad to offer this gift as a thank-you to George, who loved organs. I had hoped his widow, Ann, would know of the dedication and attend the concert, but she passed away in December 2014. The dedication concert is planned for the spring of 2016. ☞

Judy Goodman and her husband, Dr. Jay Goodman, 2006.

(left to right, in tuxedos) Dreyfoos and US Senator Lawton Chiles enjoy a fundraising party on *Prime Time*.

A series of photomurals created with PEC's LaserColor process, in use in fundraising presentations for the Kravis Center. The live model is not standing next to a completed building, but a photo of a scale model.

The 1989 "non"-groundbreaking ceremony in Lake Worth: (left to right) John Brogan, unidentified, Edward Eissey, Robert Montgomery, Raymond Kravis, and Dreyfoos; with the *Palm Beach Post's* commentary below.

AT LONG LAST, THE KRAVIS CENTER'S BLUE RIBBON GROUND-BREAKING COMMITTEE GETS THE GO-AHEAD.

(left to right) Nobel Prize winner David Baltimore and his wife, Dr. Alice S. Huang, with Dreyfoos and his then wife, Carolyn, at an MIT fundraising dinner at the Dreyfoos home, 1992.

Statue on the median of Okeechobee Boulevard in front of the Kravis Center, inscribed: "In honor and memory of Henry J. Rolfs, June 21, 1908 to May 8, 1994, Who dared to dream boldly and sustained the courage to turn his dreams into reality. He gave his all for the benefit of a greater West Palm Beach in Downtown/Uptown."

Pat Pepper Schwab in 1985, before she served on the West Palm Beach City Commission and later became mayor.

Shannon Ginn and his wife, Diane.

Cartoon of Dreyfoos (*The Palm Beach Post*).

Dreyfoos in 1991, giving a tour of the Kravis Center construction during a "Cocktails for Culture" event.

During the Kravis Center's construction: Llwyd Ecclestone, Palm Beach County Commissioner Karen Marcus, and Cultural Council CEO Will Ray.

Dreyfoos (on left) and Raymond Kravis cut the symbolic ribbon at the dedication of the Kravis Center in September 1992. From left are the building's general contractor, Winton M. "Red" Blount Jr., and architect, Eberhard Zeidler.

Helen K. Persson, primary donor of Helen K. Persson Hall at the Kravis Center.

Dreyfoos (right) inspects repairs to the Kravis Center with Jim and Judy Mitchell after the hurricanes of 2004-2005.

Abe Gosman, primary donor of
the Michael and Andrew Gosman
Amphitheatre at the Kravis Center.

The Gosman Amphitheatre.

Julian Cohen, for whom the Cohen
Pavilion is named, attends the
2003 Kravis Center Gala with his
wife, Carol.

The Cohen Pavilion during construction, 2003.

Dreyfoos (left) with singer-songwriter Kenny Rogers.

Dreyfoos (right) with radio and TV commentator Charles Osgood.

(left to right) George Michel, conductor-pianist Skitch Henderson, and Dreyfoos, in the Founders' Room at the Kravis Center.

Dreyfoos with comedian-actress Lily Tomlin.

Dreyfoos with soprano Roberta Peters.

Renate and Alex Dreyfoos with singer Jackie Evancho (then age 12), at the Kravis Center in 2012.

(left to right) Soprano Renee Fleming with Alex and Renate Dreyfoos at the Kravis Center.

(left to right) Alex and Renate Dreyfoos, and soprano Dame Kiri Te Kanawa, in 2008 at the Kravis Center.

Alex and Renate Dreyfoos with saxophonist Kenny G at the Kravis Center.

Philanthropists Leonard and Sophie Davis, 1992. Leonard was especially helpful to Dreyfoos in the early planning stages of the Kravis Center.

Yo-Yo Ma, a favorite performer at Kravis Center who Dreyfoos got to know at MIT's Media Lab. Photo by Todd Rosenberg.

Violinist Itzhak Perlman with whom Dreyfoos consulted during the design of the Kravis Center. Photo by Lisa Marie Mazzucco.

Attorney Jon Moyle and his wife, Jean, in 2000. Moyle was very instrumental during the development stages of the Kravis Center.

CHAPTER 15

Leveraging Success

(left to right, front) WPEC news anchors Steve Wolford
and Jackie Bange, and (rear) sportscaster Dan Oliver
and weatherman John Matthews.

The Climb to the Top

When WPEC switched its affiliation in 1989, it was a big event in South
Florida television, but only one within a chaotic marketplace. A fifth station,
Channel 25, signed on January 1, 1989—the same day WPEC switched from
ABC to CBS. Tallahassee-based John H. Phipps Co. and Miami auto dealer
and YPO/WPO member Alan Potamkin had secured a television broadcasting permit from the FCC while aggressively pursuing and securing the ABC
affiliation for Palm Beach, beating out a bid by WTVX.

This scramble in the media marketplace provided an opportunity for a
remake of WPEC's personality and program offerings, a responsibility Dreyfoos gave to General Manager Bill Peterson. Under his leadership, the station
introduced the first Doppler radar in the market and launched additional
newscast times. He also promoted anchor Chandra Bill, who proved to be a

great asset to the station. When Dreyfoos sold the station, Peterson stayed on until he left the area in 1999. He returned to West Palm Beach in 2001 to become general manager of WPTV-Channel 5. Chandra Bill had left Channel 12 for Channel 5, and they worked together once again.

Peterson's excellence enabled Dreyfoos to change his role to big-picture oversight. Though he would always miss George Mergens, the passing of years and the success of the Kravis Center now allowed him to focus on upgrading Photo Electronics products and manufacturing operations. Still, Peterson recognized that when he first came to work for the company, Dreyfoos was still grieving for Mergens. "His partner's office, which was next door to his, remained sealed into the '90s. It was hard for Alex."

Dreyfoos saw prestige in the CBS programming lineup and believed improved ratings would follow, but the advertising economy of early 1989 went into a slump. WPEC's affiliation change forced WTVX-Channel 34 in Fort Pierce to hand over its CBS affiliation and become an independent. Local TV ad salesmen were suddenly burdened with increased ad inventory. The *Palm Beach Post* reported, "With all the station switching going on, South Florida's TV ad market is a bit like a street-side bazaar—the prices are great, but there's no guarantee of what you're getting."

Once again, through circumstances not entirely of his own making, but by monitoring trends affecting his businesses, Dreyfoos struck gold. The station's signal propagated well beyond the Palm Beaches, reaching Broward County (Fort Lauderdale) viewers who turned away from the weaker signals out of Homestead and Fort Pierce. Most noticeable in Dreyfoos' bottom line was the effect on advertising. Businesses could now save money aiming at Broward County viewers through Dreyfoos' West Palm Beach station instead of buying advertising through Miami. "The difference in advertising rates at that time," Dreyfoos recalls, "was five-to-one," and WPEC regularly sold out its advertising inventory.

"Channel 12 really had a wonderful run as the market leader," says Peterson, "including in 1991, the first year of an advertising recession. Alex never faltered from his plan for growing the station. We convinced ourselves that we could emerge from that recession with more market share than when we entered. It was scary at times, but we prevailed and the station really did well." Dreyfoos gives Peterson the credit for building a fruitful team at

WPEC; during his reign the production, engineering, and news departments had no major issues. The staff also enjoyed working in the new facility. The 1990s market, though, was very different from the 1970s, when Dreyfoos had purchased the station. With the shakeup in network affiliations in South Florida and the emergence of new competitors—including broadcasters and, now, cable TV operators—Dreyfoos worked to steer his version of a local television operation into the future.

"Now Back to *Wheel of Fortune* . . . Already in Progress."

Back in early 1975, just after purchasing Channel 12 from John D. MacArthur, Dreyfoos had signed a deal to run the new game show *Wheel of Fortune*, knowingly taking a risk that the show would succeed. Its ratings turned out to be good, and the show became popular nationally and among WPEC viewers. According to Dreyfoos, "Industry tradition at the time said, if you were with them from the start, you could count on their loyalty and have an option on the show every year thereafter, as long as it aired." Time and circumstances changed that policy. Merv Griffin Enterprises produced *Wheel of Fortune* until 1994, when the show went to Columbia Tri-Star Productions. Not long after, Dreyfoos took a call from the show's legal representative.

"We're not able to renew *Wheel of Fortune* for WPEC," the rep announced.

"What do you mean?" Dreyfoos responded. "We've been faithfully airing your show since you started producing it in 1975!"

"The other VHF station there in Palm Beach is a Scripps-Howard station and, well, Scripps-Howard has eight TV outlets now. They have more leverage than you do. If we don't give them *Wheel of Fortune* in your market, they will not take it for any of their other stations. We can't afford to lose this contract. You've had the show at Channel 12 for a long time, Mr. Dreyfoos, but I'm sorry. We have to do this."

Dreyfoos knew the affiliation switch had been good for business, but apparently loyalty no longer had meaning in the buying and selling of TV game shows. Was the loss of *Wheel of Fortune* an indication of what was to come? The message Dreyfoos was hearing seemed clear enough; because his company represented only one station, not a group, they would always have less power than competitors who operated several. "Well, that really got me bugged," Dreyfoos remembers. "So, I thought, let's become a group. Let's buy

some TV stations. We've got to do something, so let's be aggressive about it."
He and Peterson began to look at available television properties.

As part of an ongoing effort to strengthen WPEC's economic position in
the marketplace, Peterson had already been following developments at stations around the country, whether or not they were for sale. What he observed and reported in the spring of 1994 reinforced Dreyfoos' decision to
find WPEC a few siblings.

Jewell and Delbert Lewis owned the ABC-TV affiliate, KTVK, in Phoenix.
Jewell's father, former US Senator and Arizona Governor Ernest McFarland
(one of the "Fathers of the GI Bill") had built KTVK. The station had been a
loyal ABC station since it signed on in 1955, and had grown into one of the
network's strongest affiliates, covering the entire state of Arizona. In the
spring of 1994, says Peterson, "The Lewises received a phone call from New
York that announced that they were losing their ABC affiliation because of a
group deal. The family had gone to sleep the night before with an asset worth
close to $300 million and woke up the next morning with an asset worth
about $150 million."

Although Phoenix was the first, it was a harbinger for other stand-alone
TV station operators. In the two years following KTVK's loss of its ABC affiliation, some six dozen stations in 30 television markets across the nation
would change their affiliations, a dramatic and historic shift. The evidence
was certainly piling up against remaining a single station.

Dreyfoos and Peterson devoted considerable time to analyzing how to
create a station group to protect their existing interests. "We got all the way
to due diligence for purchase of KLFY-TV, a CBS affiliate station in Lafayette,
Louisiana, as the first of what we thought could be our new group of stations," Peterson remembers.

Then one day Peterson came to Dreyfoos with news: "It may be a little
rich for our blood, but the Norfolk station I worked for is in trouble, as I expected. It'd be great if we could buy it." WTKR-TV was almost the same size
as WPEC, and they had been looking for smaller stations, but Dreyfoos told
Peterson to bring him the information.

It turned out that WTKR had hired the New York investment banking
firm of Lazard Freres & Co. to broker a sale. Ira Harris, a senior executive at
Lazard, was on the board of the Kravis Center, so Dreyfoos asked him about

the Norfolk station. Harris told him a bit, but then surprised Dreyfoos by asking, "Aren't you on the wrong side of this? Here you are in high-end Palm Beach. I think your station could command a real premium with this audience." He mentioned an impressive figure.

A Nice Number

Harris had given Dreyfoos something to think about, but before he reached a conclusion, he received an interesting telephone call. Vincent Young was CEO and owner of Young Broadcasting, a modest but growing television group he had founded with his father, Adam Young. (Young Broadcasting was to own 13 TV stations in the US by 1996, including former CBS-owned-and-operated KCAL in Los Angeles.)

Dreyfoos knew Adam, whose TV and radio ad agency was among the biggest in the nation. He was pleased to take the call.

"Mr. Dreyfoos, this is Vince Young."

"Hello, Vince. What can I do for you?"

"I'm calling you to ask about the possibility of purchasing WPEC."

"Well, we're not really interested in selling, but go ahead, Vince. What do you have to offer?"

"We believe $90 million is in the range of WPEC's value."

"Well . . . $90 million, you say?" Dreyfoos barely paused. "That's a nice number, but a number that had one more digit would really be a lot better number.'"

Before they hung up, the number had climbed to $100 million.

This brief conversation, coming after the conversation with Ira Harris, gave Dreyfoos a new perspective on the value of WPEC. He then contemplated, if someone would offer $100 million in a casual phone call, what would others offer if they knew it was for sale and had to compete to close the deal?

After nearly a year of closely studying the options, Dreyfoos gave Peterson the go-ahead to make an announcement.

For Sale: One Successful TV Station

"WPEC Channel 12 has taken a preliminary step that could lead to a sale of the Palm Beach CBS affiliate," reported the the *Sun-Sentinel* on June 28, 1995. Peterson was quoted as saying that Photo Electronics Corporation had retained Lazard Freres & Co. "to advise the station on its future strategic course," in response to "unsolicited overtures." While the station's answer to purchase inquiries had always been no, Peterson said, it was now "prudent to hire an expert" to determine the market value of WPEC. That determination would guide the station ownership in deciding whether to sell.

"Of course, all of that was code for: 'We're for sale!'" Peterson recalls with a wry chuckle, adding that Dreyfoos had informed the WPEC staff before the announcement was made public. Peterson could see that Dreyfoos was confident about his decision to sell. "Alex respected Ira Harris's accomplishments and knowledge, so he retained them to help work out the WPEC deal." Harris set up the sale as an auction, with a one percent commission for Lazard.

It was Bill Peterson and Josh Murray, however, that Dreyfoos charged with assuring that the station would sell for its full value.

"We ended up with a ton of suitors," Peterson recalls. "There were some people who just would not allow themselves to not be finalists! We ended up with 12, and that meant 12 different presentations. Josh set up a due diligence room and went through an elaborate process with the finalists, setting dates for each of them to submit their bids. Interest was much greater than we had anticipated."

Dreyfoos, Peterson, Murray, and Judy Goodman made it a game to guess who could name the winning bidder. The prospective buyers included the *Chicago Tribune*, the *New York Times*, and the Hearst Corporation. Murray's process soon narrowed it down to three others: Gannett, Meredith, and Freedom Communications. "Finally, Freedom only slightly outbid Meredith," recalls Peterson, "with several others very close behind them." In September 1995 the parties publicly announced the deal, which, after FCC approval, closed in January 1996. Freedom Communications paid $163 million for WPEC as their flagship station. It was a lot more than $90 million, and a stunning price for TV stations of that market size at the time.

For months, the media had speculated on the exact figure. The *Post* wrote, "Dreyfoos knows he benefitted from the hype surrounding the Time Warner deal to buy Turner Broadcasting System, which came during the two months he had his for-sale sign out." Dreyfoos acknowledged his luck: "Our timing, without our knowing it, turned out to be exceptional. The big boys realize this is the time to accumulate stations."

An additional effect may have been at work. The Telecommunications Act of 1996 had been in the works since at least 1992. Section 202(c) of this sweeping deregulation of the industry raised the 25 percent coverage cap to 35 percent, and eliminated the cap on the number of stations a person or entity could own nationwide.

It also couldn't have hurt that just before announcing its availability for purchase, WPEC returned from the statewide Associated Press Awards with four first-place and two second-place news awards, including Best Overall News Operation, among stations of comparable market size.

"Market size" refers to the total viewers in the market, on a county-by-county basis, that watch at least half of their TV viewing on stations in a particular market. This differs from "market share," the percentage of viewing a station has within the market. In 1973, when Dreyfoos purchased the station from MacArthur for $3.6 million, it was in the 92nd market. "When I joined the station in 1989," Peterson remembers, "it was at the 53rd market. When I left Palm Beach in 2004, it was 39th." (Peterson later became president of Scripps Howard Broadcasting, Inc.) Under Dreyfoos' ownership, WPEC had grown by 44 market ranks. Dreyfoos allows that much of the station's increase in value occurred because "people were nice enough to move under our antenna." With the growth of the Internet and other competition for viewers' eyes, prices for TV stations have since declined.

A Place at the Smithsonian

What does the Video Color Negative Analyzer, invented by Alex Dreyfoos and George Mergens, have in common with Alexander Graham Bell's first telephone, the R2-D2 and C-3PO characters in *Star Wars*, and Nazi Germany's ENIGMA coding machine? They are all part of the exhibition in the Smithsonian Institution entitled "Information Age: People, Information, and Technology." This permanent exhibition, located in its American History building in Washington, DC, was one of the largest ever assembled by the Smithsonian. The VCNA was added in 1990, an achievement the inventers could not share with each other.

The *Palm Beach Post* quoted Dreyfoos on the success of the VCNA: "We got it into a few labs and realized there was quite a market for it. We got quite a markup on it because the labs saved so much money by being more efficient, they could pay it off in a couple of years." Dreyfoos told the newspaper that he and Mergens had selected the field sequential color application as having great potential for systems that did not need a standard. In addition to color photo printing, the *Post* wrote, color television from space had used the field sequential system until digital imagery became standard in the early 1980s.

The Smithsonian's objective in displaying the machine was to provide the public with an example of the color television system approved by the Federal Communications Commission in 1950 and later replaced by NTSC color, a different standard that was compatible with existing black-and-white television receivers. The display allowed visitors to operate the machine.

Dreyfoos often notes that it was the invention of the VCNA and its success as a Kodak product that made it possible for him to buy Channel 12. Over time, PEC sold Kodak about 2,000 VCNAs and PVACs. He also insists, the VCNA would never have been possible without the combined skills of Dreyfoos and Mergens. "Neither of us alone would have been able to build a machine as capable as the VCNA. We needed each other."

Winding Down

After all of the changes in the businesses that Alex Dreyfoos and George Mergens had successfully assembled during their 23 years together, and especially the sale of their major components, it came down to decisions about the future of Photo Electronics Corporation, the original entity that had spawned everything else. These decisions needed to be coordinated with those affecting the other PEC properties.

When Bill Peterson had arrived in 1989, Judy Goodman was Photo Electronics' general manager, and Dreyfoos' son, Rob, was chief technology officer. Peterson quickly perceived his role as liaison between Dreyfoos and the manufacturing division. In fact, within a few years, Dreyfoos had made Peterson president of Photo Electronics, and the managers of all PEC assets reported to him for a time.

During these and other changes and transitions, Renate remained a strong, trustworthy part of the team, though her interaction with Dreyfoos became minimal. Unfortunately, the restructuring included decentralizing of the Human Resources Department and the elimination of positions. Renate ultimately left the company in 1991 to pursue her career elsewhere.

Peterson remembers the pivotal evolution of change for PEC:

> *At the end of '94, early '95, Alex was reviewing all of this and, as always, he was strategic and insightful in his decision-making process. Operationally, PEC was in capable hands, but clearly it was approaching an important tactical moment. What would be the future of manufacturing? The products were ingenious and very successful, but a new generation of products needed to come on line. There was hope that the LaserColor printer was coming, but technical problems remained unsolved, and major competition was on the horizon. The current products were getting older, and maintenance and spare parts were becoming a bigger part of the business than the sale of new units.*

Dreyfoos and Peterson tried to determine the future size and operation of Photo Electronics. "It was an emotional thing," Peterson remembers. "With Alex's original company, he and George had really captured lightning in a bottle with their inventions. It was hard for Alex to think about giving that up. He was winding down what he and George had built." After considered analysis, Peterson proposed downsizing the manufacturing. Fewer and fewer units were being sold as the world turned from film to digital photography. "It was really a strategic moment," Peterson remembers. "Ultimately, the decision was to shut down the facility and transfer most of the manufacturing assets to Rob, who then took the business to Seattle." Photo Electronics remained active, but only from a warehouse. The younger Dreyfoos continued to supply replacement and spare parts for the existing PEC product line. As of 2015, there were still a few VCNAs and many PVACs in service in color photography labs around the world. Robert took a job with Microsoft in 2007, and in 2014 became senior technical program manager at Amazon.

The legal entity of Photo Electronics Corporation remained, but its purpose changed. Doing business as (d/b/a) The Dreyfoos Group, it serves to manage the proceeds of selling Dreyfoos' businesses.

The Sailfish Story

When Josh Murray convinced Dreyfoos in 1977 to buy the properties that would become the Sailfish Marina and Resort, they presented a rather rustic setting, but in an exceptional location popular among big-game sports fishermen. At the time, everyone at Photo Electronics except the accounting department reported to Operations Manager Al Peloso; it was natural for the existing marina manager, whom Dreyfoos had retained, to do the same. Murray, more aggressive regarding growth than production-oriented Peloso, quickly grew frustrated. He handed Dreyfoos a handwritten two-page essay on a legal pad entitled, "How to Run the Sailfish Marina and Live Happily Ever After." Two days later, he got the answer he wanted: "Okay, Murray. You've got the marina." From then on, Murray ran the marina operation on behalf of the company.

For several years before the marina purchase, Marge Thomas had worked part-time for Photo Electronics as a computer consultant. Murray asked Thomas to write a computer program to solve problems at the marina, particularly in the Ship's Store. After looking over the operation, Thomas concluded, "No computer program is going to fix it. People are the problem." So Murray let her have a go at addressing problems her way, at first as a freelancer. Eventually he fired the marina manager and hired Thomas full-time, visiting the property once or twice weekly. "We were like a wagon train," says Marge. "Josh was the scout looking where we were going, and I was the leader. It was my responsibility to bring everyone along. I handled the nuts and bolts, the people—Josh was the big-idea man."

Among other things, the marina was notable as an early proponent of "no smoking" rules, and for their water taxi service. Thomas is specifically credited with masterminding a popular series of tee shirts and "Sunset at the Sailfish," a popular food and entertainment event on Thursday evenings.

One day, the dockmaster, Dick Haines, told Murray, "I had a girl apply for a job as a dock attendant; I think she would be excellent." Murray answered, "Hire her." Then he hired some more young women. "Up until then, the guys we had for dock attendants were mostly a bunch of kids going nowhere, trying to do as little work as they could," he remembers. "The young women were fantastic, and the customers loved them. I believe that led, at least in part, to the Sailfish Marina's initial success." Although the women wanted to prove that they could do what the men could, the mates from the charter boats would jump in to help them pump gas and carry ice and drinks from the ship's store, which they had never done for male attendants. One of the early female hires was hired as dockmaster after Dick Haines.

In the early '90s, a change in the chain of command at Photo Electronics took Murray out of the loop at the Sailfish Marina. In 1996 he returned to overall supervision of the business, and in 2000 he had the idea to redevelop the property again. Out came the old coffee shop, replaced by a major seafood restaurant.

The years of overseeing the Sailfish Marina provided numerous examples of a recurring dynamic, Murray explains:

> I would do analysis for Alex, and he would ask a question, and I would think, where the hell did he come up with that? I would peel away the onion and find something I'd missed. That's the way Alex pushed us, by asking more questions than needed. Sometimes a question would be on point with something we'd missed. Also, when we did deals with other people, we always found that we were way out in front because we'd done more homework.

Josh and Marge (Thomas) Murray married in 1994 and are grateful to Dreyfoos. "He gave us an opportunity," says Josh, "to do things we otherwise wouldn't or couldn't, like the water taxi or the (Emerald Valley) water company. Alex was always willing to fund a good idea, if you were excited about it. You had to do your analysis; it was never easy."

The corporation sold the Sailfish Marina to American Financial, Inc. in July 2004 for $31 million. The current owners credit Dreyfoos and Murray with establishing the long-term success of the operation, saying it was during their time that "the Sailfish Marina and Resort became synonymous with big-game sport fishing in the Palm Beaches and gained a national reputation as the 'Yankee Stadium' of the sport." In celebration, Alex returned again to photograph the wildlife of Africa. Having taken his daughter's family in the '90s, this time he shared it with his son's family and Renate.

WPEC . . . Photo Electronics . . . the Sailfish Marina . . . Casual observers might think, incorrectly, that financial success came relatively easily to Alex

Dreyfoos. As demonstrated here, each of his business achievements was built one upon another, over decades of persistence, determination, the right partner—and often, he plainly admits, good timing.

Dreyfoos also patently enjoys the process, and says, "I would equate productiveness with happiness. To me, that's the key. You've got to feel fulfilled." Though he believes this today, he cannot say whether he would if he'd had the personal fulfillment of his relationship with Renate all along. ✐

PEC's Video Color Negative Analyzer on display at the Smithsonian Institution.

Sailfish Marina after remodeling, 1999, with restaurant on the right.

The full PEC campus.

The completed Sailfish Marina and Resort, adjacent to the Palm Beach Inlet and the Atlantic Ocean beyond.

![The Sailfish Marina logo] The Sailfish Marina

![The Sailfish Marina logo] The Sailfish Marina

Location

The Sailfish Marina is located in Palm Beach Shores on beautiful, unspoiled Singer Island . . . with easy access from major highways and commercial or private airfields . . . directly on the Intracoastal Waterway, it is the closest marina to the Palm Beach Inlet and the Bahamas.

When you stay at the Sailfish Marina, in the heart of Florida's Gold Coast, beautiful Palm Beach and its internationally renowned Worth Avenue are only a few moments away.

And within a day's journey . . . Walt Disney World, Tampa, Miami or Fort Lauderdale.

If you want to see Florida, the Sailfish Marina is the spot to start!

98 Lake Drive, Palm Beach Shores, Florida 33404
Ph. (305) 844-1724

♻ A SUBSIDIARY OF PHOTO ELECTRONICS CORP.

—— Where the Season Never Ends ——
Palm Beach Shores, Florida

Charter Fishing

When it comes to big game fishing, the Pros at the Sailfish Marina know all the secrets.

The largest charter fleet in South Florida is at your disposal to take you to legendary "Sailfish Alley" where you can challenge seven feet or more of fighting fury.

All of the Sailfish Marina's charter boats and captains are licensed and approved by the U. S. Coast Guard. And to further insure your comfort, the Sailfish Marina provides live, ColorScan Weather Radar to let you see what you're heading into. Each and every charter boat is also equipped with the latest two-way communication gear.

When you charter at the Sailfish Marina, the only thing you have to do is land that trophy fish!

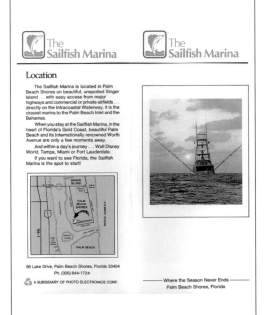

Selected pages from a Sailfish Marina brochure.

CHAPTER 16

Life Reframed

The *Silver Cloud* SWATH in French Polynesia, 2014.

For Ever and a Day

You said, "Not in a thousand years";
Then I will wait a thousand years and one.
And if you say, "Not in a million years,"
I still will wait a million years and one.
I will outwait, outlast, and outendure.
But if your Nay should be for ever,
Then I say,
"My Yea
Shall be for ever and a day."

Peter Henniker-Heaton

Reunited

Many things happened in the life of Alex Dreyfoos in the years after Renate ended their romance. He lost his dear friend and partner, George Mergens. He married a third time, and fully expected to stay married for life. He opened the Kravis Center for the Performing Arts. He transferred the manufacturing assets of Photo Electronics Corporation to his son, closed LaserColor Laboratories, established and sold the Emerald Valley Water Company, and sold WPEC.

Dreyfoos did not see Renate even from a distance for many years. Then, one day late in 1999, Connie Graham, his assistant since 1982, casually mentioned that she had run into Renate. Graham recalls: "Renate and I shared the same hairdresser for a number of years. I was at the salon one Saturday when she came in for her appointment, and we exchanged small talk. She said to be sure to tell Mr. D. hello, and gave me her business card. I didn't think that much about it.

"Probably Tuesday of the following week, I remembered to tell Mr. D. that I'd seen Renate and that she'd said hello. He had a dozen questions: 'Where did you see her? Where is she working? Why didn't you tell me yesterday?' On and on. I told him Renate had given me her business card, but I must have left it at home. He wanted me to go home to get it—he was very annoyed. I told him it would be easier to just call the hairdresser for her number, which I then did. He couldn't believe I had known how to be in touch with her all those years. *I* couldn't believe he was acting that way after all those years. I knew then how much she meant to him. He just doesn't get emotional—or irritated—and he was both."

Dreyfoos was 67 years old. He had been in love with Renate for 30 years. He promptly called and invited her to lunch, where it was obvious to both that their old feelings were still very much alive. Neither had immediate expectations about divorcing their current spouses. After serious contemplation, however, Alex proposed again, and this time Renate said yes. They spent the next few months bringing their present marriages to their ends, without seeing each other in the interim.

Dreyfoos' daughter, Cathy Carter, recalls how excited her father was to share his news. "He was just so thrilled to be back together with her, and he wanted to let the whole world know. To find that kind of happiness just really doesn't happen very often. She made my father happy, and that's all that mattered."

Dreyfoos' son, Robert, had worked with Renate for several years at Photo Electronics, where he knew her as "Renee." "Renee and Dad are great partners, because she is in perfect tune with him. They complement each other—

they always did. She would say, 'This is what's going on,' and after she gave Dad the information, he could process any issue, then take action."

In May 2000, Dreyfoos picked up Renate and flew them in his plane to his summer home on Lake Kiwassa at Saranac Lake, New York. They were married there on July 2, 2000, by Judge Karl Griebsch, witnessed by Dreyfoos' childhood friend Don Duso, and Don's wife, Sandy.

While Renate Dreyfoos is an avid reader and enjoys knitting and gourmet cooking at home, she has been equally comfortable holding an executive position at a corporation. She enjoys solitude and values her privacy, yet glides smoothly through the social arena of Palm Beach. To most outsiders, she is an enigma. To Dreyfoos, she is the consummate companion, able to adapt to most situations with charm and grace.

Before Renate came back into his life, Dreyfoos had found rewards in a long list of personal, professional, and philanthropic successes, yet with an emptiness he was helpless to fill. Their friend Rip McIntosh described it simply as "a match made in heaven, incomplete until now." In this reunion was happiness money couldn't buy.

Calming the Seas

As he reached the 21st century, Alex Dreyfoos had accomplished a major reorganization of his world and appeared to be retiring from all business endeavors. Some might have expected him to head off on an extended fishing and diving expedition, or to explore some remote part of the planet he had not yet visited. Those who knew him well understood that Dreyfoos would never stop solving and creating.

Now he had both the time and resources to pursue a different kind of business, that of giving back to a world that had been good to him. Especially since the sale of WPEC in 1996, he had made substantial gifts—to MIT, the School of the Arts, and the Kravis Center—but he wanted to do more.

Most importantly, Dreyfoos had married Renate, the love of his life. He couldn't wait to take her on an around-the-world adventure.

Upon the newly married couple's return to Palm Beach from the Adirondacks in the fall of 2000, Dreyfoos formally introduced Renate to 300 guests at an elegant dinner party at the Raymond F. Kravis Center for the Performing Arts. To the accompaniment of an orchestra playing at the top of the stairs, the new Mr. and Mrs. Alexander W. Dreyfoos—she in a plum-colored chiffon dress, he in a business suit—entered the Dreyfoos Concert Hall foyer. From this point on, Dreyfoos expected everything in his life would be smooth sailing.

Boating had been part of Dreyfoos' life since he was a child, and he had owned progressively larger vessels as his income permitted. By the time he married Renate, it was his second Burger yacht, the 114-foot *Silver Cloud*. (Dreyfoos actually calls all his watercraft "boats"; his definition of a "yacht" is "any boat bigger than your own." At this length, he was already in the league of "superyachts.")

Dreyfoos had admired this yacht in Palm Beach waters when it was the 99-foot *Grindstone*, owned by sportsman-philanthropist Fitz Dixon Jr. At the time Dixon had it built in 1985, this Burger was one of the 100 largest American yachts. Auto dealership mogul Roger Dean, the next owner, named it *Ar-De*.

"Roger hadn't had the boat long when his captain was found dead in the engine room," recalls Dreyfoos, "and then he wanted nothing to do with the boat. I made him an offer subject, of course, to a survey, which uncovered a problem that the surveyor suspected may have caused deadly fumes." Dreyfoos immediately rejected the boat as dangerous, but came to an agreement when Dean offered to replace the two engines, the source of the trouble.

At the same time, Dreyfoos added a 15-foot fishing cockpit to its length, and changed some of the boat's other features to his liking. Ever since he'd read about the completion of the Main-Danube Canal in 1992—a feat that had been tried repeatedly since Charlemagne's first effort in the year 793—Dreyfoos had envisioned a cruise of Europe's rivers. His captain, Steve Martin, determined the maximum height a boat could have while fitting under the many fixed bridges on the route. The height of the windshield was just within the maximum height.

As a result, Dreyfoos decided to have the mast removed from the bridge (which had also hindered interaction between people seated on the bridge). A bridge arch was added, providing cover, which could fold down below the maximum height as well.

Renate shared her husband's passion for ocean adventure, but severe motion sickness would prove to interfere with his ambitious travel plans. Renate reasoned, "It is difficult to enjoy the sights when being seasick." Despite her

INTERNATIONAL SEAKEEPERS SOCIETY

According to Jim Gilbert, former board president of the International Sea-Keepers Society (SeaKeepers), Dreyfoos was the first founding member of the marine conservation organization with a $50,000 commitment when Sea-Keepers was launched at the 1998 ShowBoats Rendezvous in Monaco. Drey-foos says, "I thought, someone has to be first, so why not me?"

Led by businessman Albert Gersten and environment lawyer Tom Houston, both of Los Angeles, SeaKeepers brought together concerned yacht owners from around the world who were disturbed by the worsening conditions of the oceans. The essence of their mission was to create a sensing device to monitor environmental conditions of the oceans. SeaKeepers members participate by installing on their vessels the SeaKeeper 1000, a compact, cost-effective system that automatically records weather and near-surface oceanographic information. The data is transmitted via satellite to the National Oceanic and Atmospheric Administration (NOAA) and other ocean science researchers for evaluation.

Fellow SeaKeepers members include Microsoft co-founder Paul Allen, Steve Forbes, Jim Clark, Mikhail Gorbachev, Richard DeVos, James Cameron, and Jean-Michel Cousteau.

desire to avoid such situations, she was determined to share the excitement and romance of her husband's planned voyages. To avoid her becoming ill, Renate and sometimes Dreyfoos would meet *Silver Cloud* after it crossed the Atlantic and at key points along its course. One such trip took place in the summer of 2001 on an exceptionally romantic voyage on the Rhine River.

The Rhine via the *Silver Cloud* Burger

While *Silver Cloud* traveled to Europe via Dock Express yacht transport, Alex and Renate crossed the Atlantic by air. The couple boarded *Silver Cloud* at Amsterdam in the Netherlands in anticipation of their leisurely tour on the Rhine. The cruise would give them time to reflect, to share their love of music and photography, and to be tourists in the quaint cities, towns, and villages along one of Europe's most scenic rivers.

After crossing into Germany, the historic Rhine took the Dreyfooses past Dusseldorf, Cologne, Bonn, Bingen, and into the Rhenish Slate Mountains, where Dreyfoos played a recording of Schumann's *Rhenish Symphony* as the yacht followed the river's bend at Rudesheim. Along their route they also passed

Mainz, Wiesbaden, Mannheim, Heidelberg, Strasbourg, the Vosges Mountains, and the Black Forest, stopping at Lahr, where Renate had lived as a child.

During the trip, *Silver Cloud* was outfitted with a SeaKeeper that monitored environmental conditions and transmitted them to NOAA. (See sidebar, page 321.) Dreyfoos would learn later that NOAA had called the International SeaKeepers Society to report that they were receiving apparently dysfunctional data from a yacht that appeared to be on land, in the middle of Europe, at an elevation of 1,000 feet, with very low salinity. In actual fact, *Silver Cloud* was in the middle of Switzerland's Lake Constance, a freshwater lake at 1,296 feet above sea level; the data was correct. At their annual dinner, SeaKeepers presented Dreyfoos with a NOAA map (which showed only oceanographic information and no lakes) showing his yacht at that location.

Try, Try Again

Appreciative of his wife's desire to share his passion for yachting in spite of her severe motion sickness, Dreyfoos theorized that "bigger is better" and purchased a larger vessel.

The second *Silver Cloud* was a beautiful 143-foot Feadship motor yacht, the work of the Dutch yacht builder Royal van Lent and originally launched as *Fiffanella*. Feadships were then called the "Rolls-Royce" of yachts. But Dreyfoos was not in that league at the time, and called this 1987 vessel an "oldie but goldie."

Dreyfoos had first seen this boat in Ft. Lauderdale, when he was shopping for a boatyard to build an extension to his *Silver Cloud* Burger. The yard showed him the boat, then named *Cakewalk*, which convinced Dreyfoos to hire them. He loved the boat, thinking, "I'll never be able to buy a boat like that!"

By 2002, Dreyfoos felt differently. While taking the Burger to Glacier Bay, Alaska, he followed the same waters north as a boat named *Irish Rover*, which he thought strongly resembled *Cakewalk*. Both boats ended up at the same marinas at night, and with research, Dreyfoos learned that it was indeed the same boat and was for sale; in between, *Cakewalk* had been purchased by golfer Greg Norman and renamed *Aussie Rules*. Before too long, an Australian shipyard wooed Norman into building a larger boat to fit his celebrity status, and he sold the Feadship. Dreyfoos' broker learned that *Irish Rover* was for sale and approached the broker of the new owner, but because the boat flew a foreign flag, it could not be sold in the United States or its waters.

Dreyfoos' attorney warned him to stay clear, but he was set on the boat; he didn't even need to go aboard.

By the time they reached San Diego, California, on the way back a deal had been worked out. Because Dreyfoos did not want to own both boats, he required the seller to take his Burger in trade. They switched vessels beyond the 13-mile limit into international waters. "Back in port," recalls Dreyfoos, "the Coast Guard noted that we'd switched and decided we must be doing something nefarious. They confiscated both boats. I had to sue to get mine released, though they let us stay on them at least, while we paid fines into escrow."

This was Dreyfoos' second cruise up to Glacier Bay. His friend Jack Taylor, who founded Enterprise Rent-a-Car in 1957, named his company for one of the aircraft carriers (the USS *Enterprise* or *CV-6*) he served on as a fighter pilot during World War II. When he had a 131-foot Delta built, he named it *CV-9* for the other aircraft carrier (the USS *Essex*). Dreyfoos and Taylor met through friends and shared a love for, among other things, their flying machines. Taylor was new to yachting, but *CV-9* was built in Seattle and he wanted to take it to Alaska. Dreyfoos had also planned to make that trip, with his *Silver Cloud*, so in 1995 Taylor followed him to Glacier Bay National Park.

Regrettably, Dreyfoos' purchase of the larger Feadship in 2002 did not ease Renate's seasickness. His awareness of her difficulty convinced him that it was more common than others acknowledged. "Around the islands of the Caribbean, I noticed a huge number of people who just used their shiny white boats as cocktail platforms, restaurants, and hotels in harbors. The captain has delivered the boat, while the owner has flown in to meet the ship for the party." Determined to take the lead in addressing this unspoken problem, Dreyfoos quite naturally turned to science.

He contacted a variety of experts, including yachtsman and shipbuilder John Fuglsang in Hobart, Tasmania. Fuglsang had just started a high-tech company, North West Bay Ships, to develop a line of trimaran vessels using wave-piercing technology to achieve stability. Dreyfoos rejected this method because its stability was only impressive at high speeds. It was Fuglsang who first described to Dreyfoos the advanced design concept of the uniquely stable Small Waterplane Area Twin Hull, or SWATH. At that point, it had only been used by commercial boats having to endure rough seas.

Fuglsang put Dreyfoos in touch with John D. Adams in Solomons Island, Maryland, founder of VT Maritime Dynamics, a manufacturer of computer-controlled, hydraulically actuated stabilizer systems, described as "the world leader in marine motion control solutions." In 2002 he co-founded Seakeeper Inc. (no relation to the International SeaKeeper Society) to develop gyroscopic stabilizers. Adams knew a great deal about the SWATH concept, and he and Dreyfoos began communicating with and visiting one another.

Building a SWATH Yacht

In his research, Dreyfoos found three companies that had built commercial SWATH ships, and visited all three. The German shipbuilding company Abeking & Rasmussen (A&R) had produced more SWATH design vessels than anyone else, a total of nine since 1999. Dreyfoos was especially impressed with their technical and executive director, Dr. Klaas Spethmann.

In 2004 they arranged for Renate to take an experimental ride aboard a pilot ship in Helgoland, Germany, in the very rough waters of the North Sea. Captain Steve Martin was on board, as was Adams, Dreyfoos says, "and we were all scurrying all over the boat to figure things out." Renate recalls: "Our first trial run on this SWATH was very successful. Alex watched me sitting there, knitting and reading. I felt so good, there was not a hint of seasickness. I was convinced that this was the way to travel."

That was all Dreyfoos needed to hear. He would take a major role in specifying and committing to build the world's first SWATH luxury yacht—his third *Silver Cloud*.

In Lemwerder, Germany, he met with A&R officials about building one for him. He arrived at the company's shipyard on the Weser River, north of Bremen, with Steve Martin and John Adams. Remarks Renate, "I was included in the meetings because I spoke German, and it was very interesting to watch these three men in action. I'm sure the shipbuilders were floored by Alex's knowledge and skills."

It took until early 2006 to negotiate the 53-page contract to build the new *Silver Cloud* SWATH. Then Dreyfoos' office in his West Palm Beach penthouse began to fill with plans, documents, photos, and design concepts. Dreyfoos was in his element, contemplating how to lay out the space aboard

THE TECHNICAL SIDE OF THE *Silver Cloud* SWATH

LENGTH	134' (41 m)
BEAM	58' (17.80 m)
DRAFT	13.5' (4.1 m) normal cruise 11.5' (3.5 m) harbor min.
DISPLACEMENT	600 T
FLAG	Cayman Island
FUEL	21,000 gallons
FRESH WATER	18,000 gallons max.
SPEED	14 knots
CRUISING SPEED	12.5 knots
ENGINES	(2x) 1,100 hp, turbo-charged Caterpillar C32 Diesel
RANGE	3,500 nm @10 knots

his new ship to properly serve him, Renate, and their guests, as they set off to explore the oceans of the world. When it was over, there would be 174 pages of drawings and 118 pages of specifications for the new boat.

Dreyfoos' *Silver Cloud* SWATH is among the most technically sophisticated private ocean vessels ever built. In fact, this new *Silver Cloud* may have more in common with the Space Shuttle than it does with Dreyfoos' two previous *Silver Cloud* motor yachts, the Feadship and the Burger. Accoutred with a helicopter pad, diving platform, and two tender vessels, the new ship can support long expeditionary voyages not easily accomplished aboard lesser-equipped pleasure yachts. In light of Dreyfoos' motivation, he asserts, "The most important SWATH fact to remember is that it is six times more stable than a non-SWATH."

In essence, a SWATH vessel is comprised of two submarines that travel beneath the surface waves. The bulk of the ship rides above the waves on thin vertical struts mounted to the tops of the submarines. Because a submarine experiences no motion from the action of waves, the effect of wave action on the vessel is minimal. Only a small part of the ship (the struts) is in the waves—thus the term, Small Waterplane Area. The design dramatically increases the ship's stability in heavy seas.

Abeking & Rasmussen provides a more technical explanation: "The cross-sectional area at the sea surface is approximately 1/6th that of a comparable size yacht; thus, only a minimum part of the ship is exposed to the lifting forces of the waves while 5/6th of the buoyancy is on the submarine hulls. Additional stability is provided by the SWATH's broad beam, which is twice that of a comparable yacht. The idea of SWATH was taken from the principle of semi-submersible offshore rigs, which are designed to provide a working platform with minimized motions in open seas." The theory of the design may have scared some (how will the boat hold together on these thin struts?), but Dreyfoos understood.

The basic SWATH design patent was awarded in England in 1946 to Canadian inventor Fredrick Creed. Dreyfoos explains why no successful SWATH was built between then and A&R's first pilot ships: "Great strength is required in those struts. The design was very difficult until finite-element-analysis software was available, which was provided by the aircraft industry."

Dreyfoos guided the entire process of creating his *Silver Cloud* SWATH, while A&R designed the naval architecture and exterior appearance. The SWATH design includes a Ride Control System, or stabilizers, engineered by A&R with John Adams in Maryland, which increased the inherent 6:1 stability to 10:1 when the boat was cruising, in forward motion. According to A&R's technical director, Klaas Spethmann, a typical ship is developed through four to five versions to optimize the hull. *Silver Cloud* ran through many, many iterations, mostly because there were six different buoyant bodies involved. Tank tests were performed using a model, resulting in numerous modifications.

Dreyfoos' friend Llwyd Ecclestone is famously a fellow "boat person," yet calls Dreyfoos "courageous" for taking on the SWATH—and other things. Bob Millard, another friend—elected MIT chairman in 2014—is 20 years his junior and, though a boater, not yet a yachtsman, sees a lesson in the building of the SWATH: "When I imagine the next 20 years and how I want to pattern my life, I don't see a lot I want to emulate, but Alex is, for example,

SEAKEEPER

Years later Dreyfoos would learn that John Adams, who had been so helpful with stabilizing issues for the *Silver Cloud* SWATH, had started marketing his Seakeeper gyro stabilizer in boats similar to the 39-foot T/T *Silver Cloud*, the Intrepid tender that *Silver Cloud* towed. "I wanted to support John," says Dreyfoos. "He had never taken a nickel for all his assistance. Unfortunately, though, the stringers in our Intrepid were too close together to fit his gyro." Dreyfoos asked the manufacturer to build him a new boat. Intrepid worked with Seakeeper for a successful result—an M8000 Seakeeper installed in a 390 Sport Yacht—and Dreyfoos appeared in a promotional video to spread the word. According to Intrepid, "It is the first outboard-powered boat that goes this fast and is that size that has a Seakeeper installed."

still very involved intellectually. Like with the (SWATH) boat. Most people with the money would use it to delegate the details away, but Alex jumps in and does it himself. If it interests you, you should get involved. I didn't used to do that, but now I do. Alex set a good example."

Balancing Act

The interior of the SWATH was initially laid out by Kirschstein Design Ltd. in London; Dreyfoos' captain, Steve Martin, had worked with principal Michael Kirschstein years earlier on *Sea Cloud*. Susan Schuyler Smith of Spectrum Design in Vero Beach, Florida, who had a 30-year history with Dreyfoos, took over from there. "There were challenges present throughout this job," says Smith, "but then working for Alex is always full of challenges." She wouldn't have it any other way.

First and most important, Smith explains, the weight of *everything* was critical to stabilization in the boat's design. "I was allotted so many pounds to work with, and then the helideck was added to the design, and it decreased that allowance." With the help of Lee Spencer of U & Me Transfer, Smith shipped everything from Florida in a 20-foot shipping container. "It was all weighed here—the built-ins, the tables that would be bolted down, china, crystal, linens—and then weighed again in Germany before it was put on *Silver Cloud*. Also, because the boat would be made available for charter, every single piece of fabric had to be both flame-retardant and

CAPTAIN STEPHEN MARTIN

Steve Martin has worked as Dreyfoos' ship captain since 1996 in an industry where, according to Martin, captains normally change vessels every few years. The younger man was born in Liverpool, England. His father was in the Royal Air Force, so he spent a lot of time traveling around the world, living in places like Hong Kong and Cyprus. As a youth, he took up an apprenticeship in rigging and sailmaking. For three years, he made sails for the largest square-rigged yacht in the world at the time, the 1931 *Sea Cloud*, originally built for Palm Beach socialite Marjorie Meriwether Post. While Martin was fitting the sails, the captain of *Sea Cloud* asked if he would like to work on board the ship. He soon completed his apprenticeship and, as Martin puts it, "I never looked back." Between *Sea Cloud* and *Silver Cloud*, Martin became a sailboat captain and expanded his expertise with a wide range of motorized vessels.

Martin and Dreyfoos first met when Dreyfoos was looking for an experienced captain for the 99-foot Burger motor yacht he had just purchased to replace an 81-foot model. Dreyfoos was impressed with Martin's broad skills and wide experience at sea, and their first conversation continued for four hours.

What is it like to work with Dreyfoos? Martin says, "It's like having a college professor around you 24 hours a day. He loves to share his knowledge and gets involved in anything technical. There are few ship owners with his level of knowledge. It's exciting that he is always willing to try new things, like the SWATH. He has given me the opportunity to excel."

Scotchgarded. All of this had to be in Germany six months before the boat was completed."

Dreyfoos sold the previous *Silver Cloud* (Feadship) within months of signing the contract for the SWATH, leaving his captain, Steve Martin, aground for three years. The first year of construction, he was in Germany four to six months; the second year, nine months; and nearly all of the third year. During this time he became intimately familiar with every detail of the construction. Martin describes how the balance issue looked on the German end: "An accurate record was kept of everything that went on and also off the boat, and everything was weighed: worker's tool boxes, materials—even the garbage at the end of the week."

The first phase of *Silver Cloud* SWATH's construction took place in the Yantar shipyard, in the Russian enclave of Kaliningrad (formerly Konigsberg, Germany, and home to philosopher Immanuel Kant). When the hull reached the point where it could be towed, it was moved via the Kiel Canal to A&R's shipyard near Bremen. There *Silver Cloud* was positioned in the midst of the centennial celebration of A&R's 1907 founding, with the official celebration held beneath its construction bay.

Abeking & Rasmussen estimated it would take about two-and-a-half years to build the new *Silver Cloud* and was clearly excited about being the ones to put a SWATH yacht in the water.

When Dreyfoos began this venture, he had to decide how much capital he could afford to put into the new boat. As was his lifelong habit, he employed the Case Method engrained in him at Harvard Business School. Married about five years, he and Renate had two homes with estimable expenses. The businesses had been sold and the money invested. He factored in his return on investment and the proceeds from selling the Feadship. He knew that annual maintenance of a boat was about 10 percent of its cost. He arrived at the cost. He committed to the project. He took delivery of the *Silver Cloud* SWATH in September 2008, and by November, after the stock market crashed, his personal financial worth had dropped 30 percent.

The global economic downturn had begun.

While *Silver Cloud* was under construction, Dreyfoos had sold his Eurocopter and ordered a beautiful new helicopter with a safer, fenestron tail rotor. Due to finances, he sold his place in line for the bird.

Dreyfoos had suggested to A&R that he deserved a commission on future luxury SWATH yachts that they might build for others. After all, he was contributing his time and expertise for nothing. He pointed out, "I'm giving you great promotion with this new SWATH application." Finally they responded, "Tell you what, Mr. Dreyfoos, we'll give you a one percent commission on any SWATH yachts we sell for 10 years, starting in 2006." As word of the unique SWATH propagated into the yachting community, Dreyfoos' project did indeed draw a lot of attention. As of 2015, only one small SWATH yacht was under construction, and with just one year remaining, Dreyfoos had received no commissions on the SWATH. No one was placing orders for boats at this level during these economic times, and Dreyfoos noted that A&R was asking a significantly higher price for a new one than he had paid. ☛

Alex and Renate Dreyfoos with Judge Karl Griebsch, who officiated at their wedding.

Don and Sandy Duso, witnesses to the wedding of Alex and Renate Dreyfoos, 2000.

Alex and Renate Dreyfoos at their wedding celebration, the Kravis Center.

Mary Rowell, controller for the Dreyfoos Group and a member of the Dreyfoos team since 1990, at the Dreyfoos wedding celebration.

Mike and Connie Graham, Renate and Alex Dreyfoos, and Evelyn Dreyfoos Spelman, at the celebration of the Dreyfoos' wedding, at the Kravis Center.

The *Silver Cloud* Burger as it looked when Dreyfoos purchased it as Ar-De, in 1996.

The fishing cockpit extension on the *Silver Cloud* Burger.

Flybridge of *Ar-De*—before purchase and alterations by Dreyfoos as *Silver Cloud*.

Bridge modifications to the *Silver Cloud* Burger.

The *Silver Cloud* Burger in 1999 on the Danube River in Vienna, Austria, with the boat's equipment folded down, allowing it to pass under the adjacent bridge in the down position.

The *Silver Cloud* Burger in 1999, in the fjords of Norway.

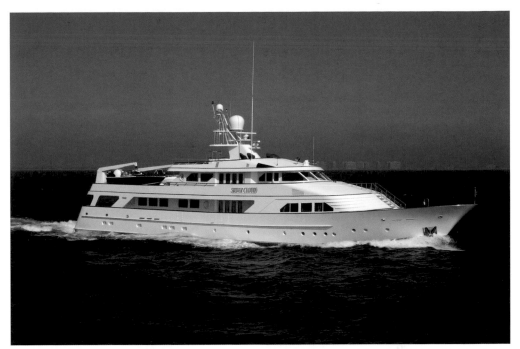

Dreyfoos took this picture of the *Silver Cloud* Feadship on the day he purchased it as *Cakewalk* in 2002. He liked the photo so much, he photoshopped the vessel name on it.

While visiting the National Naval Aviation Museum in Pensacola, Florida, Dreyfoos took this picture of Jack Taylor with a Hellcat aircraft, the type Taylor flew in World War II.

Technical Director Dr. Klaas Spethmann of Abeking & Rasmussen, 2005.

Dreyfoos' technical consultant John Adams, 2005.

Silver Cloud Captain Stephen Martin.

A 1/16 scale model hull of the *Silver Cloud* SWATH at the historic Vienna Model Basin in Austria, 2006. Waves are generated in this towing tank, while measuring behavior such as the ship's resistance and recovery from rogue waves. (Visit www.YachtSilverCloud.com for a video showing *Silver Cloud*'s motion in rough seas.)

The *Silver Cloud* SWATH in 2007 during its first phase of construction at the Yantar shipyard in Kaliningrad, Russia.

The *Silver Cloud* SWATH under final construction in Germany.

The *Silver Cloud* SWATH with a Eurocopter EC135 on the helipad.

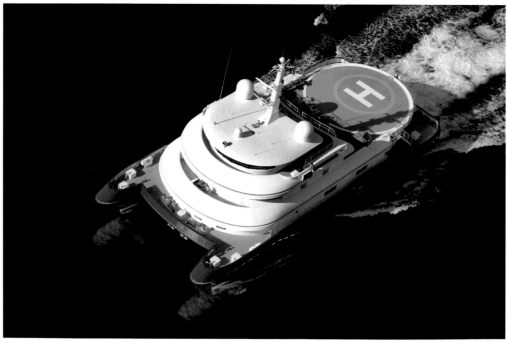

An aerial of the *Silver Cloud* SWATH.

Dreyfoos at the owner's helm station outside the master stateroom on the *Silver Cloud* SWATH in 2009.

The *Silver Cloud* SWATH in French Polynesia, 2014, with its Intrepid tender, T/T *Silver Cloud*.

(left to right) *Silver Cloud* Captain Stephen Martin, Renate and Alex Dreyfoos receiving *Boat International*'s 2010 World Superyacht Voyager's Award in London, England.

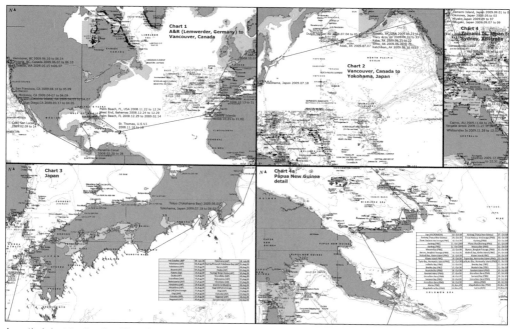

A nautical chart tracing the *Silver Cloud*'s 2008-2010 voyage, made by Dreyfoos as part of the entry for the 2010 World Superyacht Voyager's Award.

Renate Dreyfoos (left) with Henry "Rip" McIntosh and his wife, Susan.

Bob Millard, chairman of MIT in 2014, relaxes aboard *Silver Cloud*, next to its model, in 2011.

341

Dreyfoos surrounded by his family on Thanksgiving Day 2011: (left to right) grandson Mac Carter, daughter Cathy Carter, granddaughter Michelle Carter, grandsons Aron and Travis Dreyfoos, Renate, daughter-in-law Julie, and son Robert Dreyfoos.

(left to right) Cathy Dreyfoos Carter with her daughter, Michelle; son-in-law, Brian Fenimore; and son, Mac, in 2013.

Dreyfoos with grandson Aron Dreyfoos at his 2013 MIT graduation.

CHAPTER 17

Giving Back

Dreyfoos (left) and former MIT classmate Paul Gray, who became president of the institute 1980-1990. Here they celebrate their 50th class reunion in 2004, a milestone that earned them their red jackets.

Advocating for Education

Dreyfoos was not idle during the three years he waited for the *Silver Cloud* SWATH to be built. Between trips to Germany to monitor the fabrication and assembly process, he filled his schedule with philanthropic activities that focused primarily on education, the arts, and biomedical research.

Dreyfoos' patronage began before building the SWATH, or selling the Sailfish Marina, or even marrying Renate. (See page 347.) Despite these earlier gifts, however, it was the tremendous profits from the sale of WPEC that enabled him to increase his generosity.

A year after he closed on the sale of WPEC, in 1997, Dreyfoos contributed $1 million to the Palm Beach County School of the Arts Foundation. "I got involved after the high school, grades 9-12, was up and running," he carefully explains. "Dedicated parents had started the foundation to provide equipment and improvements that were not in the school budget. They came to me with the idea that if I made a million-dollar gift, people that were grateful for what I had done elsewhere in the community would also contribute to the school foundation."

Over the next 10 years, Dreyfoos was pleased to see the idea work out. After Dreyfoos' gift, others of various sizes funded scholarships and enhancements to the high school. Thanks to Leonard and Sophie Davis, the Music Library in the Media Center and the school stage were named for Clyde Fyfe. The Davis's son, Alan Davis, and his wife, Mary Lou Dauray, also created a $1 million endowment. Kravis Center donors Sydelle and Arthur Meyer made possible Meyer Hall, the school's auditorium.

With his gift to this magnet school, Dreyfoos made history. It was the largest private contribution ever made to a public school in Florida, and he continued his significant support. During a tour of the school, he learned that many classrooms lacked computers because teachers were uncomfortable with them. Dreyfoos arranged for the school to hire the IT contractor he used, at his own expense, benefiting both faculty and students.

Dreyfoos is impressed with many aspects of the school. "I like the fact that admission to the school is decided only by the applicant's talent through an audition process, without considering school grades," he notes. "The selection also cuts through economic, religious, racial, social, and legacy considerations."

In 1997 the county renamed the school the Alexander W. Dreyfoos Jr. School of the Arts (DSOA). Dr. H. David Prensky, a founding member and then executive vice president of the school's foundation, accompanied its president to broach the naming matter with Dreyfoos. A decade later he wrote:

> *[Dreyfoos] replied that he didn't think he was interested in having his name on another building. . . . I told him he may not be, but that we were very interested in exactly that. It was the only name . . . I saw as the fitting one. . . . Ever since I arrived in this community . . . every activity in it that I considered important, that made life worth living, had Alex Dreyfoos leading it or bringing it into existence.*

The Dreyfoos School of the Arts has been consistently well viewed. In

2014, *US News & World Report* ranked it #46 out of 31,242 US public high schools. *Newsweek* placed it at #39, out of 5,000 asked to compete (2013). The school attracts artistically talented students from all parts of Palm Beach County to focused study in Communications Arts; Dance; Film, Photo and Digital Media; Music (Band, Keyboard/Piano, Strings, and Vocal); Theatre; and Visual Arts. Graduates are regularly accepted at such select schools as Harvard, Juilliard, Princeton, Rhode Island School of Design, Yale—and MIT.

Individual DSOA students described to Dreyfoos, in 2007, what the school meant to them. Here are a few excerpts:

> Brittney Lewer: *"We are a community. Our common denominator is a love of art. Never have I seen a group of more passionate people. . . . Their efforts are duly rewarded. . . . [They] carry their skills with them outside of their art classes."*

> Emmaleigh Litchfield: *"I know that it is because of Dreyfoos' free and passionate atmosphere that I was able to gain so much from my high school experience. . . . DSOA has proven that an artistic education only enhances every other aspect of education. I think the secret is that we, as students, can do what we love to do first."*

> Kelsey Newman: *"We are deeply grateful for this place. . . . [DSOA] gives many students who otherwise might not have the opportunity to pursue their passions the chance to do so."*

Dreyfoos' son, Robert, believes that, in the future, the School of the Arts and the Kravis Center will best represent his father's legacy. "Those are wonderful things. Dad is visionary. He knows what is right for a community, and he knows what makes things happen. His education positioned him to do well in business, and the arts nurtured him along the way. This is all his way of giving something back."

Massachusetts Institute of Technology

A proud MIT alum, Dreyfoos has long been contributing to his alma mater with both time and resources. He is a Life Member Emeritus of MIT's board of trustees, known as the "Corporation," which has subcommittees called "Visiting Committees" in oversight of the institute's departments.

Media Lab, a laboratory of the MIT School of Architecture and Planning, is aimed at identifying and exploiting convergences among design, technology, and media. Descriptions of the lab's work are dramatic:

Where "the future is lived, not imagined."

"Actively promoting a unique, antidisciplinary culture . . . beyond known boundaries and disciplines, encouraging the most unconventional mixing and matching of seemingly disparate research areas."

"In its first decade it was at the vanguard of the technology that enabled the digital revolution."

The Media Lab embodies the blending of art and science, the very notion that Professor Hardy first introduced to Dreyfoos at MIT in 1951. In fact, Professor Nicholas Negroponte, co-founder and former director of the lab, points out that the whole idea for a media lab was hatched in 1982 aboard Dreyfoos' yacht *Prime Time*, in the company of Jerome "Jerry" Wiesner, Science Advisory Committee chair for President John F. Kennedy and MIT president 1971 to 1980.

Dreyfoos joined the Visiting Committee for the Media Laboratory/Media Arts and Sciences during construction of the lab (designed by I. M. Pei), and continued as its chair from 1988 until 2001; he remains on the Advisory Council. For nearly a decade, he also served on the Visiting Committee for Electrical Engineering and Computer Sciences.

Through his continued service to MIT, Dreyfoos has formed lasting bonds with people of like mind. Much-younger Bob Millard, like Dreyfoos, has combined art plus science, and remarks that this theme is "nascent at MIT. The word 'design' is being attached in non-traditional ways." A collector of antique scientific instruments, Millard notes that the beauty of form was once as important as function, then design became utilitarian, but now he sees it changing back; artists can be scientists and vice versa.

Another of Dreyfoos' valued relationships from the Media Lab has been Dr. Andrew B. Lippman, who he calls "a stabilizing influence on the lab since day one." Lippman's work has ranged from global digital television to wearable computers. Dreyfoos makes a point of seeking out his company whenever he visits Boston.

MIT allowed Dreyfoos to propose two chairs; he chose associate professors V. Michael Bove Jr. and Michael Hawley. Michael Bove's three MIT degrees included a PhD in media technology. Among his many achievements in research, leadership, invention, and authorship, Bove became head of the Object-Based Media Group at the Media Lab, a position he still held in 2015.

Michael Hawley, who held the Dreyfoos chair from 1993 to 2002, came to MIT from Yale (with a double major in music and computer science) for his doctoral in computer science. He also won the 2002 Van Cliburn International Piano Competition, and Hawley performed at the Kravis Center in 2004. This shared mix of art and science formed a bond between the two men. Hawley performed at the Kravis Center in 2004. Alex and Renate attended Hawley's 2009 wedding to Nina You in Bhutan, where Hawley crusades for education and healthcare. Bhutan is the subject and name of the largest book in the world (7-foot-by-5-foot), produced by Hawley, also director of the annual EG conference, described as "a conference and a community of leading innovators driving our most creative industries."

Dreyfoos continued to endow the Alexander W. Dreyfoos (1954) Professorship at the Media Lab in 2015, when Dr. Pattie Maes held the honor, as well as a PhD in computer science from the Vrije Universiteit Brussel in Belgium. Maes specializes in artificial intelligence and human-computer interaction. In the 1990s, her Software Agents research group at the Media Lab created Firefly technology, which became a company, sold to Microsoft. Its "things like this" filtering is now seen on websites such as Amazon as "Customers who bought this item also bought," to offer recommendations to users. Under Maes' leadership, concepts explored by the Media Lab's Fluid Interfaces Group, which focuses on creating intuitive devices, led to the revolutionary "FingerReader," which in effect turns printed material into an audiobook as wearers scan text. Maes also cofounded Open Ratings, a vendor evaluation service purchased by Dun & Bradstreet.

As this book went to press, the Dreyfoos chair was in transition. Dr. Maes was joining MIT's administration, and Associate Professor Dr. Joseph A. Paradiso was about to become the new Dreyfoos chair.

In 2013 the MIT Corporation named the auditorium atop the Media Lab Complex in Dreyfoos' honor, because "Alex's voice is such an important one in helping us constantly reinvent the Lab so that it remains as relevant as it was when it opened its doors in 1985."

Dreyfoos was also pleased to contribute $15 million to construct the Alexander W. Dreyfoos Building, one of the two iconic towers of the Ray and Maria Stata Center, Building 32, to honor his esteemed professor, Arthur C. Hardy. The center's other tower was named for its benefactor, Microsoft founder Bill Gates. Frank Gehry, who designed the Stata Center, was also the architect of the Guggenheim Museum Bilbao in Spain and Walt Disney Concert Hall in Los Angeles.

Dreyfoos and Renate flew to the 2004 Stata Center dedication on the plane of friends Amin J. Khoury of B/E Aerospace and his wife, Julie; the four dined with Gehry and toured his unusual building. Khoury recalls that the couples' first flight together was to Nice, France, where Dreyfoos' *Silver Cloud* was anchored, to attend the International SeaKeepers Society's annual Bal de la Mer in nearby Monaco. Khoury says he was fascinated by the work of the society, and is "continuously astonished by Alex's generosity and the number of buildings and organizations he is involved with."

Kindness

Large financial gifts attract publicity, but personal kindnesses less so. Connie Graham, assistant to Dreyfoos since 1982, has been witness to his little known deeds: "I tell Mr. D. he lives a charmed life. He always makes the close connection on flights, gets a room in a booked hotel, and receives a part for his camera or computer the day he is leaving for a three-week trip. He has even found his 'lost' passport while in a foreign country. The list is long. Now I think maybe it is karma—repaying his many acts of kindness that come straight from the heart—and because he can. These are acts that will never be publicly known, given no credit other than knowing he has made someone's life a little better. To me, above all, his kindness shines." Graham would know; Dreyfoos frequently describes her as the person who

THE GIFTS OF EASTMAN

In 1912 MIT President Richard Maclaurin enlisted the help of alumnus Frank Lovejoy, then general manager of Eastman Kodak, to solicit from his employer much-needed funds to build a new campus. After careful consideration, George Eastman wrote MIT a check for $2.5 million, with the stipulation that he remained anonymous. Maclaurin created a pseudonym of "Mr. Smith" for the donor. For eight years, while Eastman wrote even more checks, it was a game for students to guess the identity of their benefactor. In 1920 Eastman finally agreed to allow his identity to be revealed at the annual alumni dinner, but the speech Maclaurin prepared for the occasion had to be read by others. The president was ill with pneumonia, from which he died a week later. Eastman lived until 1932, when he committed suicide to escape debilitating health. By then his gifts to MIT had added up to $11 million, the equivalent of about $190 million in 2015.

Viewed from a time when the names Eastman and Dreyfoos are linked in the development of photography, and both having given much of their resources, this story probably has more meaning for Dreyfoos than for many others who studied under the Great Dome of Building 10 and the other hallowed halls built with Eastman's money. These words could have been spoken by either man, but they are attributed to George Eastman in 1923:

If a man has wealth, he has to make a choice, because there is the money heaping up. He can keep it together in a bunch, and then leave it for others to administer after he is dead. Or he can get it into action and have fun, while he is still alive. I prefer getting it into action and adapting it to human needs, and making the plan work.

Alex Dreyfoos has also put his money into action, and has put himself into the action as well—making things happen, getting them started, with his vision, his meticulous thinking, and his influence. To Eastman's words, he also adds: "Philanthropy is building, but in a different way—trusting others with the tools to carry on with your same spirit and values."

knows more about him than he does himself.

Along the way, Dreyfoos has given his time as well as his money. He served on the board of the Trudeau Institute and became an emeritus member. More recently, he joined the board of the Henry Morrison Flagler Museum in Palm Beach, which memorializes the ancestor of his dear friend, George Matthews.

invited Dreyfoos to serve on the board of trustees. When Gruss retired in 2014, MPFI's parting gift was a framed photograph taken by Dreyfoos in Germany in 1956.

Germany's Max Planck Society for the Advancement of Science was originally founded as the Kaiser Wilhelm Society, and renamed for one of its presidents in 1948. Max Planck (1858-1947) is one of 17 Nobel Prize laureates that the society has produced; another is Albert Einstein. Its mission is, in part, to produce "basic research at cutting-edge, strictly curiosity-driven and quality oriented."

In 2014, Alex and Renate Dreyfoos made a gift of a million dollars to the Max Planck Florida Foundation. "Our work is focused on advancing the world's understanding of how the brain works," said CEO and Scientific Director, Dr. David Fitzpatrick. "Mr. Dreyfoos continues to be one of our most vocal champions." In honor of the Dreyfoos' gift, MPFI will designate its central atrium at the research institute as the Alexander and Renate Dreyfoos Atrium.

Renate has been at her husband's side not just to receive thanks for their joint gifts, but also to see him receive many honors and awards, and she sees it as a wonderful culmination of his legacy. "Having had a 45-year affiliation with him on so many levels, and now to finally be with the man I love—it's just wonderful. I am incredibly proud to be Mrs. Alex Dreyfoos every day, but especially when others give him the honor and recognition he deserves so much." ☞

Principal Susan Atherley accepting a donation from Dreyfoos in 2011 for the Dreyfoos School of the Arts.

Photo shoot for a program cover for a Dreyfoos School Foundation gala; the Dreyfooses are center right. Far left are Foundation President Simon Offit and past president Dorothy Lappin.

Dreyfoos (left) in 1993 with Associate Professor Michael Hawley as he became the first Dreyfoos Chair at MIT's Media Center.

Michael and Nina Hawley with Renate and Alex Dreyfoos, at the 2009 Hawley wedding in Bhutan.

Alex and Renate Dreyfoos in the lobby of the Dreyfoos Building, 2004.

(left to right) Ray and Maria Stata, architect Frank Gehry, and Renate and Alex Dreyfoos at the dedication of the Stata Center.

Microsoft co-founder Bill Gates, announcing his gift toward the Gates Building part of the Stata Center.

The Dreyfoos Building (left) and Gates Building (right) that comprise MIT's Stata Center.

(from left) William Meyer, Dreyfoos' successor as Kravis Center chairman of the board, Kravis Center CEO Judy Mitchell, and Dreyfoos in 2011.

Dreyfoos (right) with Gary Lickle.

Jane Mitchell, the third Kravis Center chair, with Dreyfoos in 2014.

Richard Lerner, then president of The Scripps Research Institute, and his wife, Dr. Nicky Lerner, with Renate and Alex Dreyfoos, at the Kravis Center, 2004.

Scripps Florida, in Jupiter, showing the DNA pinnacle known as the "Dreyfoos spinnaker."

MIT President Rafael Reif and wife, Christine, (standing) with Alex and Renate Dreyfoos, (seated) at the Alexander W. Dreyfoos '54 Auditorium in the MIT Media Lab.

The Renate and Alexander Dreyfoos Atrium at Scripps Florida, 2014.

Scripps Trustees Amin Khoury (left) and Dreyfoos (right) join Scripps President/CEO Dr. Michael Marletta at the Institute's tenth anniversary luncheon, 2014.

Dreyfoos (right) and former Florida Governor and US Senator Bob Graham receiving Woodrow Wilson Awards, 2006.

Rena Blades, president/CEO of the Cultural Council of Palm Beach County, and her husband, John, executive director of the Henry Morrison Flagler Museum, Palm Beach.

The Max Planck Florida Institute for Neuroscience (MPFI) in Jupiter, Florida.

(left to right) Dreyfoos with his wife, Renate, with Dr. David Fitzpatrick, president of the Max Planck Florida Institute for Neuroscience, 2014.

Dreyfoos (left) with Peter Gruss, president of the international Max Planck Society, at Gruss's retirement dinner, 2013. Gruss is holding Dreyfoos' 1955 photo of Neuschwanstein Castle in Germany, a retirement gift from Max Planck Florida.

The Alexander and Renate Dreyfoos Atrium at Max Planck Florida Institute, Jupiter, dedicated in 2014.

Fellow trustees of Max Planck Florida Institute, Dreyfoos (left) and George Elmore, with Barbara Suflas Noble, president of the Max Planck Florida Foundation and vice president for advancement at Max Planck Florida.

(left to right) Former PBAU Free Enterprise Award recipients Tom Pledger (1998), Dreyfoos (1992), and Florida Senator Phil Lewis (1986).

Dreyfoos (right) with Amway founder Rich DeVos, a recipient of the PBAU Free Enterprise Award in 2000.

CHAPTER 18

A Full Life

Seven porpoises surf *Silver Cloud*'s pressure wave near Gibraltar.
Photo by Capt. Steve Martin on bridge, using *Silver Cloud*'s "Inspire" drone, 2015.

(Almost) Around the World in . . . 15 Months

While Abeking & Rasmussen was building the *Silver Cloud* SWATH, Alex and Renate Dreyfoos were planning what they had waited for since they married in 2000: an around-the-world cruise on a vessel stable enough for Renate to enjoy the ride. The first leg of the journey started from A&R's shipyard near Bremen, Germany, in October 2008, accompanied by friends. Two A&R engineers also were on board for what doubled as a "shakedown cruise" to test the new boat and make measurements along the way to document its performance. Dreyfoos and Captain Steve Martin took *Silver Cloud* up the Weser River to the North Sea, west through the English Channel, and down the west coast of Europe to Gibraltar, where they refueled and let off the two engineers. In Dreyfoos' mind, this would be the starting point of the circumnavigation.

Dreyfoos' passions for his wife and for traveling by water had given him a purpose that moved him to build the *Silver Cloud* SWATH. Solving the dilemma of motion sickness was the first step, and a substantial one in terms of time, effort, and finances—in achieving circumnavigation. It would not, however, be the only obstacle to overcome.

While Renate had no trouble with the notoriously rough waters of the North Sea and Bay of Biscay, she chose at this point to fly back to Palm Beach. Dreyfoos headed to the Canary Islands, where George Michel and George Matthews joined him for the boat's maiden crossing of the Atlantic Ocean, an extremely calm passage to St. Thomas in the US Virgin Islands. Renate flew in, along with Amin and Julie Khoury, Gary Lickle and Michele Henry, Paula Michel, and Betsy Matthews for a celebratory last four days en route to Palm Beach. Dreyfoos wanted to see how the boat would operate with all the staterooms fully occupied, simulating a maximum capacity of friends, family, or charter clients.

During an intermission at home, the proud owners held a series of parties to introduce their unique vessel, docked at the Sailfish Club, to friends and colleagues. Dreyfoos enjoyed showing off the results of what had gripped a considerable portion of his attention for more than five years. He knew it would be some time before the boat would be in these waters again. He and Renate also introduced family members to the SWATH with a scuba diving trip to the Bahamas, as Dreyfoos' grandsons had recently become certified.

For the second leg of their odyssey, Alex and Renate departed from Florida on Valentine's Day 2009 and headed for the Panama Canal. After Panama, they pointed *Silver Cloud* north along the coastline of Mexico, the United States, Canada, and Alaska. Along the way, they had more parties on board: for Scripps in San Diego; for Dreyfoos' sister, Evelyn, in San Francisco; and for friends and family in the Northwest. Not to miss the opportunity to spend a few weeks in the Adirondack Mountains, Renate chose to disembark in Alaska, agreeing to return to *Silver Cloud* when it reached Japan. Meanwhile, George Michel joined Dreyfoos in Juneau for the passage to Japan. While passing through the Aleutian Islands, they were treated to a visit from a convocation of bald eagles on *Silver Cloud* while at a fuel docking station. The large birds fought over strips of salmon thrown on the deck by dock attendants, striking poses that delighted Dreyfoos. He considered that several-hour episode to be the most exhilarating photo experience of his life.

Other friends and relatives came aboard for segments of the journey, and Renate returned in Japan. Six weeks circling its southern island gave them broad exposure to Japan's diverse culture and geography, without the downsides of travel: packing and unpacking, hectic arrangements, and lack of control. Dreyfoos was especially grateful for *Silver Cloud* here, where they could go "home" anytime to their own beds and chef.

After mainland Japan, the waters of the Pacific provided abundant opportunities for underwater photography at southern Japan, the islands of Palau, Yap, and Papua New Guinea, down the Great Barrier Reef to Sydney, Australia. As 2009 came to an end, the Dreyfooses celebrated Renate's December birthday with front-row seats for the New Year's Eve fireworks display. The rest of the winter was spent exploring New Zealand.

Since Dreyfoos' ownership of his first *Silver Cloud* worthy of the trip, one destination that had remained on his bucket list was the Republic of Seychelles, an archipelago of 115 coral islands in the Indian Ocean, east of Africa. In 1999, while scuba diving with the *Silver Cloud* Burger in the Gulf of Aqaba and around the Suez Canal, he was getting close, and made up his mind to proceed down the Red Sea, around the Horn of Africa to the Seychelles. At that time, however, Somalian and other pirates were already a threat to vessels traveling around the Horn. Dreyfoos' marine insurance company told him: "You can go if you want, Mr. Dreyfoos, but *Silver Cloud* won't be insured." That put a stop to those plans.

A decade later, Alex and Renate were in the midst of their overarching goal: completing the circumnavigation of the world on their new *Silver Cloud* SWATH. But Dreyfoos was still resolved to include the Seychelles. In the spring of 2010, having enjoyed New Zealand and Australia, he was prepared to head northwest to the Seychelles, Madagascar, and Cape Town, thereby avoiding the Horn of Africa. Their planned route from there to the Canary Islands (just south of the entrance to the Mediterranean) would achieve the circumnavigation.

Headline news, however, reported that pirates had extended their operation and were actually basing some of their piracy fleet in the Seychelles. The insurance company now refused coverage anywhere in the Indian

Ocean, and Dreyfoos reluctantly changed his plans again. *Silver Cloud* turned around and instead headed northeast to the South Pacific, where Alex and Renate explored Fiji, Bora Bora, and Tahiti.

During their long absence, Shannon Donnelly, society editor for the *Palm Beach Daily News*, kept a running weblog of their odyssey. On March 2, 2010, she reported that *Silver Cloud* was near Fiji, in the vicinity of an earthquake-generated tsunami. Donnelly had received inquiries from friends of the couple who were concerned for their safety. Donnelly happily assured them with Dreyfoos' statement: "We have had the good fortune of being at sea between New Zealand and Fiji where the ocean depth is averaging 12,000 feet, rendering the tsunami undetectable."

Continuing eastward, the Galapagos Islands, off Ecuador, afforded another treasure trove of photo opportunities. Snorkeling with its penguins, Dreyfoos was amazed by their bullet-like speed and agility underwater, in sharp contrast to their awkward motion on land. The Dreyfooses' last destination was Tropic Star Lodge at Piñas Bay, Panama, for its excellent sailfish fishing, before passing through the Panama Canal and returning to Palm Beach.

On Saturday, May 15, 2010, Donnelly reported that the ocean extensive voyage had come to an end; *Silver Cloud* had returned Alex and Renate Dreyfoos safely to Palm Beach. Over the course of their 15 months at sea, they had traveled a total of 25,800 nautical miles (approximately 30,000 statute miles).

Though Dreyfoos was discouraged that he had once again been kept from meeting his goals of circumnavigation and visiting the Seychelles, the trip had been rewarding in countless other ways. He chose to see it as a temporary delay and turn his mind to other things.

Room to Improve

Before the SWATH, Dreyfoos had been accustomed to boats designed for fishing, which typically included a rear platform close to the water for swimming, diving, lounging, and fighting and landing fish. The SWATH was not designed that way; it sat high above the water, so it used a drop-down ladder to reach only a small platform. At the time of the design, Dreyfoos thought he could accept the difference, but over the first year of living on *Silver Cloud* it bothered him not to be able to be close to water

CHARTERS

When Dreyfoos purchased the *Silver Cloud* Feadship, it had a history of being available for charter, and his captain, Steve Martin, had relationships within the charter industry. Dreyfoos continued to accommodate charters, about 10 weeks per year, which put the boat where charter clients wanted it. Many charters require only the shiny, white floating hotel sitting still, but in a beautiful setting—typically that is the Caribbean in the winter months and the Mediterranean in the summer. The Dreyfooses often enjoyed *Silver Cloud* from these areas, because Renate could not travel comfortably in open waters on the Feadship.

Dreyfoos also made the *Silver Cloud* SWATH available for charters, mostly for clients requesting the Caribbean. Because it traveled so well, however, Dreyfoos wanted to take it to parts of the world that he had not taken the Burger or Feadship.

Later changes in maritime regulations negatively impacted the benefits of chartering the *Silver Cloud* SWATH, but in 2011, a client requested it as a secondary vessel for his extensive entourage, while his family was ensconced on a much larger chartered yacht. The internationally known figure kept a low profile and requested anonymity, although Dreyfoos had met him under other circumstances.

The setting for the trip was the Amazon River. Dreyfoos took advantage of the opportunity to accompany the delivery from the Caribbean to Brazil, then a thousand miles upriver on the Amazon from Belem to a site on the Rio Negro. Before the charter group arrived, Capt. Martin backtracked to Manaus, where Dreyfoos and his guests flew home to Palm Beach.

The client had insisted on a particular kind of helicopter to use with *Silver Cloud*—the Eurocopter EC135—and apparently was able to find it (and the insurance for it) in only one place. A company that supplied charters for England's Royal Family boxed one up, shipped it to the Caribbean, and flew in an English pilot, who island-hopped it down to Brazil. That helicopter was kept busy daily, ferrying people, equipment, and supplies between the airport, *Silver Cloud*, and the primary vessel, and visiting local destinations.

At the end of the 16-day charter, Dreyfoos flew to Manaus to reclaim *Silver Cloud* for its return trip to the Caribbean. The client's helicopter was getting ready to leave. Dreyfoos invited the pilot to ride along with them, if he would grant him a favor: Dreyfoos wanted to fly "the bird." The pilot granted Dreyfoos his wish. In telling this story, Dreyfoos paraphrased the MasterCard ad, "Getting back on *Silver Cloud* after a charter—great! Piloting the charterer's queen's helicopter—priceless!"

level. Dreyfoos asked the boat's builder, Abeking & Rasmussen in Germany, to design a platform that not only moved straight down, but also extended outward. When A&R was unable to do so, Dreyfoos suggested a concept to make it work that was successful. In 2012 the retractable platform replaced *Silver Cloud*'s tender garage. The passarelle provided a staircase from the main deck. The platform became a convenient spot for swimming, scuba diving, and relaxing at the water's edge, as well as a stable docking site for boarding the tender. After reclaiming *Silver Cloud* in Germany, the Dreyfooses cruised Norway, Sweden, Denmark, and Poland, going north of the Arctic Circle before crossing the Atlantic in a southwesterly direction to the Virgin Islands and other Caribbean sites. *Silver Cloud* then made one of its infrequent visits to Palm Beach to rest before its next very long trip.

Persistence

On July 14, 2013, *Silver Cloud* departed Palm Beach, initiating a second effort to fulfill Dreyfoos' dream of circumnavigation. While the boat made its way through the Panama Canal to Cabo San Lucas, Mexico, for a charter, Dreyfoos and his divemaster, Rich Young, flew to Cancun to dive with whale sharks with friend Jim Abernethy. Over the next few months, Alex and Renate made several trips by air, in between spending time at their Adirondacks home and on *Silver Cloud* and other places. *Silver Cloud* made its way from Mexico up the West Coast to California to entertain friends and family. In November, the couple joined a CEO group to photograph polar bears on Hudson Bay, Canada, and in December flew to Hawaii for Renate's birthday and Christmas with family on *Silver Cloud*.

Continuing conversations with the insurance company achieved a partial agreement about this time. Dreyfoos could follow a route in the southern Indian Ocean, involving only a small risk, but he was not to approach the Seychelles (one of his goals) or the Horn of Africa.

Due to the ever-changing habits of pirates, final approval to enter higher-risk areas would have to wait until 30 days in advance. The activity of Somali pirates had peaked in 2011, when they hijacked 28 vessels. As 2014 began, the improved situation granted Dreyfoos a bit of optimism. He was not interested in a return to the Western Pacific if it did not achieve circumnavigation, but here was a new opportunity for success with small risk involved.

Silver Cloud was about due to have its propeller and stabilizer shaft seals replaced after six years of operation; a minor leak could become worse during the upcoming long trip. Since the only dry dock in all of Australia that could physically accommodate the boat was owned by the Royal Australian Navy, Dreyfoos asked to have the work done there by an outside contractor. The first reply was an automatic no, but Dreyfoos convinced the Navy by asking, "Would you rather rescue us from the middle of the Indian Ocean if the seals fail?"

The seal repairs, though successful, caused a critical delay in *Silver Cloud* leaving Australia, as it changed the risk assessment of the southern Indian Ocean route. While that path would have been safer from the danger of pirates, *Silver Cloud* would have been passage-making in the midst of typhoon season. Capt. Steve Martin, whose son was also part of the crew, agreed with his boss that the risk of pirates was preferable to the likelihood of typhoons.

Earlier in the trip, a representative from the security company approved by the insurer had come aboard to discuss the realities of the situation, but Dreyfoos was not scared off. To start with, the insurer preferred not to have Dreyfoos on board during the passage, which amused their client. Since the whole point was *to* be on board, costly hostage insurance was added to his coverage. No friends or family would be invited this time. After reading the entire security manual of procedures and restrictions, Renate also decided this was not a trip for her, even if the insurer had agreed. She returned to the States for the duration of this trip and the completion of the circumnavigation.

Dreyfoos could not make this journey alone, however, and whatever crew would accompany him would be sharing the personal risk. He told his crewmembers, "This is not a command performance." They had the options of taking vacation or time off, but all seven chose to stay aboard, six males and one female. Dreyfoos, not surprised, says, "They are an adventurous group."

In February, having never been to the island of Tasmania, he hired a helicopter to pick him up on *Silver Cloud* and tour the island by air before delivering him to a resort and back to the boat a few days later. Dreyfoos also

Dreyfoos had planned to summer in the Mediterranean on *Silver Cloud*. Since ISIS had now made those waters too dangerous to enjoy, the tender was sent on to the United States.

Mission Accomplished

Dreyfoos and *Silver Cloud* remained in the Mediterranean while determining its destination for painting and other refurbishing. It was decided to be at home in Palm Beach, where they arrived on July 5, 2015 almost exactly two years to the day after they had left.

To Dreyfoos, it was meaningful to once again pass Gibraltar at the mouth of the Mediterranean, as *Silver Cloud* had technically begun this circumnavigation there in 2008, at the end of its "shakedown" test cruise. When they passed Gibraltar again in 2015, *Silver Cloud* achieved port-to-port circumnavigation; however, it had taken six and a half years. A more succinct way to define the circumnavigation was from Palm Beach (July 2013) to Palm Beach (July 2015), in just under two years. Still, Dreyfoos announced the details of the repeated part of the trip: "This completes the last (exactly) 4,000 NM leg of our circumnavigation, Gibraltar to Palm Beach non-stop in (exactly) 14 days, at reduced speed in order to avoid having to stop for fuel. That computes to 11.9 knots average speed, about 1½ knots of it due to favorable currents." During the Egypt-Mallorca leg, *Silver Cloud* had also passed west of (beyond) circumnavigation on the basis of longitude to longitude.

In the 2013 to 2015 voyage, these were the major stops along the way: Palm Beach, Panama Canal, Cabo San Lucas, San Diego, Hawaii, Tahiti/French Polynesia, Fiji, Vanuatu, and the following Australia ports of call: Cannes, Wit Sunday, Brisbane, Sydney, Hobart (Tasmania), Adelaide and Freemantle (Perth). And after departing Australia: Maldives, Suez and Port Said (Egypt), Mallorca, Gibraltar, and Palm Beach. (See Appendix for a more complete list.)

Ironically, *Silver Cloud* still hadn't been to the Seychelles! Though Dreyfoos could fly there and dive in its waters, it was not safe to cross the wider waters surrounding it by boat.

A few days after leaving Fremantle, his computing mind wrote his friend George Michel in Florida, "Yesterday we passed within about 200 NM of being exactly on the opposite side of the globe from Palm Beach, about as far away from you as I could be and still be earthbound."

The two-year circumnavigation, Palm Beach to Palm Beach, covered 103,000 NM. The total miles logged on *Silver Cloud* from its launch in 2008 was 110,000 NM, the equivalent of five trips around the world. ⚓︎

Silver Cloud's mast, showing dome housing thermal and infrared cameras; and one of two cameras with zoom, scan, and infrared ability.

Dreyfoos' master suite desk onboard *Silver Cloud*. The two top monitors were linked to the Sony cameras on the mast.

Testing the spray nozzles of the seven hoses secured to the main deck, to deter anyone trying to board *Silver Cloud*.

The guards testing the bridge deck, where a shooting position was built of steel, wood, and sandbags.

Some of the security guards' gear for protecting *Silver Cloud*.

Interior doors barred with 4-by-4 posts to prevent opening from inside.

Hatch to safe area with aluminum bar that prevented opening the hatch from above, and ladder below.

Safe area between decks filled with emergency supplies, viewed from the bottom of the ladder.

Seven customs and immigration agents (Capt. Steve Martin at center) at the Maldives, when two would have sufficed. They only left after receiving quantities of soda, water, and cigarettes.

Four of the ships moving into position ahead of *Silver Cloud* to pass through the Suez Canal.

MSC Oscar lead ship in the convoy through the Suez Canal, and the world's largest container ship at 395 m (1,297 ft.) long.

CHAPTER 19

Lifelong Pleasures, Best Shared

Alex and Renate Dreyfoos aboard the *Silver Cloud* Burger, 2000.

"Sharing the High"

Spending time with friends has been important throughout Dreyfoos' busy life. With some, he has shared a passion for diving, fishing, flying, sailing, or photography. Many of his group trips have been all male, although less so once Renate was back in his life.

One of Dreyfoos' pleasures has been joining Bob Millard, Michael Hawley, and others at Big Boys Camp, a weeklong adventure at Robert M. "Bob" Metcalfe's rustic cabin on Green's Island, Maine. Like Dreyfoos, Metcalfe had a passion for technology from a young age and set his sights on MIT. After continuing his education at Harvard, while at Xerox Palo Alto Research Center, Metcalfe (with D. R. Boggs) invented what has come to be known as Ethernet, the most widely used technology computers use to talk to one another. One of his email usernames is "etherdad." Metcalfe also founded 3Com Corporation; he shares his engineering enthusiasm through writing and mentoring, and serves with Dreyfoos on the MIT Corporation.

Gary Lickle, a self-described "machine guy," is young enough to be a second son to Dreyfoos. They've been sharing the same sports interests since the 1980s, says Lickle. "The first time we really spent together was as copilots to Isla Mujeres, Cancun, for a fishing trip on Pete Benoit's 98-foot 'mother ship,' *Repeat*, where Pete hosted groups as Alex does on *Silver Cloud*. We bonded quickly." (Like Dreyfoos, Constant "Pete" Benoit had been an avid diver, fisherman, and pilot.)

Lickle calls Dreyfoos "a master at putting together people of various backgrounds and being the common denominator in discussing ideas. Probably none of us would ever spend this kind of quality time together otherwise. He has a knack for mixing it up in a very good way that opens up everybody's eyes. *Silver Cloud* is a great platform on which to do it, taking people—especially non-water people—out of their comfort zone, in places they've possibly never been before." Lickle describes the boats, planes, diving, and photography as "our drug of choice—and Alex shares his high."

Carroll Peacock also describes the delight in these trips. "Alex flew us down on his jet for three or four days on *Silver Cloud* in the Bahamas—Gary Lickle, Marshall Criser, Dick Johnson, Jim Beasley, and me. We did nothing but eat, talk, and enjoy each other. Except Alex—at his age!—did some scuba diving with Gary."

In 2013, while getting ready for another trip on *Silver Cloud*, Lickle realized he and Dreyfoos had not been diving since Bora Bora two years earlier. The younger man thought his friend, at 80, might have given up this particular activity, but when Lickle inquired whether they would be "getting wet," Dreyfoos replied, "Absolutely!" A year later, Dreyfoos hosted several groups of friends coming and going during six weeks of diving in French Polynesia.

"He's still fearless," declares Lickle, "and if you're lucky enough to be his friend, and he calls and asks what you are doing on a given day, you will want to clear your calendar." On one such occasion, the pair took Dreyfoos' helicopter west to Clewiston, Florida, for lunch, where he landed in the parking lot at Sonny's BBQ. "On the way back, he landed on Lake Okeechobee near some bass fishermen and unrolled the electric trolling motor. The shock value alone was worth canceling whatever else I would've done that day."

Through the Lens Clearly

Dreyfoos returned from the SWATH voyage with an estimated 10,000 personal photographs, one tenth of which he considered good enough to share in his web albums at Google's Picasa. He has had a lifelong fascination for capturing photographic images, not just for improving the technical process. Having special access to exotic locales on his trips with the YPO (Young Presidents' Organization), his appetite for fine photography grew. It did not hurt that he and George Mergens had built their own state-of-the-art photographic processing lab.

After years of designing the interiors of Dreyfoos' homes, planes, offices, and boats, Susan Smith sees his photos as the theme running through every project. "Some of those photos, I've worked with since 1978," she notes. "The photos tell Alex's life and travels, unlike any others I've ever seen."

About a hundred photographs anchor the ambiance of the *Silver Cloud* SWATH, all taken before the 2008 to 2010 voyage. Each photo was carefully sized, printed, framed, and weighed in the US, and then sent to Germany for installation. It was a project in itself to choose the best for each interior area, combining some in small groupings. "Alex enjoyed participating in the process," says Smith. "Finding the correct lighting to illuminate each picture, for example, was complex, choosing the size in relation to the light measured off the wall."

While sharing a meal at a restaurant in Germany, Smith wondered aloud to her friend and client, "It's so interesting to me that I can hang three or four photos of yours from different areas of the world, yet they all coordinate in some way. What is the common thing that ties them together?"

Dreyfoos knew. "I don't just take random shots. I like to take a photo that tells the entire story." As with everything else, he puts careful thought into organizing and composing each picture, and he doesn't accept limitations. When *Silver Cloud* was in Portofino, Italy, Dreyfoos climbed a nearby hill—what Floridians call a mountain—to photograph it from a certain angle. There were bushes in the way, so the next day the chief engineer carried a ladder up the hill for the photographer to stand on.

The shot of *Silver Cloud* near London's Tower Bridge was a bit more complicated. Dreyfoos was denied opening of the bridge for *Silver Cloud*, which he learned required advance application, so Capt. Martin turned the boat around to leave. When the bridge started to open for a second boat, Dreyfoos saw an opportunity. He had Martin drop him off on the riverside—where he talked his way onto the roof of a barge to improve his vantage point—and then back up *Silver Cloud* into the shot. After the second boat and its wake had disappeared, the composition was complete. "Of course," Martin adds, "when we tied up at the dock, we got a visit from the authorities for lingering so long."

One photo that came out beautifully is of the *Silver Cloud* Burger in front of Pfalzgrafenstein, a 14th-century toll castle on the Rhine River. It was anything but peaceful, says Martin. "She looks like she's cruising at a good rate, but actually we were trying to sit still, as the river was running six knots and we were in a one-way traffic lane. Every time I got positioned in front of the castle, more traffic came and yelled at me for being on the wrong side of the river."

In the 1980s, Dreyfoos went on an African safari with his old friends the Shlossmans and the Browns. According to Bernie Shlossman, "We would find an animal stalking its prey, and we'd have to sit for what felt like hours waiting for Alex to take his photograph." Not that Shlossman minded. "I took about 20 pictures. Alex took about 700. On a wall of my home, I have a dozen photos from that safari, taken and enlarged and given to me by Alex. My kids fight over who will inherit them."

Meticulous in the reproduction of his travel photos, Dreyfoos chooses one each year to adorn the 700 or so Christmas cards he and Renate send out. Some recipients collect them.

Now in a new phase of his life, Dreyfoos has the time to pursue taking his work to a more public audience. He was invited to show his work at the Palm Beach Photographic Centre in West Palm Beach and the Cultural Council of Palm Beach County; both invited him back a second year. He answered repeated requests to publish his photos with *A Photographic Odyssey: Around the World with Alexander W. Dreyfoos,* a 10-inch-by-15-inch cocktail table book of 587 of his favorite images taken over 60-plus years in 60 countries. The perspectives vary—on land, on the water, and from the air—including a large percentage of underwater photographs. The Cultural Council of Palm Beach County published the book in 2014.

For advice in this new arena, he often turns to Rena Blades, who tries to tell it like it is to this council founder and donor. "Alex always wants to know the truth, and the truth is, he's not your typical photographer. He has super high energy and a scientist personality—that's his core—constantly analyzing in a persistent way, dissecting and parsing things out, trying to break it into bits to be understood, but sometimes you can't do that. Alex is masterful in his scientific approach to the art of the image. He is an aspiring artist competing with the rest of the world, and he's vulnerable there." Still, Blades clarifies, "Alex is warm, not dryly analytical. He's absolutely fine making himself vulnerable, which is unusual with a person of his stature and accomplishments."

Michael Hawley, a former holder of the MIT Dreyfoos Chair, longtime friend, and fellow photographer recalls an occurrence at MIT: "My class took about 100,000 shots for a program on expeditions. Instead of developing them into slides set in cardboard frames, we left them uncut and asked Kodak for their best film scanner. We set up this fancy gadget at MIT, which Alex saw and loved. He went on eBay and found the same machine, missing a part or two, for a ridiculously low price, then grabbed the missing parts from my lab and set it up in his home office. There was no better way to scan film then. It was typical of Alex every step of the way." Hawley relates to that blend of art and science. "I think for both of us, our creativism began with photography and expanded as we were drawn into it and as the scientific aspects of it were added to it."

For Dreyfoos, it all comes back to the years with his father in the Adirondack Mountains with cameras.

Back to the Woods

Though Dreyfoos embraced his life in South Florida and traveling the world, a part of him has unceasingly treasured the wooded lakes in the Adirondacks that he had enjoyed as a child. Even after his father's death in 1951, Dreyfoos visited the area each year until the Air Force sent him to Germany in 1954.

His family's tent-platform on Burnt Island on Saranac Lake was supposed to be theirs forever. So it was a shock to Dreyfoos when he returned to the US in 1956 to find that his mother had taken it all away. [She had also discarded Dreyfoos' collection of about a thousand movie star photos from his father's work.] "While I was in Germany," he recalls, "my mother arranged to have the permit transferred, and then sold all of our boats, furnishings, and equipment to the local postmaster. I was furious, and by then, the state had decided not to issue any new permits." There was a modest resort at the east end of Lower Saranac Lake, where New York State had been unable to purchase to make part of the Adirondack Park. For several summers, Dreyfoos and his first wife, Joan, rented a cabin and boat for a few weeks.

Finally, in 1963, Dreyfoos asked Harry Duso for help in regaining a campsite. As Don Duso remembers, "My father advised Alex that the Potter family had a permit for Knobby Island (also called 'Green Island'), and for financial and health reasons needed to give it up: 'Buy their gear, put your name on the permit, send it in, and I will make sure it is issued to you.'"

Dreyfoos did, and Duso kept his word, even constructing an additional tent platform for his old friend. For nine years, Dreyfoos' own children enjoyed a taste of summers on the lake in the woods, even if it wasn't Burnt Island.

While Dreyfoos watched, platforms were gradually removed as aging campers gave up their permits. Although Dreyfoos had been a New York State resident when he acquired his camp, he reasoned that other residents might object to his having a camp now that he lived in Florida. After all, it was New York State taxpayers that made them possible. He also noticed that the small amount of lakefront property available was inexpensive relative to Palm Beach waterfront. So, in 1972, Dreyfoos purchased property on Lake Kiwassa, connected by waterway to Lower Saranac Lake. "It had a rundown, several-bedroom cottage," he says, "a one-room bunkhouse, and a beat-up boathouse. It also had 650 feet of lakefront with a gorgeous view of the mountains—and in the same direction as what we had on Burnt Island."

Working with conservation regulations, in 1992 Dreyfoos was able to remove, replace, and add to the structures to provide a comfortable summer home. He was inspired by the "great camps of the Adirondacks he had seen as a child, grand compounds built by grand families in the late 19th century. He and Renate often host friends and family at the retreat, including Renate's mother, who otherwise lives in St. Augustine, Florida, close to Renate's sister Elfi Norris.

When Amin and Julie Khoury visited, Dreyfoos' helicopter sat by the house on permanent floats. "He took me on a long tour of the area in his Eurocopter," recalls Amin, "telling me stories and pointing things out. I enjoyed that *he* enjoyed sharing his love and memories of the area." More memories float near the helicopter, in the 19-foot, 1937 Chris-Craft Dreyfoos found, just like the one his father had purchased for him. Dreyfoos took great pleasure in having it restored.

Gary Lickle and Michele Henry accessed the lake house easily in their seaplane. "In the Adirondacks," Gary explains, "Alex is a different person than anywhere else, a deeper person, talking about the history of his family and how he formed his desire to be on the water. It wasn't what I would've expected from the MIT grad—more rough-and-tumble in a tent. As he tells you, 'That's the point where we jumped off the log,' you can feel it. It's a different touch point with him, more emotional."

Dreyfoos still has poignant memories of whooping young boys chasing each other, his father calling the family to dinner, and the plaintive strains of his mother's cello through the trees. In the end, it didn't matter that someone else had his family's tent platform site. By the late 1970s the state eliminated the camp permit system and removed all signs of the campsites. All of the land has reverted to its natural splendor.

A Changing Diagnosis

From the simplicity of Burnt Island to exotic locales, life has handed Alex Dreyfoos some remarkable experiences. Now he adds Alzheimer's disease to the list: "I first became concerned about my memory while flying. Air traffic controllers gave me instructions by radio, which I had always easily remembered and executed. When I found myself having to write down their instructions and often asking them to repeat them, my fears went to Alzheimer's, as my mother had suffered from the disease."

Alex and Renate Dreyfoos were early subscribers to 23andMe Personal Genome Service, which reached one million members in 2015; Dreyfoos was number 424. Analysis of his DNA found APOE variant 4, the gene mutation that indicates a tendency for Alzheimer's in those of European ancestry.

An initial medical diagnosis indicated a strong probability that Dreyfoos was correct, reinforced by repeated neuropsychological tests at roughly one-year intervals. He consulted Dr. Bradley T. Hyman, director of the Alzheimer's Disease Research Center at the MassGeneral Institute for Neurodegenerative Disease. Hyman said although there were brain scans, a true diagnosis could still only be confirmed at autopsy, but he agreed that it was likely Dreyfoos had Alzheimer's.

Like many others in this predicament, Alex and Renate Dreyfoos worried about how their lives would change as the condition progressed. Then, in 2012, they heard about a breakthrough test that could determine whether or not Drey-foos had Alzheimer's disease. While serving on the scientific advisory board at Scripps, Dreyfoos met Nobel Prize winner Dr. Paul Greengard of Rockefeller University, who put him in touch with neurologist Dr. Samuel E. Gandy of Mount Sinai Hospital's Alzheimer's Disease Research Center in New York.

Dreyfoos underwent a positron emission tomography (PET) scan using a new radioactive dye that could detect telltale amyloid plaques in the brain; their presence indicates Alzheimer's. Dreyfoos recalls, "Gandy expected a positive result because of my history. Happily, they found no such plaques—he said I did not have the disease after all." Gandy said he was "shocked beyond belief. The chances of this happening—the first scan being negative in this context—are just infinitesimal." Once again Dreyfoos could enjoy each day and not worry that he needed to get his affairs in order quickly.

CBS Evening News interviewed Dreyfoos on June 19, 2012, regarding this test. When his friend Gary Lickle saw the segment, he thought, "When the world says no, Alex is always the one to figure out a way to conquer something—a cultural deficit, seasickness, and now Alzheimer's."

Wishful thinking.

At MassGeneral, Hyman wasn't convinced by the Mount Sinai results. He said the test was not sensitive enough to read small amounts of plaque. He still felt that Dreyfoos likely had Alzheimer's, but if he had only small amounts of undetectable plaque, at least the disease might be progressing at a slow pace.

Dreyfoos' sister Evelyn, one and a half years younger, has developed Alzheimer's to the point that she was moved to a memory care facility in 2015. However his own health proceeds, Dreyfoos is aware of his good fortune: "I am under the care of this brain trust of top-notch experts—who don't always agree—and I can travel to them as needed. I can take advantage of the latest research. But I cannot stop my Alzheimer's. If it is my fate, I can only face it straight on, with the most knowledge and as-sistance I can gather."

Despite Renate's great concern about Alex's health, she knows that this pragmatic approach of his to everything will not waiver. She helps him in-vestigate all the options available and speaks openly with him about the cir-cumstances. "I am prepared for a future by his side, whatever that means," she says emphatically. "We are together and will remain so."

Dreyfoos' investigation looks beyond his personal dilemma. "I will also continue to support research against what I believe will be a devastating disease for many to follow me, becoming a huge healthcare cost for our country and the world." Even a sample of the estimated figures provided by the Alzheimer's Association in 2015 is shocking:

- 1 in 9 people age 65 and older has Alzheimer's disease.

- Of those with Alzheimer's, 4 percent are under age 65, and 15 percent age 65-74.

- The first baby boomers, a large segment of the US population, reached age 65 in 2011, increasing the future number of people at risk for Alzheimer's.

- Every 67 seconds, someone in the US develops Alzheimer's. By 2050, this will increase to every 33 seconds.

- By 2025, the people over 65 with Alzheimer's may be 7.1 million, 40 percent more than at present. By 2050, the number may nearly triple.

- The number of people living past 85 will greatly increase due to medical breakthroughs, and social and environmental conditions.

- It is difficult to determine how many people die from Alzheimer's, but it increases continually, while deaths from other causes decrease. In 2015, about 700,000 Americans age 65 or older will die with Alzheimer's.

- One-third of all seniors who die in a given year have been diagnosed with dementia.

- The estimated economic value of unpaid care of people with Alzheimer's and other dementia was $18 billion in 2014. These caregivers suffer their own emotional and physical stress, loss of income, and higher mortality, which adds to the cost of a patient's illness in the long term. Long-distance caregivers also have specific challenges.

- The costs of home health care, adult day centers, assisted living, hospital stays, nursing homes, and hospice for Alzheimer's and other dementias are expected to total $226 billion in 2015 and increase to more than $1 trillion per year by 2050. This is a five-fold increase in present government spending under Medicare and Medicaid and a nearly five-fold increase in out-of-pocket spending.

Dreyfoos feels strongly that, "As death from other diseases are reduced and our population lives longer, Alzheimer's research should become a much higher priority for the National Institutes of Health, if for no other reason than the potential return on investment in terms of reduced healthcare costs."

Passion and Purpose

Dreyfoos' friend George Michel says in the Foreword, "Lots of people do things with a purpose, but I don't know anyone who does so with more passion than Alex." At a young age, encouraged by his father, Dreyfoos found passion for many things, such as mechanics, photography, and electronics. Though he may have disliked sharing his mother with her musical passion, that same passionate nature enabled him to achieve great things. His sense of purpose helped him rebuild a car so he could drive, took him to MIT, and carried him on a path of inventiveness and determination that brought great rewards to many people and institutions. His deepest passions, once developed, never waned; he devoted 13 years to bringing the Kravis Center to fruition.

On a personal note, Dreyfoos waited almost 30 years to make Renate his wife. His next purpose was to take her around the world, combining his passions for travel and photography. First he had to conquer her seasickness by finding a yacht design she could cruise on comfortably. Then he was stopped again and again because of terrorism on the other side of the world. During this time, increasing age and a diagnosis of Alzheimer's made everything more difficult. George Michel probably speaks for most people who know him well: "There was never a doubt in my mind that Alex would eventually find a way to complete the mission. To me the time, effort, cost, and risk involved in achieving circumnavigation—the passion and purpose—are more significant than the technical achievement."

A favorite photo of Renate Dreyfoos, taken by her husband in 2008.

The Dreyfoos family on the *Silver Cloud* Feadship, celebrating Christmas 2003 in the Caribbean waters of St. Martin: (left to right) Mike and Cathy Carter, Mac Carter, Michelle Carter, Travis Dreyfoos, Alex and Renate Dreyfoos, Aron Dreyfoos, Julie and Robert Dreyfoos.

Celebrating Dreyfoos' 80th birthday in 2012 are some of his then closest surviving, longest-known friends, (left to right): Llwyd Ecclestone (45 years), George Michel (64 years), and George Matthews (46 years).

Dreyfoos photographing manta rays and sharks in French Polynesia in 2014.

Dreyfoos fly fishing in the 1960s on the Raquette River, New York, and on a 2002 YPO trip to Alaska.

(left to right) Gary Lickle, Jim Beasley, Marshall Criser, Dick Johnson, and Carroll Peacock, on a *Silver Cloud* trip to the Bahamas, 2006.

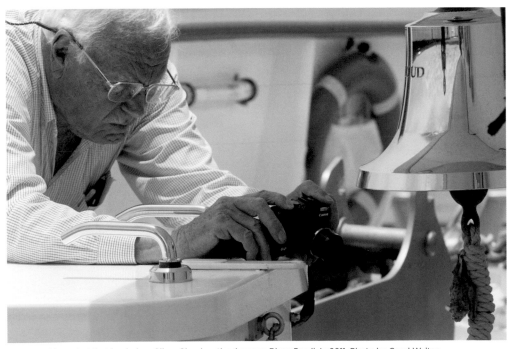

Photographing a bat that landed on *Silver Cloud* on the Amazon River, Brazil, in 2011. Photo by Carol Walton.

Dreyfoos' grandson Travis Dreyfoos shows he shares a family passion. (2015)

The following three photos by Dreyfoos come with stories typical of his going to some lengths to capture an image:

The *Silver Cloud* Burger at the Tower Bridge in London, England, 1999.

The *Silver Cloud* Burger in front of the Pfalgrafenstein toll castle on the Rhine River, Germany, 2001.

The *Silver Cloud* Feadship in Portofino, Italy, 2003.

An example of the Christmas cards sent by Dreyfoos for decades, featuring his travel photos; this 2009 photo was taken in the Aleutian Islands, Alaska.

This 2011 card is of Milford Sound, New Zealand, with a tiny *Silver Cloud* in the center.

Father and son with cameras (the father's a Graflex, the son's a Kodak Brownie Reflex) in the 1940s.

Dreyfoos' sister, Evelyn, visiting him in the Adirondacks.

Dreyfoos' AStar helicopter (top) and second 1937 Chris-Craft (see Chapter 3) "parked" by the boathouse of his Lake Kiwassa home.

Dreyfoos' Lake Kiwassa property before (bottom, 1980) and after (top, 2006) several phased renovations.

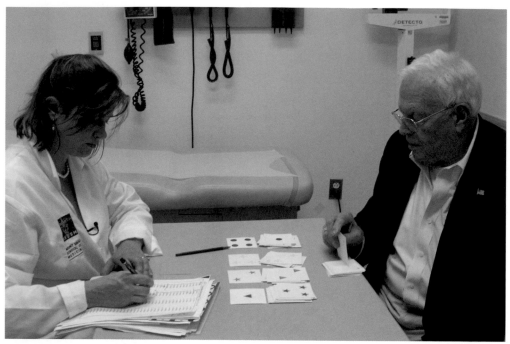

Dreyfoos taking a neuropsychological test in 2012 at Mount Sinai General Hospital's Alzheimer's Disease Research Center in New York.

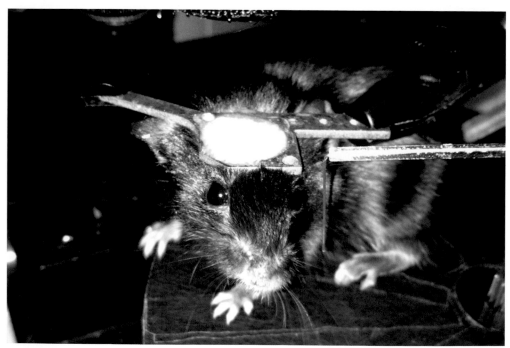

Researchers at the MassGeneral Institute for Neurodegenerative Disease bred this mouse with the APOE4 gene of Alzheimer's disease (which Dreyfoos has) and inserted a glass plate to study its brain through a microscope.

Dreyfoos in Fiji, 2014, using the Poseidon SE7EN Rebreather Scuba Dive System. He says, "With no air bubbles, the fish are not the least bit leery of me, and I can get great close-up shots."

Pink anemone fish photographed by Dreyfoos in the Maldives, 2015.

Coming Home

by Alex Dreyfoos

A watercolor painting celebrating Dreyfoos' life,
by Pamela Wallace Ohlsen, commissioned by Dreyfoos' sister,
Evelyn Dreyfoos Spelman, as a gift in 2006.

Looking out across Lake Kiwassa, I see Mt. Ampersand rising from the mist over the lake. The view here at our camp near Saranac Lake, New York, often carries me back to my youth, when our family spent summers here. The calmness of the Adirondack Mountains still eases my active mind and sets me instead to rumination.

As I consider the many years of my life, I feel satisfaction at having realized my dreams, met fascinating people along the way, and, quite simply, experienced the best the world has to offer. As if that were not enough, I have enjoyed the privilege of helping to create and raise two wonderful children, made many lifelong friends, and experienced true love.

To have been this fortunate is humbling. Is it kismet? I doubt it. I'm not a great believer in fate. I believe in determination and hard work. But even those can only get you so far. What I have come to understand—and the painstaking process of assembling and reviewing this book has supported this contention—is that there are few achievements in my career that are totally mine. Starting with my father and mother, there have always been others supporting, inspiring, and challenging me to take life to the next level. Thus, I have never assumed that my prosperity belonged to me alone.

My philanthropy and support of cultural, educational, and research institutions, as well as civic causes, represent the contributions of hundreds of people who have helped me to succeed in life. You have met many of them on these pages, and I am grateful to every one of them, and to others. I believe that three in particular, by their tremendous impact on my life, have also indirectly affected many others in positive ways, perhaps even yours. These are the "what if's" of my life, but they reach much, much further.

At MIT in 1951, Professor Arthur C. Hardy reached out to a 19-year-old student he knew only by his father's obituary. Hardy helped me see how I could combine art and science, not just for my personal good, but in what I would offer to the world. He helped guide my formal education within MIT and at Harvard Business School, from which I reaped untold benefits that permeate much of what I have achieved.

These are lights that, once lit, have never burned out.

After the Kravis Center opened and I sold the television station, I helped make it possible to improve the facilities of the public high school for the arts on the property adjacent to the Kravis Center, which is now named the Alexander W. Dreyfoos School of the Arts. As I have repeatedly presented to the powers-that-be, I would like to see the school's name changed to the Dreyfoos School of the Arts *and Sciences*, to place emphasis on the importance of both areas of study. Whether or not my efforts succeed, my own life has convinced me that this combination provides balance for the most productive of thinkers. I am not alone.

In 2010, Marc Tucker, then president of the National Center on Education and the Economy, was quoted in the *New York Times*:

> *One thing we know about creativity is that it typically occurs when people who have mastered two or more quite different fields use the framework in one to think afresh about the other. . . . But if you spend your*

whole life in one silo, you will never have either the knowledge or mental agility to do the synthesis, connect the dots, which is usually where the next great breakthrough is found.

History has given us many examples of lateral thinkers who lived in both "silos": Ben Franklin, Leonardo da Vinci, and many Nobel Prize winners, from Albert Einstein and Winston Churchill to our own Dr. Gerald Edelman at Scripps, who trained to be a concert violinist before he switched to science. This awareness clearly started long before Professor Hardy instilled it in me.

My friend and technology designer Bran Ferren, expounded on this belief at the 2014 TED Conference. Though a generation younger than me, Bran also had artistic parents but felt drawn to structural design, and also scavenged the streets of New York for electronic surplus. His personal epiphany occurred not in college, but on a visit to the Pantheon in Rome at age nine. Through this project of "unprecedented creative vision and technical complexity," said Bran:

> *I came to understand that the worlds of art and design were not, in fact, incompatible with science and engineering. I realized, when combined, you could create things that were amazing that couldn't be done in either domain alone. But in school, with few exceptions, they were treated as separate worlds, and they still are. My teachers told me that I had to get serious and focus on one or the other. However, urging me to specialize only caused me to really appreciate those polymaths . . . who did exactly the opposite. And this led me to embrace and want to be in both worlds.*

Bran offers an instruction manual for developing our future thinkers and doers where they are naturally meant to go:

> *The ingredients for the next Pantheons are all around us, just waiting for visionary people with the broad knowledge, multidisciplinary skills, and intense passion to harness them to make their dreams a reality. But these people don't spontaneously pop into existence. They need to be nurtured and encouraged from when they're little kids. We need to love them and help them discover their passions. We need to encourage them to work hard and help them understand that failure is a necessary ingredient for*

success, as is perseverance. We need to help them to find their own role models, and give them the confidence to believe in themselves and to believe that anything is possible, and ... we need to encourage them to find their own path, even if it's very different from our own.

Though I obviously support a school that can check off many of these "need to's," I would not want such talented students to be limited in their thinking.

I cannot overemphasize how much I am beholden to George Mergens—my friend, business partner, and teacher. George taught me that where a person goes to school and what degrees he (or she) earns mean nothing, compared to how he uses his innate intelligence and education. Largely self-taught, George was a natural engineer, a mechanical genius who could visualize and fabricate objects. While I, with my MIT and Harvard degrees, could conceive of and design electronic circuits, I could only describe mechanical needs by their intended functions. Friends and colleagues often asked George for his wise, humble, and thoughtful opinions.

I cherish the time that George and I spent together, sharing many common interests beyond the art and science of photography and electronics. But nothing can compare to our excitement in the discovery and engineering of solutions that resulted in new technologies. We encouraged each other through the bad times and celebrated the successful ones. With the Video Color Negative Analyzer, we did our best to push Kodak into the electronic age! That was no small success, considering Kodak's entire history was based mostly in chemistry. We obviously didn't push them far enough, as not fully pursuing the potential of electronics has left them, unfortunately, in bankruptcy.

Sometimes George had to temper my enthusiasm. Of the two of us, he was the patient, conservative one who put careful thought into everything he did.

If I had never met George Mergens, you would be reading a different book. The development and evolution of the VCNA would have taken a different turn, and many of the endeavors that ultimately benefitted from its introduction might not have occurred. I miss my friend George, and I am forever thankful to have shared some of the best moments in my life with him.

George's tragic and untimely death shook the foundations of all that motivated me. Without him, it was difficult to consider how I could continue on the path of creativity and invention we had started together. I found myself avoiding anything that reminded me of him. Our common undertakings had been aimed at inventing something new or increasing the value and profitability of our enterprises. But none of that was important when George was not there to share in the process. I decided to invest in the local community that had given George and me so much support over the years. My first goal was to devote myself to building the Raymond F. Kravis Center for the Performing Arts in West Palm Beach.

Pouring myself into cultural and civic causes also masked the pain of my longing for the woman I knew I would always love, even in absentia. Had Renate and I married earlier, I daresay I would have turned all my attention to her. Would I have started, quit, or moved more slowly with a performing arts center? Nevertheless, there were many very talented and capable people involved in the effort, and who's to say who else might have grabbed the ball and run with it?

What if?

Maybe I should believe in kismet at least a little bit, because Renate and I did finally marry, and she has given me the personal fulfillment of which I had long dreamed. Since our marriage, we have explored the oceans and wonders of the world together. We have yet to tire of each other's company after tens of thousands of nautical miles covered in our expeditions. Everything turned out exactly as it was meant to be after all. ⇐

— THE END —

PHOTO BY GARY LICKLE

Appendix

The Ancestry of Alexander W. Dreyfoos

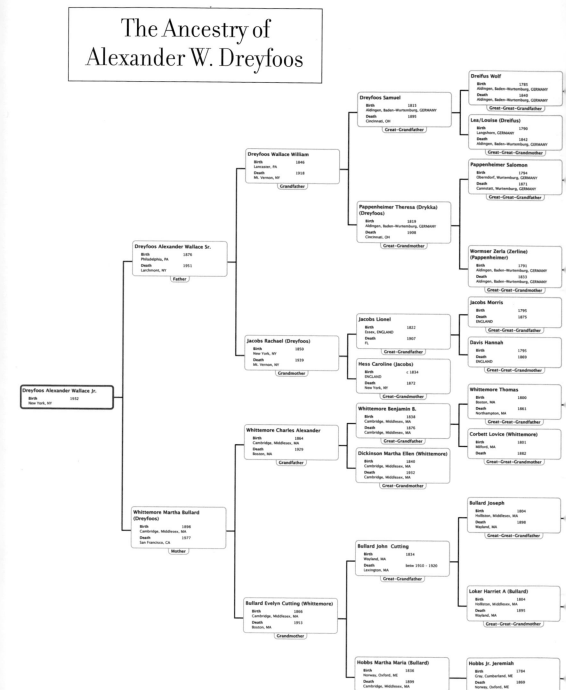

Dreyfoos Alexander Wallace Jr.
Birth 1932
New York, NY

Dreyfoos Alexander Wallace Sr.
Birth 1876
Philadelphia, PA
Death 1951
Larchmont, NY
Father

Whittemore Martha Bullard (Dreyfoos)
Birth 1898
Cambridge, Middlesex, MA
Death 1977
San Francisco, CA
Mother

Dreyfoos Wallace William
Birth 1846
Lancaster, PA
Death 1918
Mt. Vernon, NY
Grandfather

Jacobs Rachael (Dreyfoos)
Birth 1850
New York, NY
Death 1939
Mt. Vernon, NY
Grandmother

Whittemore Charles Alexander
Birth 1864
Cambridge, Middlesex, MA
Death 1929
Boston, MA
Grandfather

Bullard Evelyn Cutting (Whittemore)
Birth 1866
Cambridge, Middlesex, MA
Death 1953
Boston, MA
Grandmother

Dreyfoos Samuel
Birth 1815
Aldingen, Baden-Wurtemburg, GERMANY
Death 1895
Cincinnati, OH
Great-Grandfather

Pappenheimer Theresa (Drykka) (Dreyfoos)
Birth 1819
Aldingen, Baden-Wurtemburg, GERMANY
Death 1908
Cincinnati, OH
Great-Grandmother

Jacobs Lionel
Birth 1822
Essex, ENGLAND
Death 1907
FL
Great-Grandfather

Hess Caroline (Jacobs)
Birth c 1834
ENGLAND
Death 1872
New York, NY
Great-Grandmother

Whittemore Benjamin B.
Birth 1838
Cambridge, Middlesex, MA
Death 1876
Cambridge, Middlesex, MA
Great-Grandfather

Dickinson Martha Ellen (Whittemore)
Birth 1840
Cambridge, Middlesex, MA
Death 1932
Cambridge, Middlesex, MA
Great-Grandmother

Bullard John Cutting
Birth 1834
Wayland, MA
Death betw 1910 - 1920
Lexington, MA
Great-Grandfather

Hobbs Martha Maria (Bullard)
Birth 1836
Norway, Oxford, ME
Death 1899
Cambridge, Middlesex, MA
Great-Grandmother

Dreifus Wolf
Birth 1785
Aldingen, Baden-Wurtemburg, GERMANY
Death 1840
Aldingen, Baden-Wurtemburg, GERMANY
Great-Great-Grandfather

Lea/Louise (Dreifus)
Birth 1790
Langshorn, GERMANY
Death 1842
Aldingen, Baden-Wurtemburg, GERMANY
Great-Great-Grandmother

Pappenheimer Salomon
Birth 1794
Oberndorf, Wurtemburg, GERMANY
Death 1871
Cannstatt, Wurtemburg, GERMANY
Great-Great-Grandfather

Wormser Zerla (Zerline) (Pappenheimer)
Birth 1791
Aldingen, Baden-Wurtemburg, GERMANY
Death 1833
Aldingen, Baden-Wurtemburg, GERMANY
Great-Great-Grandmother

Jacobs Morris
Birth 1795
Death 1875
ENGLAND
Great-Great-Grandfather

Davis Hannah
Birth 1795
ENGLAND
Death 1869
Great-Great-Grandmother

Whittemore Thomas
Birth 1800
Boston, MA
Death 1861
Northampton, MA
Great-Great-Grandfather

Corbett Lovice (Whittemore)
Birth 1801
Milford, MA
Death 1882
Great-Great-Grandmother

Bullard Joseph
Birth 1804
Holliston, Middlesex, MA
Death 1898
Wayland, MA
Great-Great-Grandfather

Loker Harriet A (Bullard)
Birth 1804
Holliston, Middlesex, MA
Death 1895
Wayland, MA
Great-Great-Grandmother

Hobbs Jr. Jeremiah
Birth 1784
Gray, Cumberland, ME
Death 1869
Norway, Oxford, ME
Great-Great-Grandfather

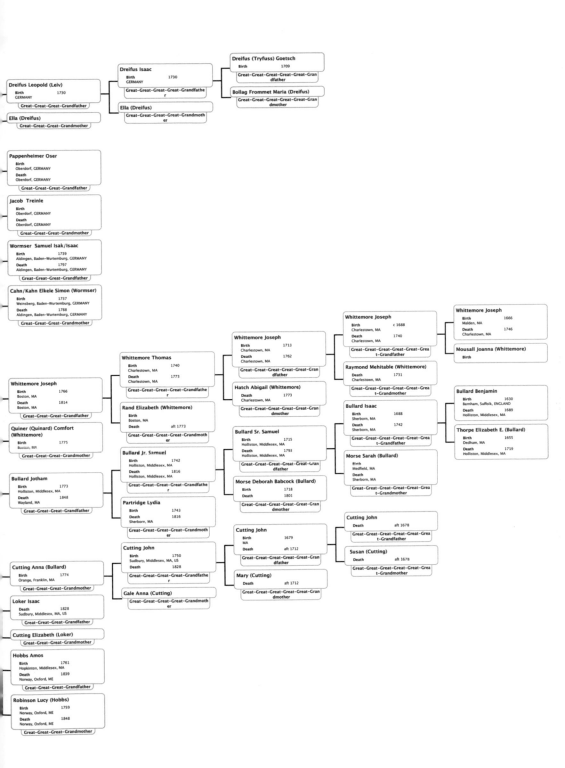

Dreifus Leopold (Leiv)
Birth 1730
GERMANY
Great-Great-Great-Great-Grandfather

Ella (Dreifus)
Great-Great-Great-Great-Grandmother

Dreifus Isaac
Birth 1730
GERMANY
Great-Great-Great-Great-Grandfather

Ella (Dreifus)
Great-Great-Great-Great-Grandmother

Dreifus (Tryfuss) Goetsch
Birth 1709
Great-Great-Great-Great-Great-Grandfather

Bollag Frommet Maria (Dreifus)
Great-Great-Great-Great-Great-Grandmother

Pappenheimer Oser
Birth
Oberdorf, GERMANY
Death
Oberdorf, GERMANY
Great-Great-Great-Great-Grandfather

Jacob Treinle
Birth
Oberdorf, GERMANY
Death
Oberdorf, GERMANY
Great-Great-Great-Great-Grandmother

Wormser Samuel Isak/Isaac
Birth 1739
Aldingen, Baden-Wurtemburg, GERMANY
Death 1797
Aldingen, Baden-Wurtemburg, GERMANY
Great-Great-Great-Great-Grandfather

Cahn/Kahn Elkele Simon (Wormser)
Birth 1737
Weinsberg, Baden-Wurtemburg, GERMANY
Death 1788
Aldingen, Baden-Wurtemburg, GERMANY
Great-Great-Great-Great-Grandmother

Whittemore Joseph
Birth 1766
Boston, MA
Death 1814
Boston, MA
Great-Great-Great-Great-Grandfather

Quiner (Quinard) Comfort (Whittemore)
Birth 1775
Boston, MA
Great-Great-Great-Grandmother

Bullard Jotham
Birth 1773
Holliston, Middlesex, MA
Death 1848
Wayland, MA
Great-Great-Great-Great-Grandfather

Cutting Anna (Bullard)
Birth 1774
Orange, Franklin, MA
Great-Great-Great-Grandmother

Loker Isaac
Death 1828
Sudbury, Middlesex, MA, US
Great-Great-Great-Grandfather

Cutting Elizabeth (Loker)
Great-Great-Great-Grandmother

Hobbs Amos
Birth 1761
Hopkinton, Middlesex, MA
Death 1839
Norway, Oxford, ME
Great-Great-Great-Grandfather

Robinson Lucy (Hobbs)
Birth 1759
Norway, Oxford, ME
Death 1848
Norway, Oxford, ME
Great-Great-Great-Grandmother

Whittemore Thomas
Birth 1740
Charlestown, MA
Death 1773
Charlestown, MA
Great-Great-Great-Great-Grandfather

Rand Elizabeth (Whittemore)
Birth
Boston, MA
Death aft 1773
Great-Great-Great-Great-Grandmother

Bullard Jr. Samuel
Birth 1742
Holliston, Middlesex, MA
Death 1816
Holliston, Middlesex, MA
Great-Great-Great-Great-Grandfather

Partridge Lydia
Birth 1743
Death 1816
Sherborn, MA
Great-Great-Great-Great-Grandmother

Cutting John
Birth 1750
Sudbury, Middlesex, MA, US
Death 1828
Great-Great-Great-Great-Grandfather

Gale Anna (Cutting)
Great-Great-Great-Great-Grandmother

Whittemore Joseph
Birth 1713
Charlestown, MA
Death 1762
Charlestown, MA
Great-Great-Great-Great-Grandfather

Hatch Abigail (Whittemore)
Death 1773
Charlestown, MA
Great-Great-Great-Great-Great-Grandmother

Bullard Sr. Samuel
Birth 1715
Holliston, Middlesex, MA
Death 1793
Holliston, Middlesex, MA
Great-Great-Great-Great-Grandfather

Morse Deborah Babcock (Bullard)
Birth 1718
Death 1801
Great-Great-Great-Great-Great-Grandmother

Cutting John
Birth 1679
MA
Death aft 1712
Great-Great-Great-Great-Grandfather

Mary (Cutting)
Death aft 1712
Great-Great-Great-Great-Great-Grandmother

Whittemore Joseph
Birth c 1688
Charlestown, MA
Death 1740
Charlestown, MA
Great-Great-Great-Great-Great-Great-Grandfather

Raymond Mehitable (Whittemore)
Birth 1731
Charlestown, MA
Great-Great-Great-Great-Great-Grandmother

Bullard Isaac
Birth 1688
Sherborn, MA
Death 1742
Sherborn, MA
Great-Great-Great-Great-Great-Grandfather

Morse Sarah (Bullard)
Birth
Medfield, MA
Death
Sherborn, MA
Great-Great-Great-Great-Great-Grandmother

Cutting John
Death aft 1678
Great-Great-Great-Great-Great-Grandfather

Susan (Cutting)
Death aft 1678
Great-Great-Great-Great-Great-Grandmother

Whittemore Joseph
Birth 1666
Malden, MA
Death 1746
Charlestown, MA

Mousall Joanna (Whittemore)
Birth

Bullard Benjamin
Birth 1630
Barnham, Suffolk, ENGLAND
Death 1689
Holliston, Middlesex, MA

Thorpe Elizabeth E. (Bullard)
Birth 1655
Dedham, MA
Death 1719
Holliston, Middlesex, MA

425

Alexander W. Dreyfoos
Awards and Honors

1980 The Palm Beach Post: Business Leader of the Year

1985 Palm Beach Chamber of Commerce Board of Directors Special Award

1991 Nova University Entrepreneur Hall of Fame

1992 Florida Master Entrepreneur of the Year (Ernst & Young and Merrill Lynch)

1992 Palm Beach Atlantic University American Free Enterprise Award

1992 Palm Beach Chamber of Commerce One and Only Award

1992 The Palm Beach Post Man of the Year

1994 Northwood University Outstanding Business Leader

1995 Town of Palm Beach United Way Alexis de Tocqueville Distinguished Citizen Award

1996 Florida Atlantic University Entrepreneur of the Year

1997 MIT Marshall B. Dalton Award

1997 MIT Bronze Beaver Award

1999 Lynn University Honorary Doctor of Science Degree

1999 The Palm Beach Post 100, for the book, *Our Century: Featuring the Palm Beach Post 100: the People Who Changed the Way We Live* (2000)

2001 Junior Achievement Inaugural Business Hall of Fame Award

2005 American Diabetes Association Valor Award

2006 Woodrow Wilson Center Award for Public Service

Alexander W. Dreyfoos
Awards and Honors

2007 Cultural Council of Palm Beach County Lifetime Achievement Award

2007 Kellogg School of Science and Technology, The Scripps Research Institute: Honorary Doctor of Science Degree

2007 City of West Palm Beach: Key to the City

2007 Palm Beach County Commission and City of West Palm Beach: proclamations declaring March 23, 2007, Alexander W. Dreyfoos Day

2008 Association of Fundraising Professionals: Lifetime Achievement Award

2010 Palm Beach Centennial Ambassador (from the Town of Palm Beach Centennial Commission) recognizing 42 successful citizens "rich in the resources that matter most, like friends and family," who also had close connections to the island for at least 50 years.

2012 Palm Beach Civic Association William J. "Bill" Brooks Community Service Award; Dreyfoos notes, "In terms of recent years, I am particularly proud of this" (named for the 17-year general manager of former rival, WPTV-Channel 5), bestowed on residents whose contribution has significantly improved the quality of life in the community.

2013 Historical Society of Palm Beach County Archival Evening Honoree

2013 Ellis Island Medal of Honor, which recognizes community leaders who have used their abilities to change the lives of others around the world.

2014 Chamber of Commerce of the Palm Beaches: Community Leader of the Year

2014 National Society, Sons of the American Revolution: Gold Good Citizenship Medal

The National Society of the
Sons of the American Revolution

INSTITUTED JULY 4, 1876   ORGANIZED APRIL 30, 1889

Dear Compatriot:

Congratulations on becoming a member of the National Society of the Sons of the American Revolution. As you know, we in SAR are dedicated to carrying out patriotic, historical, and educational programs in our home communities. Now, you, as a member of this Society have the opportunity to join your fellow Compatriots in carrying out these Society objectives.

Enclosed are the following: your Membership Certificate and a record copy of your Membership Application.

Perhaps, you have a brother, a son, a nephew or a cousin whom you would like to sponsor for membership in SAR. The brochure included herein provides the information necessary for you to prepare your relative's papers for membership in your Society. Or, maybe you have a friend whom you would like to sponsor for membership in SAR. Again, this brochure will assist in this endeavor.

There is another way to assist in identifying prospective members. One of the better ways is for new or current members to complete the enclosed prospective member request sheet, better know as a census sheet. Please consider those men that you know who may qualify for membership and provide the information requested. In turn, the information will be forwarded to the appropriate state secretary for additional contact. Your efforts will be of tremendous service to the Society.

Again, congratulations on becoming a member of SAR. I am confident you will enjoy your membership and will display your Membership Certificate with great pride. Wear your Rosette proudly!

Very truly yours,

Nathan White

President General, NSSAR

National Headquarters • 1000 South Fourth Street • Louisville, KY 40203 • (502) 589-1776 • Fax: (502) 589-1671
www.sar.org

Alexander W. Dreyfoos
Biographical Timeline

1932 . . . . Born in New York, New York, soon moved to Larchmont

1951 . . . . Father died

1954 . . . . BS degree, MIT

1954 . . . . Married Joan Jacobson (divorced 1975)

1954–56 . . . . USAF, Wiesbaden, Germany

1956 . . . . Daughter born, Catherine Marcia Dreyfoos

1957 . . . . Met George Mergens

1958 . . . . MBA degree, Harvard Business School

1958 . . . . Son born, Robert Whittemore Dreyfoos

1963 . . . . Established Photo Electronics Corporation

1964 . . . . Invented Video Color Negative Analyzer (VCNA)

1969 . . . . Moved to Florida

1973 . . . . Purchased WPEC-TV12 TV station

1973 . . . . Invented LaserColor printer

1977 . . . . Purchased properties for Sailfish Marina

1978 . . . . Founded Palm Beach County Council of the Arts

1981 . . . . Married Barbara Williams (divorced 1986)

1986 . . . . George Mergens died

1986 . . . . Married Carolyn Buckley (divorced 2000)

1988 . . . . Established Emerald Valley Water Company

1991 . . . . Sold Emerald Valley Water Company

1992 . . . . Kravis Center opened

1996 . . . . Sold WPEC-TV12

2000 . . . . Married Renate Jaspert

2004–5 . . . . Sold Sailfish Marina

2008–10 . . . . Begin circumnavigation on *Silver Cloud* SWATH

2013–15 . . . . Complete circumnavigation on *Silver Cloud* SWATH

Kravis Center Board of Directors
as of the opening in November 1992

Note Members of the early founding board are indicated by *. Additional members were added from time to time until the opening, when rotations of 1-, 2-, and 3-year terms began.

Alexander W. Dreyfoos, Chairman*

Robert M. Montgomery, Vice Chairman*

Shannon R. Ginn, Second Vice Chairman

Merrill L. Bank, Board Secretary and Treasurer*

Robert S. Puder, Associate Treasurer

Judith B. Goodman, Assistant Secretary/Treasurer

John J. Brogan*	Raymond F. Kravis
William C. Clark	A. L. Levine
Julian Cohen	William C. Lickle
Joseph E. Cole	Bernard A. Marden
Patricia Cook	Helen K. Persson
Leonard Davis*	Thomas R. Pledger
A. Ephraim Diamond	Philip Rauch
E. Llwyd Ecclestone, Jr.	Wiley R. Reynolds III
George T. Elmore	Charles E. Schmidt
Alfonso Fanjul, Jr.	Carl Shapiro
Murray H. Goodman	Florence Starkoff
Marshall Hess	Natalie G. Stone
Grace E. Hokin	Sidney Stoneman

Ex Officio

Nancy Graham, Mayor, West Palm Beach

Carol A. Roberts, Commissioner, Palm Beach County

Silver Cloud Circumnavigation
2013—15

NOTE: The many days at sea in Cabo San Lucas, French Polynesia, Fiji, etc. were spent scuba diving. *Silver Cloud* was at anchor much of the time in open water; little distance was covered then.

FROM	DEPARTURE	TO	ARRIVAL	DAYS ON THE SEA	DISTANCE NM
West Palm Beach, FL (USA)	7/14/13	Christobel (PAN) Eastside Panama Canal	7/18/13	5	1301
Christobel (PAN) Eastside Panama Canal	7/19/13	Flamenco Island (PAN) Westiside Panama Canal	7/19/13	1	44
Flamenco Island (PAN) Westiside Panama Canal	7/21/13	Cabo San Lucas (MEX)	7/27/13	7	2105
Cabo San Lucas (MEX)	8/2/13	Charter Cruising Mexico & back to Cabo San Lucas	8/16/13	14	360
Cabo San Lucas (MEX)	8/19/13	Cruising Mexico & back to Cabo San Lucas (MEX)	9/2/13	15	560
Cabo San Lucas (MEX)	9/4/13	San Diego, CA (USA)	9/7/13	4	721
San Diego, CA (USA)	10/30/13	Honolulu, HI (USA)	12/7/13	9	2247
Honolulu, HI (USA)	12/18/13	Kona, HI (USA)	12/18/13	1	146
Kona, HI12/21/13 (USA)		Maaleae Bay, Maui, HI (USA)	12/21/13	1	77
Maaleae Bay, Maui, HI (USA)	12/28/13	Kewalo Basin, Honolulu, HI (USA)	12/28/13	1	86
Kewalo Basin, Honolulu, HI (USA)	3/29/14	Papeete, Tahiti (Fr. Polynesia)	4/7/14	10	2386
Papeete, Tahiti (Fr. Polynesia)	4/26/14	Cruising Tuamoto Archipalego & back to Papeete	6/23/14	28	1126
Papeete, Tahiti (Fr. Polynesia)	6/26/14	International Dateline (180*W)	7/1/14	6	1615
International Dateline (180*W)	7/2/14	Port Denarau (FIJ)	7/3/14	2	326
Port Denarau (FIJ)	8/1/14	Cruising Fiji Islands & back to Port Denarau	9/18/14	49	938
Denerau (FIJ)	9/29/14	Port Villa, Vanuatu	10/1/14	3	527
Port Villa, Vanuatu	10/2/14	Cairns (AUS)	10/6/14	5	1315
Cairns (AUS)	10/23/14	Whitehaven Beach, Witsunday Islands (AUS)	10/24/14	2	295

CONTINUED ON NEXT PAGE

FROM	DEPARTURE	TO	ARRIVAL	DAYS ON THE SEA	DISTANCE NM
Whitehaven Beach, Witsunday Islands (AUS)	10/25/14	Brisbane (AUS)	10/27/14	3	559
Brisbane (AUS)	11/2/14	Sydney (AUS)	11/4/14	3	526
Rozelle Bay, Sydney, NSW (AUS)	11/10/14	Cambell's Cove, Sydney (AUS)	11/10/14	1	10
Cambell's Cove, Sydney (AUS)	2/16/15	Hobart, Tasmania (AUS)	2/18/15	3	636
Hobart, Tasmania (AUS)	2/21/15	Melbourne (AUS)	2/23/15	3	482
Melbourne (AUS)	3/1/15	Fremantle–Perth (AUS)	3/7/15	7	1725
Fremantle–Perth (AUS)	4/11/15	Gan Anchorage (MAD)	4/22/15	12	3057
Gan Anchorage (MAD)	4/22/15	Mulaku Atoll Anchorage (MAD)	4/23/15	1	238

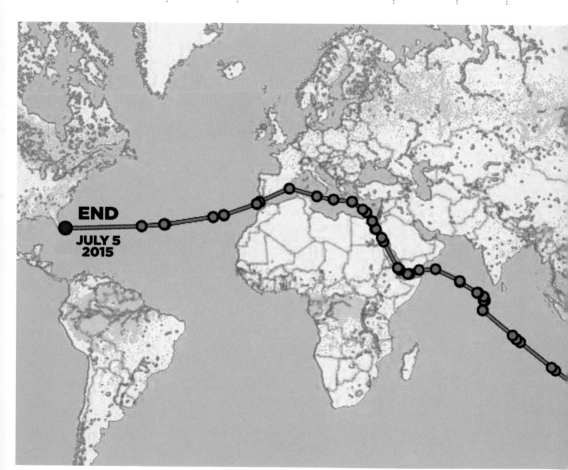

END
JULY 5
2015

FROM	DEPARTURE	TO	ARRIVAL	DAYS ON THE SEA	DISTANCE NM
Mulaku Atoll Anchorage (MAD)	4/25/15	Feliohe Atoll Anchorage (MAD)	4/25/15	1	46
Feliohe Atoll Anchorage (MAD)	4/26/15	Male, South Anchorage (MAD)	4/26/15	1	119
Male, South Anchorage (MAD)	4/29/15	Hughada (EYT)	5/08/15	10	3030
Hughada (EYT)	5/8/15	Suez (EYT)	5/09/15	1	188
Suez (EYT)	5/10/15	Palma, Mallorca (ESP)	5/16/15	7	1776
Palma, Mallorca (ESP)	6/18/15	Fuel Dock, Gibraltar (GIB)	6/20/15	3	445
Fuel Dock, Gibraltar (GIB)	6/20/15	West Palm Beach, FL (USA)	7/5/15	17	4000
		TOTAL		**236**	**33012**

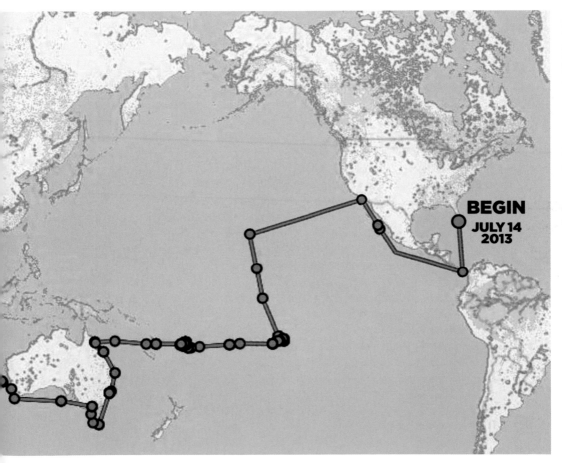

BEGIN
JULY 14
2013

Bibliography

BOOKS

Abramson, Albert. *The History of Television, 1942 to 2000*. McFarland & Co., 2002.

Andersen, Robin, ed. *Battleground: The Media*, Vol. I. ABC-CLIO, 2008.

Bickhoff-Boettcher, Nicole, Gertrud Bolay, and Eduard Theiner. *200 Jahre juedisches Leben in Hochberg und Aldingen, 1730-1930: Remseck am Neckar.* Gemeinde Remseck am Neckar, 1990.

Bronowski, Jacob. *Science and Human Values*. Faber and Faber, 2011.

Burlingame, Dwight, ed. "Eastman, George (1854-1932)," *Philanthropy in America: A Comprehensive Historical Encyclopedia*, Vol. 1. ABC-CLIO, 2004.

Burrows, William E. *By Any Means Necessary: America's Secret Air War in the Cold War*. Farrar, Straus and Giroux, 2001.

Conway, Flo and Jim Siegelman. *Dark Hero of the Information Age: In Search of Norbert Wiener, the Father of Cybernetics*. Basic Books, 2006.

Crabb, Kelly Charles. *The Movie Business: The Definitive Guide to the Legal and Financial Secrets of Getting Your Movie Made*. Simon and Schuster, 2005.

Davis, William Thomas. *Bench and Bar of the Commonwealth of Massachusetts*, Vol. 1. Boston History Co., 1895.

Die Deborah, May 1, 1863; May 8, 1863; July 3, 1863; cited by Elizabeth Plaut.

Ede, Sian. *Art and Science*. I. B. Tauris, 2005.

Edwards, David. *Artscience: Creativity in the Post-Google Generation*. Harvard University Press, 2010.

Florida, Richard L. *The Flight of the Creative Class: The New Global Competition for Talent*. Harper Collins, 2005.

Green, William and Gordon Swanborough. *The Great Book of Fighters: An Illustrated Encyclopedia of Every Fighter Aircraft Built and Flown*. MBI Publishing, 2001: "The Lockheed P-80 Shooting Star was the first operational jet fighter of the USAF. The jet saw extensive combat in Korea with the Air Force as the F-80. As one of the world's first successful turbojet-powered combat aircraft, it ushered in the 'jet age' in the USAF and other Air Forces worldwide. One of its claims to fame is in training a new generation of pilots, especially in its closely-related T-33 Shooting Star."

Harvard Law School, Quinquennial Catalogue of the Law School of Harvard University.

Henniker-Heaton, Peter. *Jubilee and Other Poems*. E.D. Abbott Co., 1979.

Kalmus, Herbert T. and Eleanore King Kalmus. *Mr. Technicolor.* MagicImage Filmbooks, 1993.

Kemp, Martin. *Seen/Unseen: Art, Science, and Intuition from Leonardo to the Hubble Telescope*. Oxford University Press, USA, 2006.

Kennedy, Richard S. *Dreams in the Mirror: A Biography of E. E. Cummings*. W. W. Norton & Co., 1994).

Kriplen, Nancy. *The Eccentric Billionaire: John D. MacArthur—Empire Builder, Reluctant Philanthropist, Relentless Adversary*. American Management Assn., 2008.

Kuhn, Thomas. *The Structure of Scientific Revolutions*, 4th ed. University of Chicago Press, 2012.

Proctor, Theresa Bixler. *Erosion of Riparian Rights Along Florida's Coast*. FSU, 2004.

Putnam, Robert D. and David E. Campbell. *American Grace: How Religion Divides and Unites Us.* Simon & Schuster, 2010.

Sadler, Roger L. *Electronic Media Law*. Sage Publications, 2005.

World of Invention (Gale Group, 2005).

BIBLIOGRAPHY

NEWSPAPER ARTICLES

Chicago Tribune, 1993
Miami Herald, 1980, 1982, 1992
The Miami News, 1984
The New York Times, 1991, 1994, 2007, 2010
The Palm Beach Post, 1962-64, 1972-74, 1978-85, 1986-92, 1995-96, 2003, 2007, 2009
Palm Beach Daily News, 1972-74, 1978-79, 1982, 1986-89, 2008, 2010
South Florida Sun-Sentinel, 1988, 1990-91, 2008.

OTHER PERIODICALS

"Aboard the *Silver Cloud*: Landfall: Romantic Rhine," *ShowBoats* (Oct. 1, 2005).

"Alex W. Dreyfoos Jr., Electronics Engineer: Under the Banyan Tree." *Forbes* (May 15, 1978).

"Alexander Dreyfoos." *Studio Light: A Magazine of Information for the Profession* (Aug. 1928).

"MIT Media Lab Auditorium Named to Honor Alexander W. Dreyfoos '54," *MIT News* (Dec. 6, 2013).

"New Kodak Developments," Business, *Time*, Vol. 65, No. 1 (Jan. 3, 1955).

"*Silver Cloud*: A Divan for Renate," *Boat Exclusive* (Apr. 2009).

"What? Color in the Movies Again?" *Fortune* 10 (Oct. 1934).

Bartlett, John et al. "Important Decision Regarding Right to Pictures," *Bulletin of Photography*, Vol. 12 (1913).

Bray, Ralph. "The Origin of Semiconductor Research at Purdue." *Purdue Physics* newsletter, 1989, http://www.physics.purdue.edu

Gilbert, Jim. "Interview with Superyacht Owner Alex Dreyfoos." *Boat International* (July 2013).

Gray, Frank et al. "The Production and Utilisation of Television Signals." Trans. *AIEE* 46 (June 1927).

Gray, Frank. "The Use of a Moving Beam of Light to Scan a Scene for Television." *OSA* 16 (Mar. 1928).

Kane, Martin. "Something New in Fishing Tournaments at Palm Beach." *Sports Illustrated* (Jan. 28, 1963).

LaPook, Jonathan. "New Test Can Diagnose Alzheimer's, but Raises Questions." *CBS Evening News Online* (June 19, 2012).

Pulling, Nathaniel H. "Arthur C. Hardy: Profile of a Scientist." *Color Measurement Digest* (Feb. 1958).

Reiss, Spencer. "Frank Gehry's Geek Palace." *Wired* (May 2004).

Schultz, Kevin M. "Protestant-Catholic-Jew, Then and Now," *First Things* (Jan. 2006), www.firstthings.com.

Vallée, Robert. "Norbert Wiener (1894-1964)," International Society of Systems Sciences. Université Paris-Nord, 2001, www.isss.org/lumwiener.htm.

Van de Water, Ava. "A Tailor-Made Home for a Self-Made Man." *Palm Beach Life* (Dec. 1985).

SELECTED ELECTRONIC SOURCES

Anderson, Richard B., autobiography, http://freepages.history.rootsweb.ancestry.com.

Broadcasting Yearbook, 1957-1965 and 2003, www.americanradiohistory.com.

Broadway Photographs, http://broadway.cas.sc.edu/content/studio-apeda.

Film Reference, www.filmreference.com.

Florida, Richard L. Interview by Lou Dobbs, Apr. 14, 2005, for CNN.com.

Kaufman, Rabbi David. "A Brief Introduction to Why I Perform Interfaith Marriages,"
    July 29, 2008, updated October 2013, interfaithmarriage.blogspot.com.

Lindsay, David. "Eastman Becomes a Mystery Donor to MIT" People & Events, PBS,
    http://www.pbs.org/wgbh/amex/eastman/peopleevents/pande15.html.

MIT Media Lab 25th Anniversary (video), Oct. 15, 2010, www.media.mit.edu.

Oppenheim, Roy. "The Swiss Roots of The Guggenheim." Peggy Guggenheim Collection,
    http://www.guggenheim-venice.it/inglese/museum/guggenheim_roots.html

Papers of Elizabeth Strauss Plaut, Leo Baeck Institute, Center for Jewish History, http://cjh.org.

Sewell, AnEta. Interview by Barbara Cheives, posted Sept. 2, 2010, Arts Radio Network,
    www.artsradionetwork.com.

Stein, Herb. "The Stein Saga" autobiography, https://sites.google.com.

PUBLIC DOCUMENTS

Bradbury's Pleading and Practice Reports, Vol. 5. Banks Law Publishing Co., 1920.

Decisions of the United States Courts Involving Copyright 1914-1917 (1918).

FCC 47 Code of Federal Regulations Statute 73.3555 (1985).

FCC 94-322. Further Notice of Proposed Rulemaking re: Review of FCC Regulations Governing
    TV Broadcasting (1995).

FCC Media Ownership Rules: Current Status and Issues for Congress. Library of Congress. (up-
    dated Aug. 3, 2006).

FCC Notice of Proposed Rulemaking re: Review of FCC Regulations Governing TV Broadcasting
    (1992).

Minutes. City of West Palm Beach Bicentennial Committee, Jan. 23, 1974.

Purdum, Elizabeth D. *Florida Waters: A Water Resources Manual from Florida's Water Management
    Districts.* Southwest Florida Water Management District (2002).

Reports of Cases Decided in the Commission of Appeals of the State of New York, Vol. 221 (1918).

Resolution 2230.3.22.4-R-39-74. City of West Palm Beach (adopted Jan. 23, 1974).

Telecommunications Act of 1996.

OTHER SOURCES

Alzheimer's Association. "2013 Alzheimer's Disease Facts and Figures." *Alzheimer's & Dementia*,
    Vol. 9, No. 2.

Landmark Campaign Newsletter No. 2, Nov. 1986.

Report of the Committee on Educational Survey. MIT Press, Dec. 1949.

Secretary's Report: Harvard College, Class of 1885.

Index

Note: Italics indicate photographs

INDEX